Contents

Continued overleaf

France in revolt: 1995-2005

Jim Wolfreys

'In recent years,' remarked the sociologist Emmanuel Todd in November 2005, 'French political life has been nothing but a series of catastrophes. And each time the ruling class's lack of legitimacy becomes more flagrant'.[1] He was speaking in the aftermath of the rioting which had set dozens of France's run-down suburbs ablaze for a full three weeks, providing an unrelenting nightly reminder of the anger felt by urban youth at years of impoverishment, discrimination and repression, and their frustration at the political establishment's disregard for them and their neighbourhoods. If the 8,000 cars torched during the uprising spoke of the lack of more effective political tools at their disposal, then the government's response, exhuming emergency powers from France's colonial past, was an eloquent indication that the options open to a regime in crisis were narrowing after a decade of revolt against social inequality.

Jacques Chirac's 1995 presidential election victory had been based on a promise to heal France's '*fracture sociale*', a phrase borrowed from a report on social exclusion written by Todd himself. But it soon became clear that the Gaullists' vision of a 'France for all' amounted to the same neo-liberal free for all served up by governments of left and right since the early 1980s. Within six months of Chirac's victory his prime minister, Alain Juppé, had produced a plan designed to overhaul the social security and pensions system established in the aftermath of the Second World War.

The response of the labour movement to Juppé's offensive was nothing short of astonishing. On 24 November railway workers went on strike, groups of them going into sorting offices to call on postal workers to do the same. As the strike gained momentum, they in turn urged telecom workers to follow, who were then joined by those in the electricity and gas industries, along with hospital staff. With the movement driven largely from below and organised through mass meetings of strikers 'all together', irrespective of sectional or union affiliations, demonstrations in support of the strikes were held on an almost daily basis until mid-December, mobilising 2 million people nationally at their peak. By 15 December the government had withdrawn its pension reforms. Although the government was still able to push through the cuts in social security, Juppé never recovered from the strikes. His administration stumbled on for a further 18 months and then the man generally expected to assume the leadership of the mainstream right after Chirac simply drifted into obscurity.

November/December 1995 was a turning point, not just in France but internationally. It marked the end of a long cycle of defeats for the labour movement, and the beginning of an ongoing period of resistance to neo-liberalism which has found expression in a series of anti-capitalist protests, beginning in Seattle in November 1999, and in the development of a critique of contemporary capitalism that traditional social democratic parties were no longer capable of providing.

This article is about what has happened to the movement in France during the ten years since 1995. It begins with an assessment of the crisis facing a ruling elite whose parties and institutions are no longer capable of mobilising mass popular support for its policies, before looking at the potential—and the limitations—of a movement which has proved capable of resisting the establishment, but has not yet been able to offer a viable alternative to it.

The bitterest pill

During the 1980s France's two main political parties, the Socialists and the Gaullist RPR, adopted the neo-liberal policy model pioneered in Britain and the US. But resistance proved hard to break down. University students, nurses, and railway and bank workers fought back in the late 1980s, as did school students, and Air France and France Telecom workers in the early 1990s. This resilience combined with a broader political identification with certain aspects of the so-called 'Republican social model', based on the establishment and consolidation of the welfare state in the immediate post-war period. As a result no party was able to mobilise widespread support for 'popular capitalism' and dominate French political life sufficiently to achieve the comprehensive imposition of neo-liberal reforms demanded by employers. Indeed, no government has been able to win a second term in France for nearly 30 years.

The cross-party consensus that there is no alternative to an unbridled market economy has progressively alienated every mainstream party from its activist base and electorate. The historic Socialist election victory of 1981, which put an end to 23 years of right wing rule, was followed by 'alternation', whereby parties of left and right take turns in office. This was held up as a sign of the 'maturity' of the political institutions of the Fifth Republic.

But these institutions are now in crisis. Alternation pits parties against each other, but since the intensification of competition between the major parties is no longer primarily based on ideological differences it takes other forms, most of which tend to erode further the legitimacy of these parties. Networks of corruption became increasingly necessary to underpin the operations of declining organisations. For much of the post-war period collusion between the major parties, intent on freezing the Communists out of government, had kept corruption 'in-house'. But deeper internal divisions, and the decline of the Communist 'threat', meant that whistle-blowing was increasingly used as a means of undermining opponents and rivals. Revelations from within the RPR, for example, have made it an open secret that the Paris city hall was turned into an elaborate slush fund for the party over a 20-year period following Chirac's election as mayor in 1977, while various leading Socialists, along with prominent figures in both mainstream right wing parties, have been forced to resign their posts following dozens of high profile trials and scandals.

By 1995 internal rivalry within the RPR had reached such a pitch that Chirac's position as the uncontested figurehead of the party was challenged by his prime minister Edouard Balladur, who managed to group the most committed neo-liberal elements of the mainstream right, like Alain Madelin and Nicolas Sarkozy, around his campaign. Chirac was reduced to standing on a 'social' platform that implicitly rejected the very neo-liberal model he himself had convinced the mainstream right to adopt in the 1980s. Two years later Lionel Jospin, a key figure in persuading Socialist Party activists to abandon plans for sweeping social reform in the 1980s, performed a similar trick to become prime minister. He placed himself at the head of a 'plural left' coalition with the Communists and Greens, and promised to turn the demands of the so-called 'social movement' into policy. The response by the CNPF employers' association was aggressive. Its outgoing president, Jean Gandois, emerged white with anger from a meeting at which Jospin had made plain his government's intention to honour its commitment to a 35-hour week. 'We have been duped,' he claimed, and called on his successor to be 'a killer'. The association duly changed its name from a confederation to a 'movement' (MEDEF),[2] and proceeded to fight a long, and largely successful, campaign to undermine the 35-hour week.

By 1998 frustration at the pace of neo-liberal counter-reform led several leading ruling class figures openly to advocate electoral alliances between the mainstream right and the fascist Front National. Such was the extent of political polarisation in France that four years later Jean-Marie Le Pen was able to beat Jospin into third place in the presidential election all on his own, going through to a second round standoff against Chirac. The Socialist Party, with only symbolic reforms to compensate for mass unemployment and the privatisation of public services on an unprecedented scale, had failed for the first time to achieve the objective which had inspired its formation in 1972—to compete for the presidency. Alternation was in disarray, and Chirac posed as the champion of 'the Republic in danger' after getting the first round support of under 14 percent of registered voters. The millions who flocked to demonstrate against Le Pen summed up the meagre choice before them with the slogan, 'Rather the crook than the fascist.'

There was basic continuity between Jospin and Juppé on economic and social policy. But there was a significant difference between the ability of the ruling elite to set the agenda in France and elsewhere. The difference was confirmed by the introduction of a 35-hour week, although it brought little significant change to most working lives (one study estimates that it has reduced total working hours by around 3 percent),[3] by the scale of opposition to its attacks on the education system and by the waves of protest involving various networks and associations of the social movement. Francis Fukuyama expressed the concern of the elites internationally:

> The United States and Great Britain had Ronald Reagan and Margaret Thatcher. Both broke the old order and laid the basis for new growth. The following generation saw the arrival of Bill Clinton and Tony Blair.

> Fundamentally, they applied the same economic and social recipes, under a left guise. Nothing of the sort has ever happened in France... France's handicap is that it has not yet found an actor or a party which will subject it to this cathartic exercise.[4]

Desperately seeking such an actor, Chirac turned to the unlikely figure of Jean-Pierre Raffarin, a portly *notable* from the west of France with no outward signs of personality or charm, whose rather unimaginative advisers presented him as the embodiment of 'the France from below'. Raffarin, like Chirac and Jospin before him, found that pretending to be something he was not could only get him so far. He emerged victorious in the summer of 2003 from a hard fought struggle by public sector workers to ward off his attacks on their pension rights, famously declaring, 'It's not the street that governs.' But the extent of popular opposition to neo-liberalism proved fatal to him two years later. He became the scapegoat for the political establishment's failure to persuade a simple majority of the population to back the proposed neo-liberal constitution for the EU in the May 2005 referendum.

The weakness of the regime was clearly exposed. After defying the street in 2003, Chirac was now faced with the choice of disregarding the ballot box or standing down. Since nobody was forcing him to stand down he found a new prime minister, Dominique de Villepin, an ally and a lifelong stranger to elected office, and a new interior minister, Nicolas Sarkozy, a rival whose contempt for Chiraquism was undisguised. 'It is no longer the Paris city hall,' Sarkozy had declared in 1995. 'It's the antechamber of the morgue—Chirac is dead, all that's missing are the last shovels of earth'.[5] The composition of the government—with Sarkozy shadowing De Villepin and the centre-right UDF coalition refusing to take ministerial office—was a vivid reflection of longstanding divisions within the ruling class over how hard and how fast to push the neo-liberal offensive. The difficulties experienced by successive governments in asserting a neo-liberal agenda lay with the Republican social model, according to the hardline conservative right:

> The blockage of the state and the political sphere is directly related to the hard core of the ruling class under the Fifth Republic, which is based on osmosis between political leaders, top civil servants and the union leaders. From this comes a consensus, which goes beyond political cleavages, in favour of retaining a social-state model.[6]

Sarkozy has no qualms about denigrating this model when he feels it necessary to do so. He departed from the Gaullist party line at the height of the referendum campaign to declare, 'The best social model is the one which gives everyone a job. So it's no longer ours!'[7] And just as George Bush can leave New Orleans to its fate while heaping praise on Rosa Parks and the civil rights movement, so Sarkozy can denounce France's urban youth as a 'dirty rabble' whose neighbourhoods should be cleaned out with a power hose, and at the same time propose abandoning the allegedly 'colour blind' Republican model of integration in favour of ethnic monitoring, affirmative action and voting rights for immigrants. Sarkozy represents, for sections of the French right, Fukuyama's missing link in French politics, the neo-liberal enforcer. Members of his entourage make no bones about what their desire for 'a right without complexes' represents:

> I've always been conservative. I like order. I believe in individual initiative and effort and, where the economy is concerned, in the invisible hand of the market. For example, I'm for the total privatisation of the state education system.[8]

Sarkozy may receive standing ovations when addressing the MEDEF, but his political base on the right is much narrower than that enjoyed by Juppé a decade ago, and the right's level of support nationally far lower than it was then. And yet, following its humiliating defeat in the EU referendum, the government was still able to announce the privatisation of the motorways and the closure of unprofitable railway lines, and to impose a new 'employee contract' by decree. This gave employers, for the first time, the right to sack workers during the first two years of their contract without any justification.

How then, given the chronic weaknesses of the French right, and the apparent strength of the 'social movement' since 1995, has it been possible for such measures to be implemented along with other similar attacks, notably on pensions and social security?

The weight of the world

The past decade has witnessed the huge capacity for mobilisation in France—the strikes and demonstrations of 1995, the comparable movement against pension reform in 2003, the wave of protests against the Front National between the two rounds of the 2002 election, the political campaign against the EU referendum, and the various mobilisations of associative, trade union and *altermondialiste* networks, such as the gathering in Millau in support of José Bové in June 2000, and against the WTO at Larzac in 2003.[9] But there have also been periods of very low levels of struggle. In 1997, for example, strike action in the public sector was at its lowest ebb, while the following year saw the fewest number of strike days ever in the private sector.[10] Moreover, changing perceptions of class and of the role of workers in society have allowed those who want to dismiss the movement to present it as a directionless reaction against progress and modernisation, despite the return of the social question:

> Neo-leftism no longer has a social reference point—instead it identifies with all kinds of victims, with no unifying principle and with nobody giving a general meaning to action. The working class had a universal mission and a positive contribution through its work, to collective life. Today, there is no longer a central cause.[11]

In the 20th century, as Gerassimos Moschonas argues in his study of European social democracy, the working class became both more involved in politics and more visible 'than any previous dominated class'.[12] By contrast,

> Today's workers (internally divided and socially weakened), junior employees, insecure labourers, the unemployed, young people in search of their first job, people who have taken early retirement, single-parent families, the inhabitants of deprived neighbourhoods, minorities of every sort (principally immigrant workers), the 'have-nots' more generally—these people represent a heterogeneous set of situations, not a more or less 'compact' self-confident social force.[13]

This, argues Moschonas, makes the crisis of representation affecting workers, discussed below, double-edged. On the one hand, he argues, the labour movement has lost the 'sociological and symbolic centrality' of the first half of the 20th century. But on the other this serves as a justification for social democracy's abandonment of its attempt to politicise working class culture—and the exhaustion of its capacity to do so accelerates a crisis of working class political representation which appears to confirm the notion that it is a social force in decline.[14] Falling union membership, flexible working practices and the globalisation of the economy are frequently taken as evidence that 'analyses based on the domination and exploitation by capital of the world of work' are no longer relevant. This, in any case, is how the MEDEF justified its plans for a 'social refoundation', unveiled in January 2000, which amounted to an attack on pensions, training, and the health and social security systems, and a call for the state to retreat further from industrial relations in the face of more deregulation.[15]

Drawing new generations into union activity is clearly not straightforward, with one in four under-25s unemployed and nearly half of all young workers on short-term contracts. Unemployment and job insecurity inevitably take their toll on confidence and organisation over time. But these difficulties should not be taken as evidence that the working class is in decline or that lives are now shaped by individual rather than collective concerns. Important changes are nevertheless affecting the composition of classes in society, with political consequences. Up to 13 million people in France are categorised as either 'workers' (*ouvriers*[a]) or 'employees'. What has changed over the past 20 years is that the number of those classed as 'employees' now outweighs the number of 'workers' by 15 percent. But although their jobs may differ in name, the working conditions, wages and exposure to unemployment of employees on modest incomes bear little difference to the experience of manual workers. By the mid-1990s poor families in France were more likely to remain poor than in the 1980s, and rich families less likely to become so.[16]

Around 7 million people, 28 percent of France's active population, are officially classified as 'workers'. The proportion of industrial workers within that category has declined at the expense of workers in the tertiary sector—those employed as chauffeurs, or in warehousing, cleaning or packing. This is far from being evidence of a creeping individualism rendering collective solutions outdated. The opposite is more likely to be the case: 'Their relationship to others (both employers and other workers) is more direct, more specific, much less mediated by the prism of categories, and therefore much more pressing and important for each person'.[17] Similarly, while the biggest change in the composition of white collar work is the rise in the number of people employed by private individuals (like nannies or childminders)—who now make up roughly the same numbers as

---

a: In French, as in some other south European languages, there are two words for 'worker': a general term, *travailleur*, and *ouvrier*, which refers to the narrow category of manual workers.

those who work in administration—the shift in category from worker to employee among low wage earners is neither proof that society is becoming more middle class nor that individualism is rife: 'Often isolated in a succession of ephemeral working relations, employees have no less need of social fraternity than the new workers'.[18]

This is not to underestimate the disorientation felt by those whose working lives are subject to insecurity and flux. One of the most important political developments of the past 15 years has been the ability of the Front National to win a significant number of votes from young workers, those most likely to endure precarious working conditions and to be least integrated into the political or trade union culture of their parents' generation.[19] Unions are today confronted by something which has always been a feature of the labour movement—the working class is diverse, and subject to changes and upheavals in its internal composition: 'Moving to more complex, multidimensional models of class does not imply that classes are dying'.[20] Structural upheavals in the world of work present obstacles to effective organisation, but do not prevent it. The fact that young workers in particular are subject to insecurity and unemployment inevitably makes it harder to organise them into unions, but 70 percent of those employed on a short-term basis will eventually be offered indefinite contracts. And those employed as domestic cleaners, hotel workers and childminders may be going into jobs with little or no tradition of union organisation, but so were the barbers, school teachers and typographers who joined the ranks of the CGT in the early years of the 20th century.[21]

Indeed, one of the features of struggles over the past decade has been the mobilisation of workers who have generally found it difficult to organise—the homeless associations which occupied empty housing in central Paris in the mid-1990s, the unemployed associations which put the Jospin government on the back foot in the winter of 1997/8, the *sans papiers* whose demand for residency rights led to a wave of protests drawing in unprecedented public support in the mid-1990s, and the successful strikes by young workers in recent years precisely in sectors of typically insecure employment with few traditions of union organisation—McDonald's, Virgin and the hotel group Accor. In the spring of 2005 workers sustained strike action for five weeks at the Carrefour supermarket chain, where conditions were notoriously poor and union membership very low.

Unions are confronted by the problem of their own organisational fragmentation along political lines, as well as by employers' attempts to break up established patterns and networks of solidarity in the workplace.[22] These divisions have increased over the past two decades following the expulsion of left wing activists from the CFDT, who set up the independent SUD trade union in the post and telecom industry, a process which has spread to virtually the entire public sector. But one of the defining characteristics of the 1995 strikes was the impulse towards unity from below which saw, for the first time, united contingents of all the main trade union federations and joint mass meetings of workers from different sectors. This was the basis of the dynamic driving the movement—strike action which spread through rank and file activity, drawing in wider support expressed in regular and significant demonstrations, giving further impetus and confidence to the strikers until Juppé was forced to back down.

Some have seen the movement as a way of locating the defence of jobs and working conditions organised by strike committees or *coordinations* within the wider context of a globalising economy.[23] 'For the first time in a rich country,' declared *Le Monde* in December 1995, 'we are witnessing today what is in reality a strike against "globalisation", a massive and collective reaction against financial globalisation and its consequences'.[24] Certainly, in France and elsewhere, the aftermath of December 1995 saw the development of anti-capitalist groups and associations whose protests followed a trajectory which sometimes paralleled, and sometimes overlapped with, labour movement struggles. In Italy, for example, the CGIL union called for a general strike on 23 May 2002 against the Berlusconi administration. Over 13 million workers took part, and the CGIL went on to link up with the social forum movement which had developed in Italy following the Genoa protests against the G8 summit, notably playing a prominent role in the 2002 European Social Forum in Florence. Similarly in Spain, the trade unions which organised the June 2002 general strike of 10 million workers also played a part in the protests at the EU summit in Seville two days later, as they had in Barcelona the previous spring when 500,000 demonstrated. For some the conclusion is clear: 'The establishment of an explicit correlation between opposition to the neo-liberal projects of national governments and denunciation of the authority of global "governance" derives from thorough trade union work'.[25]

Why did the dynamic of 1995, leading to a convergence of these 'two calendars of mobilisation',[26] fail to function in the same way in France in 2003? The movement failed to gather sufficient momentum to defeat Raffarin, although demonstrations took place on an even greater scale than in 1995, with national mobilisations of 2 million taking place on four separate occasions, a total number of strike days five or six times higher than in 1995, and action spreading through the education system in much the same way as it had on the railways against the Juppé plan. The veteran commentator on French trade unions René Mouriaux puts this down to political weaknesses—the lack of a set of straightforward aims around which the movement could unite, the failure of the union leadership to develop radical alternative propositions to the government, and its inability to win over rank and file members to the positions it did develop. More generally, a global vision was lacking, a unifying political goal. Despite these shortcomings, however:

> The victory of the right over pensions does not seem to have smashed popular mobilisation, and the experience of 2003 will give rise to reflections which in all probability will lead to a richer formulation of an alternative response to the neo-liberal offensive.[27]

He was right. Two years later the movement found a way of taking on all the mainstream parties and mobilising the overwhelming support of workers at the polls against the neo-liberal EU constitution. A feature of this extraordinary movement was how strikes and demonstrations—against attacks on public services and the 35-hour week, and government plans to abolish the Whitsun bank holiday—gave impetus, confirmed by the opinion polls, to the broader political campaign against the constitution. The result was the most significant political victory against neo-liberalism to date.

Political alternatives

The past ten years have been characterised, then, by moments of intense struggle interspersed with periods of relative calm. Some have noticed the coincidence between low levels of strike action and election campaigns—a more plausible cause lies in economic factors, with struggle more intense when the economy picks up.[28] Revolt against long-term social inequality can take unpredictable forms in a context of political instability and disaffection, where the rate of unemployment has remained virtually unchanged at 10 percent for two decades.

Over 700 of France's suburbs, with a combined population of 4.5 million people, are officially considered areas 'in difficulty'. In Clichy-sous-Bois, where the rioting started in autumn 2005, one in four people are unemployed. It is estimated that 30 percent of households in the area are unable to afford council housing. Youth unemployment in the Seine-Saint-Denis suburbs north of Paris runs at between 25 and 40 percent.

The rage and frustration which led youths to burn schools and job centres, which for them had become symbols of the poverty and discrimination excluding them from 'Republican' society, is not a reaction confined to France's impoverished suburbs. In 2000, for example, textile workers threatened with redundancy at the Cellatex plant in Givet occupied the factory and took charge of the 56,000 litres of sulphuric acid and the 46 tonnes of carbon sulphide stored inside, threatening to blow it up, and eventually discharging thousands of litres of acid into the streets.[29] Others have made attempts to generalise conflict by linking it up with wider issues. During the power cuts caused by strikes against plans to privatise the French gas and electricity industries in 2003, electricity workers went into working class estates and reconnected supplies onto the cheapest rates. The so-called 'Robin Hoods' who carried this out did so under the slogan 'Our energy is not for sale'.[30]

Mass strikes and protest movements have always been a feature of the French labour movement, whatever the level of trade union organisation. The strike waves of June 1936 and May 1968, as in the winters of 1986 and 1995, spread and developed through rank and file action, and were led by strike committees rather than the trade union bureaucracy. Only when it came to bringing these movements to a close did the leadership of reformist organisations make their influence felt.

The singularity of the 1995 and 2003 strikes was that these organisations, and in particular the French Communist Party (PCF), were weaker than ever before. This did not mean, however, that the movement was spontaneously able to develop an independent political strategy. Indeed, one of the ironies of December 1995 was that it effectively carried the Socialist Party back to office in 1997, while the 2003 movement was stifled by the trade union leadership and followed by a surge in support for the Socialist Party in the following year's regional and European elections. But the period opened up by the strikes of 1995 has confirmed that disaffection with the compromises and pessimism of the social democratic and trade union leadership, apparent since the railway strike of 1986, is translating into alternative organisational forms. The spread of the *coordination* movement in the workplace and the development of grassroots associations, a consequence of the decline of trade union organisation and of the Socialist and Communist party machines, expresses a desire to challenge their leadership by activists keen to take things into their own hands. This pattern has been repeated wherever a breach has been left by social democratic organisations.

The most obvious example has been the rise of the Trotskyist left. Lutte Ouvrière (LO) and the Ligue Communiste Révolutionnaire (LCR) have established themselves as major national organisations, each winning more votes than the Communist Party at the last presidential election, with a combined 10 percent of the poll. Their spokespeople, LO's Arlette Laguiller and the LCR's Olivier Besancenot, are household names. But the pattern has also taken other forms. Intellectuals have acted as a substitute for political leaders at various moments in French history. The inability of socialists to offer independent leadership from the mainstream Republican left during the Dreyfus affair at the turn of the 20th century meant that many of their polemical duties were taken up by a novelist, Emile Zola. During the Algerian War it was a philosopher, Jean-Paul Sartre, who spoke out when the left was silent, and in the aftermath of the 1995 strikes the sociologist Pierre Bourdieu took a lead in putting anyone who compromised with the neo-liberal consensus on the defensive. Bourdieu also understood the need to equip activists with arguments, setting up a publishing house to this end in a move followed by other grassroots associations. The role played by ATTAC and the Fondation Copernic in refuting mainstream arguments on the EU constitution was at least the equal of the Communist Party's efforts during the referendum campaign. ATTAC has developed from an association set up to call for a tax on financial speculation into an activist network of up to 40,000 people dealing with the full spectrum of political issues. It is one of the most striking examples of how the thirst for political alternatives and for the tools to achieve them is generating ways to counteract the decline of the reformist party machines which shaped the outlook of the left for most of the 20th century.

These networks of activists have been at the core of major mobilisations drawing millions into action. But just as every mobilisation has confirmed, in different ways, the decline of social democracy, so they have also revealed the limits of the social movement's capacity to seize the political initiative. Jospin, as we have seen, capitalised on the right's disarray in 1995 to rein in significant sections of the anti-neoliberal left behind his plural left project in the aftermath of the strikes. That project collapsed in 2002, forcing Jospin into a dramatic withdrawal from politics on election night. But the so-called 'left of the left' was also wrongfooted by Le Pen's defeat of Jospin, and found itself simply echoing the Socialists' plea for the millions who demonstrated against Le Pen to vote Chirac. Many activists then reacted to being outmanoeuvred by Raffarin and the leadership of the main trade union federations in 2003, despite a massive and sustained movement against his pension reform, by voting for the Socialists rather than for the far left in 2004. Similarly, after the victory of the left in the 2005 EU referendum, Chirac's survival was largely due to the absence of a concerted campaign to force his resignation.

The revival of the Socialists' electoral fortunes in the wake of protest movements reinforces something underlined by Moschonas—that the link between social democracy and its popular electorate is deteriorating but has not broken. On the one hand, for the first time in a century working people have been deprived of effective political representation. But on the other, the organisational and institutional infrastructure of social democracy remains, 'even if its centre has largely fissured and its contours have altered', and social democratic parties no longer act as 'producers of meaning' in defence of the interests of those on modest incomes. Political traditions take a long time to establish and a long time to break down. The decline of social democracy is not a linear process, but turns around an 'impossible' identity based on the tension between a residual social democratic sensibility, along with its surviving structures, and the social-liberal embrace of the market which is undermining them. This 'dual impossibility of both breaking with and adopting the logic of solidarity' means that social democracy continues to exert a pull on a popular, working class electorate, while at the same time contributing to the marginalisation of workers in public life.[31]

So while social democracy is no longer able to mobilise around a programme of social transformation, it is able to maintain a level of electoral support by default. And, as we have seen, changes to working lives and the concerted attempts by employers (and political forces like the FN) to break up networks of collective organisation and solidarity can make the compromises of trade union leaders appear 'realistic'. All this undoubtedly has an impact on levels of confidence and combativity in the workplace. This is particularly true in the private sector, where a number of defeats have taken place in recent years (Danone, Marks and Spencer, Michelin). At the same time, however, falling trade union membership and the decline of social democracy should not be seen as primarily sociological phenomena, based on the 'disappearance' of the working class. The erosion of support for the Communists and the Socialists over the past decade has political roots, reflecting disaffection with compromises made in office. But social democracy has never been as coherent a political force in France as in Britain, historically divided between the Socialist and Communist parties. The same applies to the crisis of France's main trade union confederations. The fact that a fragmented trade union movement organises no more than one in ten workers means that its leadership is influential, but not as monolithic or as heavily bureaucratised as elsewhere. Frustration at the unions' leadership of the strikes against pension reform in 2003, dissipating the movement by separate rather than consecutive days of action on nine different occasions, led workers at a mass meeting in Marseille in June 2003 to jeer and whistle at CGT leader Bernard Thibault, greeting him with cries of 'General strike!' And it was this same anger, rather than any underlying sociological factors, which led an estimated 100,000 people to leave the CFDT in the wake of the 2003 movement.[32]

Since 1995 movements of striking workers, the unemployed, *sans papiers* and the homeless have reasserted their status as actors in their own right rather than the victims of the market's hidden hand. The slogans of the movement, '*Tous ensemble!*' (All together), 'Our world is not for sale', 'Another world is possible', although very general, nevertheless express confidence in the power and solidarity of those fighting back against neoliberal attacks. Moreover, the electoral performance of the Trotskyist left shows that it is possible to build an electoral base on a platform which counters the pessimism of social democracy by stressing working class potential for self-activity.

The movement and its political expression appeared to be unfolding according to parallel or consecutive rhythms until the May 2005 referendum. The linking up of the LCR and the associative network of the radical left with the PCF and parts of the Socialist left during the referendum campaign made a longer term anti-neoliberal alliance a tangible possibility.

But a tendency to remain aloof from the movement is still a problem for some elements of the far left. LO reacted to the riots of November 2005 by counterposing the youth of the suburbs to the working class, as if the two were somehow separate entities. Worse, the organisation also echoed the racist stereotyping of the riots as the work of 'yobs' and petty criminals, attacking those involved for having no social conscience, and deploring, with no trace of irony, their lack of solidarity.[33] LO's refusal to initiate or engage consistently in political campaigns (anti-racism, anti-fascism, the social forum process, the EU constitution referendum) means that its interventions are generally made in reaction to events, be they those laid down in the electoral calendar, or when strikes and protests flare up. The organisation's ability to play a dynamic role in the development of the movement is therefore very limited.

The difficulties experienced by unions in organising among the young mean political issues can take on a much greater importance in establishing links between different groups of workers. Had anti-war activists gone out of their way to work with Muslims in building a united anti-war movement, for example, real potential existed for establishing genuine cooperation between the political left and immigrant-origin youth—something which has generally evaded the anti-racist movement in France. Instead the movement limited the prospects for such cooperation by putting terrorism on an equal footing with US imperialism, and choosing not to march through areas with large black and Arab populations. Such errors were then compounded when sections of the left chose to put the defence of secularism in schools before the fight against racism, supporting the imposition of a 'Republican' dress code which forbids Muslim girls to wear the hijab to school. This was a failure to fulfil one of the basic functions of the radical left, to mount an effective defence of stigmatised minorities under attack. It had wider repercussions. There is no guarantee that the left would have found it possible to provide an alternative arena for the expression of the revolt by the youth of the suburbs last year if it had offered genuine, practical solidarity to them during the hijab affair or actively attempted to involve them in the anti-war movement. But at the very least the left would have been better placed to engage in the political discussions about what to do next which took place in the suburbs after the rioting.

'In this splintered, reactive conflictuality, frequently conveying reactions of anger and revolt,' wrote one commentator in the wake of the 2003 strikes, 'there still exists a risk of spontaneous aggregation and open social crisis'.[34] The expression of this anger is taking place in a situation characterised by chronic political instability and in the broader context of the class recomposition outlined above. It puts great responsibility on the left to engage consistently with struggles of all kinds and to find ways of working with people who may have different ideas about how change can be brought about. More broadly, the revolutionary left, as elsewhere in Europe, has a dual task. It is, first, to unite with those wanting to fight neo-liberalism and to provide coherent political and electoral alternatives to mainstream social democracy. The magnificent campaign against the EU constitution organised by the radical left in the spring of 2005 showed that the potential for such an alliance exists in France on an even greater scale than those already build in Britain and Germany. And it is, second, to maintain and to build independent revolutionary currents within the wider movement in order to prove in practice that consistent, viable and effective opposition to neo-liberalism can only be achieved by those seeking to replace capitalism with a social order offering the equality and emancipation which social democracy has never been able to deliver, in any of its guises.

NOTES

1: *Le Monde*, 13 November 2005.

2: Mouvement des entreprises de France.

3: Canada has experienced a similar fall without a 35-hour week. See P Askenazy, *Les Désordres du travail* (Paris, 2004).

4: F Fukuyama, in *Quelle ambition pour la France?* (Paris, 2002), cited in P Ariès, *Misère du sarkozysme: Cette droite qui n'aime pas la France* (Paris, 2005), p251.

5: Cited in P Ariès, as above, p47.

6: N Baverez, *La France qui tombe* (Paris, 2003), cited in P Ariès, as above, p35.

7: *Le Monde*, 14 May 2005.

8: E Mignon, *Le Monde*, 3 September 2004, cited in P Ariès, as above, pp118-119.

9: For a more detailed narrative of these movements, see the following articles in *International Socialism*: J Wolfreys, 'Class Struggles in France' (Autumn 1999); 'The Centre Cannot Hold: Fascism, the Left and the Crisis of French Politics' (Summer 2002); and 'How France's Referendum Caught Fire' (Summer 2005).

10: J-M Pernot, 'Pleins et déliés de la contestation. Du repli de la grève au mouvement sur les retraites', in S Béroud and R Mouriaux, *L'année sociale 2003-4* (Paris, 2004), p122.

11: M Wieviorka, 'L'air du temps est favourable au movement surfant sur les peurs et les inquiétudes', *Libération*, 14 October 2005.

12: With, notes Moschonas, the possible exception of the Enlightenment bourgeoisie. G Moschonas, *In the Name of Social Democracy: The Great Transformation: 1945 to the Present* (London, 2002), p305.

13: As above, pp307-308.

14: As above, pp308-309.

15: E-A de Sellière, *Le Monde*, 27 January 2000.

16: E Maurin, *L'Egalité des possibles: La nouvelle société française* (Paris, 2002), pp10-11.

17: As above, p36.

18: As above, p46.

19: See N Mayer, *Ces Français qui votent FN* (Paris, 1999), pp75-97.

20: M Hout, C Brooks and J Manza, 'The Persistence of Classes in Post-Industrial Societies', *International Sociology*, vol 8, no 3, 1993. Cited in G Moschonas, as above, p308.

21: J-M Pernot, *Syndicats: lendemains de crise?* (Paris, 2005), pp313-314.

22: M Pialoux and S Beaud, *Retour sur la condition ouvrière* (Paris, 1999).

23: N Parsons, *French Industrial Relations in the New World Economy* (Oxford, 2005), p167.

24: *Le Monde*, 7 December 1995.

25: E Agrikolianski, O Filleule, N Mayer (eds), *L'altermondialisme en France: La longue histoire d'une nouvelle cause* (Paris, 2005), p311.

26: As above.

27: S Béroud and R Mouriaux, as above, pp22-23.

28: J-M Pernot in S Béroud and R Mouriaux, as above, p122.

29: C Larose, S Béroud, R Mouriaux and M Rabhi, *Cellatex: Quand l'acide a coulé* (Paris, 2001).

30: S Béroud, *Les Robins des Bois de l'énergie* (Paris, 2005).

31: G Moschonas, as above, pp300-301.

32: G Filoche, 'Les braises durables du mouvement social', www.legrandsoir.info/article.php3?id_article=2730).

33: *Lutte Ouvrière*, 4 November; 11 November 2005.

34: J-M Pernot in S Béroud and R Mouriaux, as above, p134.

The riots did not take place in a 'political desert'

Abdellali Hajjat

The deaths on Thursday 28 October 2005 in Clichy-sous-Bois (north east of Paris) of two French kids of immigrant workers, Zyad Benna and Bouna Traoré, set off riots in working class outer city areas (*banlieues*) that have been the most significant (both geographically and symbolically) in the history of France. Their deaths and the gassing of the local Bilal mosque were the spark that ignited the powderkeg that for two decades has been growing in size in the *banlieues* of the big cities. Police violence is no rarity in these areas, which have become used to endless identity checks, to strong-arm arrests based on the way people look, and to police custody where anything goes. Such daily occurrences explain why the two youngsters from Clichy-sous-Bois were running away.

From the first riots in the Minguettes at Vénissieux (near Lyons) in 1981 onwards, revolt has been confined to a particular area, that of the victims, but what recent events demonstrate for the first time in French history is that it was a police 'blunder' that ignited such a blaze of urban violence. The minister of the interior played a circumstantial role, but the structural role was 20 years of government, both 'left' and right, culminating in the failure of French *banlieues*.

The causes of this popular fury are social and political, not ethnic or religious. It is not a question of some 'failure to integrate', a meaningless

---

This article first appeared on Oumma.com on 30 November 2005.

phrase these days, in that there is a dangerous tendency to privilege culturalist explanations (if they don't integrate, it's because of their 'cultural difference'). This uprising could only develop in a complex of economic, social, political and spatial inequalities generated by the crisis of post-industrial capitalism and anti-social public policy. In the 'country of the rights of man', which prides itself on how well the 'French model of integration' works (as opposed, falsely, to the US or British 'multicultural' model), working class neighbourhoods are on the way to ghettoisation (a phenomenon symmetrical to the less talked about ghettoisation of rich neighbourhoods.) But the fire would not have flared up so much if Nicholas Sarkozy, the minister of the interior, had been less provocative. He did not hesitate to condemn the young inhabitants of working class neighbourhoods, talking about 'scum' to be 'hosed clean' in a way that would have been denounced as incitement to hatred and ethnic cleansing if the words been uttered by the leader of the National Front. Also open to question were his claims that Zyad Benna and Bouna Traoré had been involved in burglary, and that the teargas had not been thrown by the police but by the young people themselves. But Sarkozy is not alone in his contempt for working class neighbourhoods. When certain 'left' leaders use the terms 'little savages' or '*banlieue* Le Pens' they embark on the same logic that turns classes into dangerous classes.

Certainly there was wide discussion in the French media about the social and political causes of the riots (unusually they mostly avoided making a mishmash with the 'threat of fundamentalism', unlike Sarkozy). But what some left-wing sociologists and/or journalists have also stressed is the way in which working-class neighbourhoods, where most French or foreign descendants of post-colonial immigration live, have become a political 'vacuum' or 'desert'. They claim that France has been the stage of 19th century style *jacqueries* (directionless rampages) led by 'lumpen subproletarians' 'lacking class consciousness'.The implication is that, if there had been a political force organising the revolt, its entire subversive potential could have been geared to a revolutionary logic. Comfortable in their position as journalists or academics, they unhesitatingly bemoan the 'handicap' suffered by the rioters, who cannot in the end fit into the framework of Marxist thought—as opposed to workers conscious of belonging to the working class. But to explain this lack of political representation they ignore the question as to why the French left has proved unable to act as a political horizon for the inhabitants of working class neighbourhoods, especially one that determines the activity of militants who are immigrants or have a post-colonial immigrant background.

The working class *banlieues* are not a 'political desert', but they are moving in that direction as the autonomous movement of immigrants disintegrates. Since the end of the 1960s this movement has had to confront obstacles that have reduced its capacity to act autonomously. Its dynamic has been repressed, absorbed and manipulated. Only if we go back over the abortive revolts of the immigrants and their children can we understand the present vacuum in working class *banlieues*.

There have been numerous attempts at politically organising the post-colonial immigration in France—from the Movement of Arab Workers (MTA, 1970-76,) to the Immigrant Movement of the Banlieues (MIB, founded in 1995), via Divercité and left wing Muslim associations such as the Union of Young Muslims (UJM). The activism of immigrants (or their descendants) found expression in a set of political images that corresponded to economic, political and urban changes in French society—the pre-1962, anti-colonialist 'wretched of the earth', the 'immigrant worker', the '*sans papiers*' (immigrants lacking documents), the '*beur*' (French-born children of North Africans), the 'Muslim', etc. Contrary to the miserabilist view conveyed by some sociologists, the uprising in the *banlieues* has a rich history of over 20 years of political experience.

Repression

Not every local organisation or post-colonial immigrant organisation has a politically subversive language. In reality there is a divide between, on the one hand, mutual help organisations of a social and/or religious nature, anti-illiteracy organisations, organisations to help with civic duties, etc, which are heavily dependent on municipal subsidies, and, on the other, organisations with clearly spelt out political aims, generally of the radical, anti-colonialist, anti-Zionist left. The public authorities have favoured the former because they play an obvious role in 'sterilising' local revolt. The latter have always been subject to repression by national and local government, which uses different methods depending on political context.

Thus the MTA—an organisation with hundreds of members that was close to the Maoists in La Gauche Prolétarienne, had deep roots in the 'Arab' areas of Paris and Marseilles, was fiercely anti-Zionist and was the forerunner of immigrant struggles—was literally decimated by the repressive policies of the interior ministry of the Giscard d'Estaing government (1974-81). Its capacity for organising a 'general strike' against racism in September 1973 was perceived as a threat to public order and its foreign militants were systematically harassed, deported or imprisoned, above all because of their support for the Palestinian cause and for organising strikes by *sans papiers*.

The struggles over Sonacotra (the government-appointed body for running immigrant hostels) of 1974-80—for improved living conditions in an institution of social and political control directly inherited from French colonisation in Algeria—had to cope with a de facto alliance between the French government, associations based on countries of origin (Algeria, Morocco, Senegal, etc), the trade unions (CGT, CFDT, etc) and Sonacotra itself. This alliance made it possible for hundreds of militant immigrant workers to be expelled forcibly. Mobilisations against racist and/or police crimes suffered particularly from police repression after the murder of Djilali Ben Ali in the Goutte d'Or area of Paris (1971), Mohammed Diab at Versailles (1972), Thomas Claudio at Vaulx-en-Velin (1990), Youssef Khaïf at Le Val Fourré (1991), Abelkader Bouziane at Dammarie-lès-Lys (Seine-et-Marne, 1997), etc. All these protests against racist police acting with impunity and mostly ignored by the mainstream media were subject to attack under cover of legal actions for libel or disturbing public order—and generally in the form of fleets of riot police wagons or operations by special crack police forces. Since 9/11 and the rise of Islamophobic psychosis, some Muslim organisations in Lyons have experienced another kind of repression—the removal of subsidies following a memo from the intelligence services of the interior ministry, the impossibility of getting insurance or opening a bank account, etc. The repression directed at the dynamic of these political movements has played a key role in destabilising immigrant activists.

Absorption

The second phenomenon responsible for depoliticisation is political absorption. The most significant example was the March for Equality in 1983. Following the hospitalisation of Toumi Djaïdja after being shot by a policeman at Les Minguettes, a new organisation, SOS Avenir Minguettes, decided to organise a peaceful march modelled on Gandhi's marches, with the support of a section of the Catholic Church personified by Father Christian Delorme and associated networks of the Socialist Party. The simple, humanist demand was the right to life. 'Stop shooting us like rabbits,' demanded the marchers. Setting off from Marseilles with some 30 people on 15 October 1983, the march paraded through Paris on 3 December with more than 100,000 demonstrators. Nothing like this had been seen before in the anti-racist movement. It had a dynamic effect in the *banlieues*, but very quickly the activists from a post-colonial immigrant milieu who had organised '*collectifs jeunes*' to welcome the march realised how the march had become an instrument of the Socialist government. They realised that though the left welcomed the generous and all-embracing slogans it turned a deaf ear when its political power was challenged and the Palestinian question was raised. The high point of manipulation of the '*beur* movement' came at the time of the second march for equality, Convergence 1984, which was submerged in a tide of little yellow hands, 'Touche pas à mon pote' ('Don't touch my mate') from SOS Racisme.

The 1980s generation of militants were caught in a bind. On the one hand, there were possibilities of upward social mobility and the political opportunities offered by the Socialist government. On the other, there was the desire for autonomy shown in a refusal either to compromise with established power or to subscribe to treating immigrant struggles as a form of folklore. The municipalities in working class *banlieues* began to take the demands of this politicised youth seriously after the mobilisations and riots of the 1980s. But a fatal divorce[a] with the left began to operate in these areas.

Many activists from a post-colonial immigrant milieu tried to work in non-governmental political parties (the Greens, the Ligue Communiste Révolutionnaire, etc), but the experience quickly led to a dead end. The contradictions between the language of politics and militant practice led them to abandon these parties. Such, for example, was the case of Sakina Bakha, elected to the regional council of Rhône-Alpes, who was able to observe the xenophobic and/or paternalistic practices of some of those elected from the so-called left. The far left might bemoan the absence, or minimal presence, in their ranks of activists from a post-colonial immigrant milieu and from working class localities, but the recent political history of immigration shows that these parties are more part of the problem of weak politicisation in these areas than the solution to it. The political and trade

a: Cf O Masclet, *La gauche et les cités: Enquête sur un rendez-vous manqué* [*The Left and Working Class Estates: Inquiry into a Failed Encounter*] (Paris, 2003).

union left have abandoned these working class areas and the *altermondialist* movement has never set foot there. The issue of the headscarf, and the wave of Islamophobia that followed, helped consolidate an anti-*banlieue* consensus, which prevented any real enlargement of their activist base.

It was in this context of growing disillusion with the left that these areas witnessed the birth of numerous Muslim-based organisations towards the end of the 1980s. Some completely glossed over political questions and devoted themselves to cultural matters. Others, fewer in numbers, such as the UJM in Lyons (formed in 1987), maintained a language of political demands. However, if Muslim organisations have roots in certain working class estates, the movement of conversion to Islam is marginal and the vast majority of the inhabitants are untouched by any tendency to religious politicisation.

The third obstacle to politicisation is what one might define as activists escaping from their immigrant milieu through culture. From the late 1970s to the present, the 'immigration media' have flourished on the French media scene. The idea at the outset, from the first free radio stations (Radio Soleil in Paris, Radio Gazelle in Marseilles) to the Im'média agency directed by Mogniss H Abdallah, was to go onto the offensive against the autism of the French media over immigration questions. The majority of these media outlets, which had been created by activists (from the MTA or from the *beur* movement), may have been conceived as political tools to express the challenge of working class districts. But what is noticeable is their slow process of autonomisation from the political sphere to become media outlets 'like any other'. The challenge brought by hip-hop, which has been and remains an essential vector of politicisation in French suburbs, has undergone the same process of political sterilisation under pressure from radio stations (Skyrock in particular) and the record companies financing groups that conform to the dominant ideology of profit and sexism. Standardised commercial hip-hop has access to the means of production and distribution out of all proportion to the few rare groups, such as La Rumeur, which have managed to preserve the radical spirit of their origins.

Petty bourgeoisification

The fourth element explaining this desertification is contained in a paradox—the political consciousness of local activists emerged alongside an accumulation of scholarly and cultural capital (a higher level of study than the average, a more refined understanding of French society, etc) which predisposed them to move away from working-class areas. At the same time, the conditions under which politicisation took place became less favourable. While education in the 1980s made upward social mobility more likely, in the 1990s the deterioration in state schooling, the withdrawal of subsidies from organisations, and anti-social public policies prevented the political renewal of a minority of the young inhabitants on the estates. The growing insecurity of French society affected working-class areas much more strongly, and even the potential activists. After a youthful commitment to activity in associations, a commitment often synonymous with 'individual sacrifice', many decided to 'behave'—because the status of 'professional activist' lacked social stability, and because of the absence of tangible political perspectives. It is not uncommon, therefore, to find such people occupying positions as representatives or advisers to departmental councils and town halls, or following some other career where their experience and understanding of working class areas can be 'given value'. Most no longer live in run-down estates but in the better off areas that surround them.

The phenomenon of 'petty bourgeoisification' also affects the cadres of the protest organisations, who are ironically nicknamed 'bo-bar'—bourgeois barbus, or 'bearded ones'. The French government's policy of socially and politically incorporating the Muslim faith gave a breathing space to those Muslim activists cut off from the dynamics of opening up to the social movement that the network Collectif des Musulmans de France embraced. Here again, the incapacity of a section of the altermondialist movement not to fall for the hysterics over Islamic fundamentalism (crystallised in the Ramadan affair at the 2003 European Social Forum) strongly compromised the integration of its activists into legitimate politics, which will prove to be highly contentious in the struggles to come.

Unsurprisingly, in the light of the political and social phenomena that have distorted the political space of working-class districts, the political formation of the young inhabitants of the estates is almost non-existent. The riots in 2005 amply demonstrate this, and in appealing to the 'elders' we are witnessing a real political regression. With the municipalities destroying local involvement with their restrictive budgetary policy, they are resorting to calling for new ethnic 'firefighters' to calm or pacify people. What the riots have clearly shown is how difficult it is for 'elders' to exercise influence over young adolescents on the estates—some activists, whether religious or not, were even threatened physically in the worst of the fires. The rupture between the generations, between the activists with their origins in those areas and the working class kids, is unmissable. This rupture is a major obstacle to constructing a political force in working class *banlieues*.

Political routes

This catastrophic situation is a real challenge for the radical left. It knows it is handicapped by its lack of representativeness and is seeking 'transmission belts' within the estates. But it is also a challenge for the autonomous immigrant movement, which is radically questioning its history and political direction. No new major political initiative to fill the political chasm in working class districts can succeed unless the contentious 20-year relationship between the left and the estates is reviewed. A critical scrutiny of the history of immigrant struggles in the working class *banlieues* is the indispensable condition for moving forward and for avoiding a repetition of the same political errors. The riots are a summons to immigrant activists in these areas to take up a historic responsibility, without which no clear left-wing alternative project is possible.

Painful though this view may be, the route to politicisation is not closed. Unexpectedly, the 2005 riots were the product of young people with no history of the police or the courts. They felt the need to express themselves violently against injustice and police highhandedness. Contrary to the lies peddled by Sarkozy (who had all the figures from his security services), it was not a matter of fighting criminality in working class districts. The state of emergency was declared in order to repress a protest that was becoming more and more political—which was literally questioning the state's monopoly of violence. It was not the Republic, the nation or democracy that was being questioned, but the state as an institution of repression and subjection of the oppressed in this country.

Research to establish the personal development of every rioter would be of interest. We might be surprised to discover that the 'depoliticised', the 'maladjusted' and the 'wretched', who are often spoken of condescendingly on the left, are really very clear about the way society functions. One of the positive aspects of the 2005 riots will have been the strengthening of political consciousness by those living on the estates and/or by activists from a post-colonial immigrant background. As with the 1960s riots by blacks in the US, the uprising is a phenomenon with a hook to the future—you can make the public listen, you can change the world, you are not condemned to inertia and to waiting for the Messiah. You can take your destiny in your own hands.

The working class *banlieues* have seen a political dynamic come to life. In Vénissieux and in Clichy-sous-Bois spaces have been created for discussion in one form or another. Yesterday's activists, sickened by political involvement over the last 20 years, are coming back to the fore in local situations. Despite differences between local situations, one can draw up the same assessment—it is possible for a significant political force to exist in working-class areas, and it could be given concrete form in the municipal elections in 2008. For this dynamic to take hold in the months to come, what is required for its consolidation is to go back over the political history of these districts and/or of post-colonial immigration (its successes and failures), to take stock of the phenomena explaining the political desertification, to reflect on the practices of the activists (above all on the way power is managed at the heart of a movement), and to create a clear political project for the future. This presupposes overcoming the breach between the generations (by transmitting over 20 years of experience) and above all taking one's time. The autonomous immigrant movements and movements in working-class *banlieues* have for too long followed political timetables imposed from the outside—social forums, the headscarf affair, and legal actions have been just so many events diverting attention. It is better to sow the seeds of mobilisations to come than to stumble, as at present, over dry and arid soil.

At the risk of being criticised for using hyperbole, what needs underlining is that the riots are something unique in the history of France. They have to be the electric shock galvanising the formation of a new political generation in working class suburbs.

Dossier: Reform and revolution in Venezuela

Venezuela has caught the imagination of people internationally. Three times in three years the country's upper class, supported by the Bush administration, tried to get rid of Hugo Chavez—once with a coup, once with a lockout and finally with a recall referendum. On each occasion mobilisations of the lower classes defeated them. Since then accounts of real positive reforms from the 'Bolivarian Revolution' have been greeted with enthusiasm in a world where its seems that only neo-liberal counter-reforms are the order of the day. And the enthusiasm has been heightened by Chavez's upstaging of Bush at November's Summit of the Americas.

But enthusiasm often slides into a way of looking at Venezuela which is the obverse of that in the mainstream media. They depict what is happening in terms of one man—and much of the left accept that depiction. It is an approach which is inadequate for understanding real social and political struggles. Such struggles necessarily involve a multiplicity of actors—and not just individual actors, but social forces, classes in motion as masses of people see for the first time the chance of lifting the weight of oppression from their lives. From these emerge contradictory notions of what should be done and where society should be going.

The process in Venezuela is far from over. There have been significant reforms, but not yet revolution in the classic sense of the term. The ruling class remains intact, symbolised by the continuing existence of the Venevision and Globovision media empires that backed the attempted coup against Chavez. And most of the old state remains in place, putting a brake on further reform even when this is called for from the president. It certainly does not provide a guaranteed mechanism for transforming society in the interests of the mass of workers, the urban poor and the peasantry.

This is producing a growing debate inside the popular movements as to the way forward—a debate which parallels that of workers' movements of the 20th century over reform and revolution.

Here we present the views of some of the protagonists. On the one hand there are interviews with Chavez's vice-president, Vincente Rangel, and with Marta Harnecker, often described as an important adviser to Chavez. On the other there is an interview with one of the country's new left wing union leaders, a statement by certain social movements, and a text from two members of the recently formed Party of Revolution and Socialism.

In the laboratory of the revolution

An interview with Marta Harnecker

Marta Harnecker is a Chilean journalist and activist, exiled in Cuba after the coup of 1973, who is now working in the Ministry of Popular Participation in Venezuela. A book of her interviews with Hugo Chavez has recently been published in English. This interview is translated from ***Siete sobre Siete*** *in Uruguay.*

What stage is the Bolivarian Revolution at?

At the stage of the deepening of the revolution—of an effort to make the state apparatus more efficient, fighting against corruption, purifying the police and the organs of state security, and working to deepen participatory democracy and to implement a different economic logic, a humanist logic based on solidarity.

What have been the most important steps in the political process since Chavez defined the socialist direction of the Bolivarian Revolution?

I might surprise you when I say that there has not been any step relevant to that definition. What is happening is that practice has been showing the leadership of the process that the humanist logic based on solidarity that they have been implanting at every level, especially on the economic terrain, has been clashing with the capitalist logic of profit with every step taken.

For example, you cannot create agricultural co-operatives or produce basic industrial products successfully if the state does not take on a big role in the buying and selling of such products. You can't control the impact of the increase in monetary circulation resulting from the enormous number of grants the government is giving to all the Venezuelans studying in the various *misiones* if you don't find a way of controlling the prices of the products that make up the basic diet of the poorer section of the population. How can you resolve this within a capitalist logic where the motor of the system is profit and not the satisfaction of human need?

An emergency measure adopted when the opposition wanted to stop the process through the attempt to make the mass of the population give in through hunger during the lockout at the end of 2002—the purchase of foodstuffs for improvised popular markets—showed the way. Today there are hundreds of popular markets across the whole country, accounting for 40 percent of food consumption, offering products much cheaper than the private commercial establishments. Their prices have been maintained through state subsidies at the same level as at the beginning of the experiment. Moreover, this is encouraging firms to produce stuff domestically that had previously been imported, by assuring them a market for their products and avoiding intermediaries.

As you can see, 'socialism' in Venezuela did not start when Chavez announced it at the beginning of 2005, but considerably earlier. And I speak of socialism in quotation marks because in reality what is happening in Venezuela is not socialism but a road which can lead to a society ruled by a humanistic logic based on solidarity, in which all human beings can achieve their full development.

Chavez does not deny that at the beginning he thought it was possible to resolve the deep economic and social problems of Venezuela through a third way—he believed it was possible to humanise capitalism, but history has shown him this is not possible.

The insistence on socialism as the only road comes, paradoxically, at the same time as efforts are being made to incorporate the private sector in the economic plans of the government.

This is something contradictory for the classic vision of socialism as a society in which all the means of production must be in the hands of the state, eliminating the roots of private property. In this classic vision the emphasis is put on property and not on control of the means of production.

When Chavez speaks of the socialism he intends to be built in Venezuela he always makes it clear he means 'socialism of the 21st century', and not a copy of previous socialist models.

What is central in Venezuela today is getting rid of poverty. A short while ago I heard a young leftist criticise the vice-president of the republic as a reformist because he had said the main enemy was poverty, and that it was necessary to eliminate poverty instead of talking of the necessity of eliminating the bourgeoisie! What is the point of attacking private enterprises at the moment? These are radical slogans that have little to do with an analysis of the real situation. Does this young man not understand that to get rid of poverty it is necessary among other things to create productive employment, and that the reactivation of the private sector has been the principal source of employment in the country in recent months? Why doesn't he ask himself why the Venezuelan bourgeoisie, which threw everything into trying to get rid of Chavez in the past, is desperate to collaborate with the government today?

Even Lenin himself did not think it was necessary to eliminate private property in order to begin to construct socialism. Few people have read one of the first decrees of the newly established Soviet government—the decree over private publicity, which started from the premise that those private capitalists disposed to collaborate with the government would have to have space to publish their advertisements. It was not the socialists who marginalised the capitalists in Russia—it was the capitalists who marginalised themselves by refusing to collaborate with the Soviet government and opting for civil war.

In analysing this problem one must not forget the question of the correlation of forces. So long as the bourgeoisie feels strong and believes it can dominate the situation through ballot boxes or weapons, it is understandable for it not to be disposed to collaborate with a revolutionary project that goes against the logic of capitalism. But what can the Venezuelan bourgeoisie do when it has suffered a triple defeat—the failure of the military coup in April 2002, its failure to achieve its objective through the lockout at the end of that year, and its failure in the referendum of 2004? There remains no alternative for it other than to leave the country or to collaborate with the government in return for credit facilities and an assured market.

But isn't there a danger in coexistence with the bourgeoisie?

Clearly there is a danger. The logic of capital will seek to impose itself. This means a constant struggle to see who defeats who. We are at the beginning of a long process. The control of political power, control of the exchange rate, a correct credit policy so that capitalists who receive loans accept conditions determined by the government—these are the formulae used by the Bolivarian government to make the medium and small Venezuelan businesses promise to collaborate with the government's programme, of which the axis is the elimination of poverty. These were precisely the sectors most affected by neo-liberal globalisation.

But we must not forget that we come from a society in which the logic of capital rules, with a culture which inclines both the owners of capital and the worker to work for individualist objectives. So socialism can only triumph over capitalism if it puts under way, together with the transformation of the economy, the transformation of people. To the extent that people see the positive effects of the new attempted economic model oriented to the new humanistic logic of soldarity, to the extent that they see the defeat of individualism, consumerism and the profit motive in their everyday practice, they will arrive at the same conclusions that Chavez has—the only alternative to the harmful consequences of neo-capitalism is socialism. It is significant that recent opinion polls show that 40 percent of the population already consider socialism something positive. This is a great advance, considering the ideological bombardment to which they have been subjected. The practical effects of the measures of solidarity adopted by the government are weapons more powerful than all the media missiles launched by the opposition.

And, being clear that we are dealing with two contradictory economic models, it is fundamental that an important part of the resources of the state go to finance and develop the state sector of the economy, since control of strategic industries is the best way to ensure the triumph of the new humanistic logic of solidarity and adequately to fulfil the national plan aimed at eliminating poverty.

The search for collaboration with private capital must only take place to the extent that it allows advance in this sense.

This definition implies a conceptual change in what constitutes 'socialism' in the 21st century and in a Latin America under severe US hegemony. What theoretical innovations are most urgent?

More than theoretical innovations, I think there were many elements to be found in the classic Marxist thinkers that were ignored or forgotten. 'Socialism in the 21st century' would have to take them up again at the same time as having to invent new solutions to the new problems created by the change in the world in these last years. One of them, socialism, is the most democratic society. Lenin said, 'Capitalism equals democracy for the elite, socialism democracy for the great majority of the people.' Another is the theme of workers' control. You can have state property, but without workers' control it is not socialism. On the other hand you can have private property under workers' control and perhaps that can be closer to socialism than the first case. Yet another—every country must find its own road to socialism. That which can or cannot be done will depend to a great degree on the correlation of forces in the country and at the global level.

If we want to be effective radicals, and not just radicals in words, we have to commit ourselves to the daily work of building up the social and political forces that enable us to bring about the changes we want. How much more fruitful politics be would if those who go in for words were committed to this daily militancy instead of seeing their writing as militancy.

A view from the top

Interview with José Vincente Rangel

José Vincente Rangel is one of the members of the Venezuelan government with decades of political experience. It began in the Movement for Socialism (MAS), the party formed by ex-guerrillas who split from the country's Communist Party in the 1970s. But while MAS and many of its former leaders are now aligned with the country's right wing opposition, Rangel has become one of the more important of Chavez's collaborators, first as minister of defence and foreign affairs, and then as vice-president since the attempted coup in April 2002. This interview first appeared in the German weekly ***Freitag****.*

Why is Chavez risking a clash with the United States?

We don't think the US is now necessarily in a position to look for a conflict with a country that wants to be respected. Chavez has clearly distinguished between the US government and its people. It is not as easy to isolate Venezuela as it was in 2002. We have developed many international relations, more than ever before in our history. If there is anybody that is isolated in the world, it is the US, or at least the Bush administration. For a long time many governments have been making concessions to the arrogance of power of the US. They are afraid of the US and so do not say what they think. In our case, we do not have any fear for the future.

What are the objectives of your foreign policy?
We want a multipolar world, without the hegemonies that exist at present. For that reason we propose a refoundation and democratisation of the UN, which functions according to the logic of the world order established after the Second World War. The Organisation of American States, the OAS, was until a few years ago a sort of backyard of the US. Today that is no longer so. A second central aim of our foreign policy is the struggle against poverty—the most important present-day problem, which has to be at the centre of all policy.

In recent years Venezuela has promoted the establishment of a petroleum consortium involving various state enterprises and, with Petrocaribe, has formed a petroleum federation in the Caribbean. In addition, various states receive Venezuelan oil at advantageous prices. How do these measures fit into the foreign policy you have just outlined?
These measures are making concrete a policy of integration. For decades there has only been the rhetoric of integration in Latin America. Today the integration of Latin America and the Caribbean has a political dimension. Venezuela is a power in terms of energy. We dispose of considerable reserves of petroleum and are the sixth country in the world in terms of gas. And the situation is favourable to us geostrategically. Venezuelan oil is four days from the US market, Saudi oil four weeks. Each country has comparative economic advantages—Argentina has enormous agrarian production, Brazil its industry, and ourselves our enormous energy reserves. But what matters for us is not only our petroleum, but that we act in solidarity and seriously in the interest of Latin American and Caribbean integration.

Hugo Chavez in an interview on the US TV channel ABC spoke of a Plan Balboa for US interventions against Venezuela. Do you think that the US would risk a second military intervention after everything that has happened in Iraq?
There are two logics as regards this. One is contained in your questions and says the US already has enough difficulties in Iraq to get involved in other, perhaps bigger, ones. But often imperialism does not behave in particularly rational ways. If it did, it would not have invaded Vietnam. There is something like a logic of desperation. And the Bush government, it becomes clearer every day, is very desperate. There are few things more dangerous than an erratic giant.

Rationality would advise the US not to attack Venezuela. But an irrational attempt at intervention is conceivable and we have to be prepared. Part of this preparation consists in making public possible scenarios for intervention.

The Venezuelan state, as the owner of the CITCO network of petrol stations in the US, has announced that it will offer heating oil at advantageous prices to community organisations, schools and old people's homes in poor areas of the US. What is intended by this?
Three much wider objectives are linked. We want, in the first place, to build three new refineries in the US, since the refining of oil is the bottleneck that is at present making prices shoot up. In the second place, we want to extend the network of petrol stations to 14,000. And thirdly, we want to give an impulse to the social component—that is, to something completely foreign to US enterprises. It is possible to offer schools and hospitals in poor neighbourhoods heating oil and petrol at concessionary prices without the Venezuelan state suffering losses as a result.

Brazil is the most important partner in the Latin American integration that you propose. But President Lula has not lived up to the expectations you had of him. If the Workers Party loses the next Brazilian elections, will this make things much worse for Venezuela?
The result of the Brazilian elections remains open. Furthermore, I don't think what is taking place in Latin America can be explained very well by the existence of this or that government. What is involved is a social process that puts neo-liberalism in question. Politicians who ignore this will be cast aside. Just think of presidents like De la Rua in Argentina, Lucio Gutiérrez in Ecuador or Sáchez de Lozada in Bolivia. In this sense I am an optimist.

The opposition in Venezuela is hardly to be seen now. Rather it is the state itself that appears to be the principal obstacle to the 'Bolivarian process'. The apparatus puts obstacles in the way of the democratisation and self-administration that the communities seek. Your government, conscious of that, has deliberately instituted the misiones—numerous social programmes—outside the ministries. Wouldn't you have to destroy the state completely and create something completely new if you were thinking seriously of the emancipation of the Venezuelan people?
That is the pure truth. I subscribe completely to your critical observations. I live inside the monster and know what it is like. We have inherited the whole anachronistic bureaucracy of '*Puntifijismo*'—of the old dominant Social Democratic and Christian Democrat duopoly that still exists protected by the law. We cannot simply dismiss the functionaries. We have suspended people

we know to be corrupt, and the Supreme Court has declared these dismissals illegal. And that is how it is—those decisions show that we are in a state based on the rule of law.

The *misiones* are an attempt to get over the wall of bureaucracy—or at least to make it more permeable. We have achieved something in this respect—the creation of an alternative economic structure and an alternative bureaucracy. But we have to be on our guard to make sure the new bureaucracy does not result in something as bad as or even worse than that of the old republic. At the end of the day, the problem is not only with personnel which come from the old traditional parties, but with a political culture. The corruption is a state within the state—it reproduces itself continually. It is a difficult process, but also a very stimulating one, for the Venezuelan Revolution is not violent but respects the democratic rule of law.

Aren't the governmental parties of the left a problem even greater than that of the bureaucracy? Despite the revolutionary rhetoric, they inspire anything but confidence. There is an absurd struggle for positions and influence, and, as everywhere else, a great deal of corruption. Or at least, this is what is said by people who come from the urban movements who have to deal with administrations run by the parties of the left.

There is probably some truth in that. You must not forget that the *Bolivarianos* are part of the population. We are not dealing with Martians who have come to Earth to make a revolution. I think the accusations of corruption are often made lightly, but without doubt there have been many cases among the left. You cannot deal with the matter with concepts like angel and devil. That is to say, on my side are those dressed in white, and over there those who are corrupt. A process of transformations like ours is not a pure phenomenon. There is also corruption among us and a perverse obsession with positions.

Don't you have to break the structures of the state and democracy completely to change anything? Finally, is not representative democracy itself the cause of the problem?

We want to create a participatory democracy in which the people are the protagonists and exercise direct control over the public budgets. Here also the political culture plays a decisive role. If people are not conscious politically they can easily be manipulated. The attempt is being made to inspire a population who have not known anything of politics for 50 years to take their own decisions.

Venezuela: A glossary of terms

Leyes Habilitantes Presidential decrees introducing economic reforms such as the division of uncultivated land among the landless, granting shanty town dwellers ownership of the land they lived on, and reorganisation of management of the state oil monopoly, PDVSA.

PDVSA Oil monopoly nationalised in mid-1970s.

UNT New union federation formed from workers' organisations that opposed the 2002 coup and 2002-03 lockout.

MAS Party in some ways similar to Eurocommunism formed by ex-guerrillas in the early 1970s. Joined political mainstream in 1990s and split after joining anti-Chavez opposition. Important figures on both left and right of present-day Venezuelan politics come from it (Rangel was its presidential candidate in 1973).

Causa R Former left wing party with influence in unions that joined right wing opposition.

PTT Small pro-Chavez social democratic party.

CPV Small pro-Chavez Communist Party.

COPEI Christian Democrat Party, pillar of old pre-Chavez political establishment.

AD Social Democrat pillar of pre-Chavez political establishment.

Puntofijismo Arrangement by which pre-Chavez COPEI and AD parties alternated in office and divided patronage to supporters between them.

MVR Movement for the Fifth Republic, main Chavista party, high level of parliamentary support, but weak in terms of mass organisation.

Bolivarian circles Network of activist Chavista groups, merged into campaign groups to fight referendum 18 months ago and reported to be of little significance today.

Misiones Local centres for providing health, education and other welfare provision, financed by oil revenues and operating outside control of state bureaucracy.

The Party of Revolution and Socialism

Interview with Stalin Perez Borges

Stalin Perez Borges, trade union leader and longstanding Trotskyist militant, is at the heart of the revolutionary process in Venezuela. He is one of the four 'national coordinators' of the new—and today majority—trade union confederation, the UNT. He is also a member of the 'initiating committee' of a new party, the Party of Revolution and Socialism.

The following interview, conducted by Fabrice Thomas and Yannick Lacoste, was first published in the 22 September 2005 issue of ***Rouge****, weekly paper of the LCR (French section of the Fourth International).*

Can you give us your analysis of the present stage of the process that is under way in Venezuela?
The revolutionary process is continuing, but there are contradictions at work, and it is being undermined by corruption and inefficiency. In the recent elections for municipal and neighbourhood councils there were clashes between the rank and file of the 'Chavist' parties and sections of the party leaderships which bureaucratically imposed their candidates.

For the moment, the confrontation within the revolutionary process with these conservative bureaucratic governmental sectors is essentially verbal. But we think that it can in the future become much sharper, and lead—especially if the confrontation with imperialism becomes more tense—to a considerable deepening of the revolutionary situation.

What is the situation on the trade union level?
With the crises of the coup d'etat against Chavez in April 2002, the oil blockade by the bosses at the end of 2002 and the beginning of 2003, and the open treason of the old confederation, the CTV, the workers understood the need to take their trade union organisations into their own hands.

It is on the basis of this taking place on a nationwide scale that a new trade union confederation, the National Workers' Union (UNT) was established. The UNT has been considerably strengthened. It is now the confederation which comprises the majority of trade union organisations in the country.

It is difficult for the moment to give a figure for its real strength, but we can say that we have more than a million members and that the immense majority of unions are affiliated to the UNT. There are four tendencies. We are waiting for the next congress to know whether the bureaucratic sector—a reformist current which includes many corrupt and incompetent leaders—has the majority.

There is also the current of the 'Bolivarian Workers' Force', which is close to the government and which is also a reformist current. And then there is the 'classist current', many of whose cadres have been involved in the recent formation of the Party of Revolution and Socialism (PRS).

Can you tell us a bit more about the PRS?

The formation of the PRS is a consequence of this battle in the UNT. In most of the meetings that were organised across the country, the majority of those who intervened demanded the formation of a force distinct from those which today support Chavez—that is to say the MVR, the PPT, Podemos, the Communist Party and some others.

Seeing this need, we decided to establish the PRS. We think that in the present situation the workers need a political organisation which defends their interests, which is for class independence, and which has a well-defined anti-imperialist project.

Within our trade union current some people reproach us for having this project. We have to carry out both tasks—build the UNT as a trade union confederation that is independent of political parties and from the government, and build a political party for the workers.

The discussion around the formation of the PRS is at present being conducted by five distinct political groups. Other organisations will be able to broaden out our political platform, and we hope to announce the official launching of the PRS at the beginning of next year. We want to plan a founding congress. We already have a paper, *Opcion Socialista* (*Socialist Option*).

This project has involved us in organising a number of events. On 9 July we held a national meeting which brought together 450 people in Caracas. We have organised and will be organising other meetings throughout the country to proclaim the need for a new organisation. We have produced a political platform to serve as a basis for discussion.

What difference is there between the PRS and the official Chavist parties that exist at present?
The organisations in the leadership of the process are reformist, Stalinist or ultra-left, and they do not help to fight against the bureaucratic character of the state. It is necessary to ensure the transformation that the popular masses are demanding, which requires greater participation by ordinary people. The population has acquired—this is a characteristic of the process—a certain amount of power. It is no longer possible for leaders, ministers or bosses to impose anything on them.

This fight against bureaucracy, corruption and reformism is beginning to show results that are significant for the future of the country. To take one example, co-management—in other words, workers' control and direct participation by the workers in the running of a state enterprise or a private enterprise.

Some members of the government think that co-management is a risk, because enterprises that are strategically important, for example PDVSA (the nationalised oil company), must remain under the control of the country's leaders. In reality, they are afraid of participation by ordinary people. We are working a lot on these experiences of workers' control. Giving power to ordinary people can be the leap forward that is needed for the pursuit of the revolutionary process.

Chavez says that we have to give people power. Well, power is controlling your factory, controlling your community and controlling the people you elect. That's why we think that the PRS can have a strong influence on the workers. We are placing great hopes in the building of our organisation, in order to enable Venezuela to advance rapidly from pure statements of intention to real anti-imperialist measures.

Socialism for the 21st century and the Latin American revolution

Miguel Angel Hernandez and Emilio Bastidas presented their views at a seminar in Rio de Janeiro last summer. They are activists in Venezuela's Party of Revolution and Socialism (PRS). It was launched last July with, they say, 'a significant representation of the country's working class vanguard' from the UNT union federation and was 'co-directed' by two of its best known leaders, Orlando Chirino and Stalin Peréz Borges. 'There was also an important participation of leaders of the popular movements and students, including dissident sections of the official Chavista parties.' This article first appeared in Spanish on the website publication ***Rebelión****, and has been translated and edited by Chris Harman.*

Venezuela brings out important aspects of the political debate taking place in the left in Latin America and internationally. Like the rest of Latin America it has been the setting for the neo-liberal policies of privatisation and IMF-monetarist prescriptions, for the crises and fall of governments which have implemented them, for the implosion of the structures of the bourgeois democratic regimes relied on by imperialism and the bourgeoisie, for confrontation with US imperialism, for the development of powerful mobilisations and revolutionary triumphs, and also, very fundamentally, for the crisis of revolutionary leadership.

Without doubt, the most outstanding events have been the conclusive defeat suffered by US imperialism with the overturning of the Venezuelan coup of April 2002, the defeat of the bosses' lockout and the counter-revolutionary sabotage of the oil industry from December 2002 to February 2003, and the defeat for Bush and the bourgeois opposition in the referendum attempt to remove Chavez in August 2004.

What was decisive in Venezuela was the movement of the oil workers in retaking control of the PVDSA during the bosses' sabotage at the end of 2002. The triumph of the working class against the 63-day lockout was the real basis of everything happening in Venezuela today, even more than the defeat of the coup of 11 April 2002. But the workers' struggle did not stop after the defeat of that lockout. It continued through 2003 with the beginning of taking over factories that the pro-coup bosses declared bankrupt, claiming they had lost money as a result of the stoppage they themselves had organised. As a result of the mobilisation and perseverance of the workers, some have now been taken over by the government, as is the case with Invepal (a paper factory) and Inveval (maker of valves for the oil industry).

A veritable revolution is taking place within the workers' movement—what we call an 'anti-bureaucratic political revolution'. The old bureaucracy of the CTV collapsed, and every day there are referendums in which new leaders defeat bureaucrats who have controlled the unions for 20 or 30 years. And the process does not stop there. Often the new leaders do not measure up to the task and are replaced by still newer leaders emerging from the heat of the struggle. This revolutionary deepening has given rise to the new union federation, UNT, without doubt the biggest mass organisation in the country. What is more, within it the revolutionary classist and democratic current is consolidating itself, with comrades Orlando Chirino and Stalin Perez Borges at its head.

The pendulum of working class struggle is swinging from light industry located in the centre of the country to its heavy battalions, especially its electrical sector and the basic industries (aluminium, iron and steel). They are beginning to undergo the experience of co-management—which in some cases, especially the Alacase aluminium enterprise, is taking on connotations of workers' control (the election of directors by an assembly, the opening of the company books, the participation of workers in the organisation of production), presaging its spread to other sectors. The working class calls this 'revolutionary co-management' to distinguish it from the European example. Meanwhile in the electrical industry the workers are fighting and resisting their own government officials, including the minister, who are rejecting co-management.

All this has opened up discussion on the way forward to fundamental solutions for our people.

We say in the political declaration of the PRS:

> We are conscious of the advances made and positions conquered in the last six years of the revolutionary process. We are conscious of the significance of the *misiones,*[1] of the widening of democratic freedom, as with the inclusion of socio-economic questions in the *Leyes Habilitantes.*[2] However, we are also clear that much is still lacking when it comes to providing a structural response to the deep problems that exist among the poorest sections of our country. It is necessary to move forward to the expropriation of the big enterprises that are in the hands of the bourgeoisie and imperialism.

> There can be no socialism without expropriation of the big private means of production. None of the parties holding ministries or parliamentary seats are ready to carry the struggle against imperialism through to its ultimate consequences. Their practice amounts to introducing timid reforms to capitalism or taking ad hoc measures that do not resolve and cannot resolve the problem of exploitation and oppression. Every day it becomes clearer that under these parties the revolution will become blocked and we will not advance to socialism... This means we have urgently to put an unambiguous socialist project for a workers' government before the masses.

By contrast, Heinz Dieterich, a German-Mexican sociologist, who is an adviser to both Chavez and Subcomandante Marcos of the Zapatistas, defines clearly what 'socialism for the 21st century' means for him:

> There will be a long phase of coexistence between big and small enterprises. It requires a minimum of 30 years, in which all forms of property are necessary, for neither the state nor the enterprises alone can resolve the problems... This first phase has nothing to do with socialism... Proposals, like those from sections of the traditional left who continue thinking of a government of workers and peasants as if we were in the 1960s, are stupid' (*El Nacional*, 27 July 2005).

So the debate over the perspectives for revolution, over socialism and its objectives, is a red hot issue, not only in Venezuela but also for Bolivia, Ecuador and Argentina—for any country where the revolutionary process has overthrown governments and put the political regime into question. There have even been schemes like those of Heinz Dieterich or Martha Harnecker (sent by Fidel to advise Chavez) in Brazil and Uruguay where there has been the electoral triumph of the centre-left. The forgotten debate of the 1970s, lived out in all its intensity with the experiences of Chile and Nicaragua, is coming to the fore again.

Francis Fukuyama's 'End of History' had a very short life. Chavez raised 'socialism for the 21st century' as an alternative to capitalism for the first time at the World Social Forum in Porto Alegre (in Brazil) because of his need to respond to the left sectors and the radicalised masses of Venezuela. Now he is popularising it internationally. In doing so he has brought the old debate back into vogue.

Venezuela has been converted into the new Mecca of the worldwide left, given the crisis of Stalinism, and that Cuba and Castroism do not enthuse people as they used to. And the prestigious voice of Chavez projects a politics of 'socialism in the 21st century'. What is involved is not only a push to the left, to the side of revolution, with an apparently radical discourse, but also a designation of the content and characteristics of the socialism appropriate for the present century. But this designation has nothing to do with the scientific socialism elaborated by Marx, Engels, Lenin, Trotsky and Rosa Luxemburg, and even less with what is required by the masses on a world scale.

The socialism of President Chavez is a 'socialism' with something missing. It would be a species of capitalism in which the collaboration of classes would prevail. It would aim for the impossible, for a supposed social function for capital alongside a hypothetical more democratic distribution of wealth. This proposal is a chimera that has never materialised in any part of the world. Capital exists to reproduce itself without limits. It does not have any heart or any fatherland. It does not seek to satisfy need, but to guarantee an increasing rate of profit.

There has been developing for some time in Venezuela an ever-greater understanding between government and important sections of business and the multinationals. It takes concrete form in particular agreements favoured by the oil bonanza and has led Vice-President Rangel to affirm that 'now the government can count on sections of business that it could not before.'

There are flagrant contradictions and limitations to the Chavez project. The great challenge in front of us is how to clarify this for the masses. There are politically organised sections who believe that Chavez is heading towards socialism but that those immediately below him are opposed to this. They do not understand that there is a tight nexus between what the president 'says' and what his ministers 'do', as together they produce a politics that disorients and confuses, preventing the revolutionary sectors occupying space politically. Important groupings with a significant presence among the popular sectors and the youth are prisoners of this confusion and, without meaning to do so, have converted themselves into the best proponents of this government policy. They are creating expectations among the population that this government is 'ours', that it is of the workers and the people, that there exists a 'popular power' whose base it is only necessary to strengthen, that we are advancing to socialism and that it is only a question of getting rid of a number of government bureaucrats and remnants of the old political order who have disguised themselves as 'Bolivarians'.

This is a complex matter, but we are intensely optimistic, given the dynamic and depth of the Venezuelan revolutionary process.

The mass of the workers and the people have taken up Chavez's proclaimed 'socialism for the 21st century', interpreting the notion in the heat of the revolutionary process, and amplifying it so as to provide an answer to their immediate needs.

People are beginning to move forward from what is said to what is done: from words to street mobilisations; from verbal criticism to direct demands on officials and the president himself—demands to make the agrarian reform concrete; in defence of workers' co-management; against police abuse. We are assisting in practice in this new phase of the revolutionary process, as well as participating in the debate over socialism as a formula for overcoming capitalism.

For the PRS, deepening of the revolutionary process means, among other things, encouraging workers' and popular mobilisations while confronting the 'socialism' of Chavez with the demand for an emergency economic plan which takes advantage of the bonanza in the price of oil. We call: for a national plan of infrastructure and housing constructions so as to create employment for millions of people; for granting the same big wage increase to workers in public and private enterprise as the 60 percent that has gone to the armed forces; for no payment on the external debt, with a national referendum so that the people can pronounce on this; for an oil constituent process that permits discussion over hydrocarbon policy, the business portfolios of the PDVSA state oil company and the annulling of concessions to the multinationals.

Our proposal to build a revolutionary organisation has caused reactions from other political sectors in Venezuela, especially from some functionaries of the Chavez government. They insist that our proposal is 'inopportune' and that we should wait at least until the end of 2006. We have also faced objections from people who once worked to build a revolutionary organisation and then abandoned that so as to be part of 'broad' organisations. They argue that the Leninist conception with which we want to build the PRS is 'self-proclaimed' and closes us off from new sectors which could be interested in the process of building a new organisation.

But we have been drawing in leaders of the workers' movement and genuine leaders of the popular and student movements, finding with great surprise that they do not object to the building of a revolutionary party or demand that we hold back from democratic centralism. There are trade union, popular and peasant sectors which have been undergoing the experience of everyday struggle and are just breaking with the bureaucratic methods of the government parties or from being volunteers in the *misiones*. They find it easy to understand the need for the method of democratic centralism so as to win victories. These experiences are very significant for us, taking into account the immense influence that Chavez has over the popular sectors and the workers. Many activists from different regions and sectors have welcomed the construction of an organisation that struggles for socialism without bosses or bureaucrats, and a workers' government.

NOTES

1: Health and education services for the working class and the poor, provided by the government and financed out of oil revenues but without going through the old state bureaucracy.

2: The laws passed in 1999-2000 which granted certain reforms and caused the bourgeoisie to turn against Chavez.

Manifesto of the popular organisations

From ***Opción Socialista****, October 2005*

The reconfirmation of President Chavez in office in the referendum of August 2004 gave new breath to the struggle of the mass of the population to make the conquests of the revolutionary process concrete and effective. It spelt defeat for an offensive by the coupist and pro-imperialist oligarchy against the background of an economic situation marked by the bonanza of high oil revenues.

President Chavez responded to these hopes with the slogans of 'Deepen the revolution', 'Revolution within the revolution', and for a 'Leap forward'. More recently he has brought into debate the proposal to go beyond capitalism and to advance towards 'socialism of the 21st century'.

However, the feeling of the people, palpable in the community, in the workplaces and in the street, is that despite the important advances brought about by the *misiones* and the other social welfare policies, all this is not enough to resolve the principal structural problems underlying poverty, a product of capitalist exploitation from which the people are still suffering.

People complain that the ministries and the functionaries of the state institutions do not really implement the policies and measures announced by the president, that they do not give material effect to social and economic changes, or to the measures contained in the various *Leyes Habilitantes*. They notice resistance to breaking with capitalism. There is beginning to be frustration and a lack of confidence in the revolutionary commitment of the circles around the head of state, which he seems unable to control. Growing numbers of struggles demand a deepening of the revolution against the shackles of bureaucratism and corruption. The tendency is for more protests and mobilisations by distinct sectors demanding fulfilment of promises and effectiveness from governmental organisms.

People block roads, demanding homes. Communities take over hospitals protesting at the deficiencies of the health service. Sections of workers protest in the face of obstacles to the application of 'revolutionary co-management' and workers' control that managers and the 'parasitic technobureaucracy' put in their way. Peasants march in Caracas against the impunity of hired killers and for the agrarian revolution, denouncing the obstruction of the bureaucracy and corruption when it comes to the application of the land law. Indigenous people have opposed the invasion and destruction of their environment by multinationals out to mine coal with authorisation by organisms of the state. Young people have raised their voices, faced with the crimes and abuses of the old, unpurged, police.

President Chavez has provided justification for these protests and has said the organised people must demand that the 'negligent functionaries get out'. But the parties with ministers in the government and parliamentary representation have not shown any sign of the political capacity or will to resolve all this and to guarantee moving towards socialism of the 21st century.

This internal weakness of the revolutionary process leaves us even more vulnerable faced with the threats of imperialism, which continues to hold positions in important areas of Venezuela's productive and financial apparatus (oil, gas, minerals, electricity, telecommunications, industry, etc), and to encourage conspiracy with the alarming and prolonged impunity of the coupist right, its means of communication and its instruments of violence.

This is happening in contradiction to the anti-imperialist language and policy of defence of national sovereignty that President Chavez presents in the face of Latin America and the whole world. We have an internal enemy concealed in the process, a veritable Trojan horse that is opening the door to the interests of the right and the capitalist oligarchy, so exposing our flank to imperialism.

People are reacting to all this, for we continue to be immersed in a revolutionary process that is part of a class struggle, between the exploited and the exploiters, between the possessing classes and the dispossessed, between the poor and the rich.

All of these struggles point towards the deepening of the revolution within the revolution. They are struggles that are taking place, for the time being, in a dispersed and disarticulated manner. What is urgently needed is a greater unifying force from the social organisations and political fighters.

The first steps are already being taken to channel the struggles around the unity and solidarity of workers, peasants and the oppressed.

A united front is necessary, a big alliance of the social movements in struggle so that we can share objectives and actions, reinforcing each other mutually as class brothers in the mobilisations, and in the construction of popular power in the face of the offensives that the agents of capital are maintaining inside and outside our frontiers. The unity and strengthening of the struggle and popular mobilisation are our main levers for continuing to push the revolution forward. It is the only way of guaranteeing the promised 'leap forward' and of ensuring the Venezuelan revolutionary process truly goes towards the 'socialist revolution' instead of being reduced to a 'caricature of revolution', to use a phrase of Che's.

Fundamental to this is the role played by the working class as the leading class in the anti-capitalist revolutionary process—in alliance with the peasants and the organised popular communities—in order to conquer effectively the instruments of power, since we do not yet have in our hands the great decisions adopted by the organisms of the state.

As we unify the struggle, it is necessary that the social movements advance the development of popular power at all levels, with citizens' assemblies, with popular committees of different sorts, with popular constituent processes in all areas of social life, with communal and local councils. There has to be a conquest of genuine representation at the heart of state power and inside the National Assembly—representation that is really subject to and in permanent consultation with the popular movement, the workers, the peasants and the revolutionary rank and file, so opening the way to the direct exercise of government by the workers and the people.

The spokespeople must come from below, strictly linked to the social struggle and organisational processes, coming from and reflecting the discussions taking place at the base. Any other way would leave us still captives of the bureaucratic apparatus, freezing and pushing back the revolution as has happened in the past in the other countries.

Adherents Committee of Urban Lands (CTU), Committees of Health, Bolivarian Circles of various districts of Caracas, collectives pushing for social control, volunteers with the ***misiones****, members of the Popular Revolutionary Assembly of Coche, broadcasters from community radio stations affiliated to ANMCLA and from Radio Ali Primera de El Valle, Antiescualidos.com, members of Catio TV, base groups from La Vega, Carficuao and Petare, UTOPIA, Tupamaros de El Valle, M13-PNA, Movimiento 13 de Abril Comuneros, Party of Revolution and Socialism (PRS), participants in Conexion Social, the Venezuelan network against Debt, Organised Popular Anticorruption and Intervention (AIPO), militants of MOBARE, militants of the MDD, militants of the MEP Youth, members of the Bolivarian Association of Lawyers, the Revolutionary Marxist Current, among others.*

Resistance and sectarianism in Iraq

Haifa Zangana and Sami Ramadani answered questions from Anne Ashford on the situation in Iraq as the third anniversary of the occupation approaches.

I'd like to start with the question of sectarianism. How do you see the problem?
Haifa Zangana: This identifying people by whether they are Sunni or Shia is something which we did not have in Iraq at the beginning of the 1980s. People didn't do that in society, and not in writing, not in history or in literature. It would be very difficult to find a reference book which deals with Iraqis by dividing them into sects.

Someone like Gareth Stansfield focuses on the idea that previously the Sunnis dominated the mechanics of government. Would you say that this is a false picture?
HZ: I think it is totally artificial, because if we applied that to Britain, and we started digging into the background of this person—is he Protestant, Catholic, Church of England—we might draw out certain patterns of who is ruling what, which could be conveniently adopted by a selective process.

If you look at the 52 playing cards of the Ba'ath leaders who were wanted by the US immediately after the fall of Baghdad, you'll find that 38 of those leaders out of 51 are Shias. So who was ruling Iraq? I think this idea is a complete fabrication, it has been made intentionally, and it can be traced back to the beginning of the 1980s during the Iraq-Iran War. The statistics presented to us now say that the majority of Iraqis are Shias, so it was the Shias who were fighting the Iranians, who are of course also Shias. They were also in the government.

This Shia-Sunni division of Iraqi society is a complete fabrication.

There is no such thing. There is class struggle, there is the oil, there are many other factors that you can really talk about in Iraq, but definitely not sectarianism. It has totally been manufactured in recent years. If you go back to the media, and look immediately after the invasion—have a pile of newspapers and read articles—you'll see that it was only a few newspapers which used to identify Iraqis by sect. Now every single Iraqi is presented as Sunni or Shia.

If I go for an interview on Channel 4, for example, they say immediately, 'Haifa Zangana, are you Shia or Sunni?' I'm a bloody Iraqi! But the process is gradual, and we really have to examine the source of it, to understand what's going on. We shouldn't fall into this trap.

Sami Ramadani: On the communal, street level, there aren't these sharp divisions between people. People don't go killing each other because they are on the wrong side of the religious divide, or even national divide.

The wars against the Kurdish people, for example, were not communal wars whereby hundreds of thousands of Arabs went to fight Kurds, but rather a repressive state that was launching a chauvinist war against the Kurdish people, and it was the state against the people. Progressive Arabs from the South used to flee and use Kurdistan as the safe area to conduct their struggle against the regime. Thousands of soldiers used to flee to the Kurdish forces, for example, at the height of these wars.

There has never been a sectarian conflict in Iraq on the communal, street level. Saddam's regime had obvious sectarian dimensions, especially after the 1991 uprising, which was centred in the South, and since most of the South is Shia, it appeared to be a campaign against the Shia. Iraq is not an apartheid society, and never was. Saddam's regime rested on using social strata and security services from across the sects and nationalities of Iraq. Saddam's regime could not have ruled the South or Kurdistan without people from the South and Kurdistan participating in that. So there was a social base, a narrow social base of course, that backed that fascist set-up, but it was a social base that was drawn from all sects and religions and nationalities.

Take a town like Fallujah. It was a very strong bastion of anti-Saddamism, because back in 1996 there was a coup attempt and he traced it to people in Fallujah, and in 1998 he ordered the imams of mosques in Fallujah to sing his praises and pray for him and they refused, so he started punishing people in Fallujah. And until today the Ba'ath is very weak in Fallujah—that's why the resistance there is led by religious forces. This is an important point—he lashed out at any source of opposition, regardless of religion, sect or nationality.

Do you think that the occupying forces have actually tried to create sectarian divisions, and if so how have they done that?

SR: Generally speaking they have encouraged it, even before the occupation, because they dealt with the Iraqi opposition forces at the conference in London and a couple of other pre-occupation conferences increasingly in terms of who is a Kurd, who is an Arab, who is Shia, who is Sunni, who is Turkoman, who is Christian, and so on. And they deliberately tried to foster this—that was quite evident. They continued that after the occupation, to an even greater extent. So any institution that they had a hand in forming had to be divided on a sectarian basis—even the army units they wanted to set up earlier were run on a sectarian basis. Paul Bremer's Iraqi Governing Council is a prime example of how they wanted to divide Iraqis.

A so-called 'balance' between the different communities basically enshrines very rigid sectarian and ethnic divisions, even down to the lowest level appointments or committees. This is completely alien to the country's general traditions, over hundreds of years.

HZ: For example, the Supreme Council for the Islamic Revolution in Iraq (SCIRI) really represents a certain class of Shias. Muqtada al-Sadr represents another class—the poorest of the poor. SCIRI is more or less the middle class and the people who supervise the holy places. There are dynasties. Families such as al-Hakim, al-Sadr and al-Khalisi are in charge of the holy places, and a fifth of the money goes religiously to them from Shia tithes—*khums*. I see it as a class struggle, rather than anything else, because after all it's one religion, Islam. There is not really much difference if you come to the texts—what matters is who is in control of what. They are political parties, using this sect or another. This is something new, these parties based on sectarianism.

If you read all their programmes they will be exactly the same in the end, because they are all very caring about the Iraqi people, national unity, against sectarianism, and so on. People are telling us from Iraq that the ministry of the interior is divided into three floors—each floor follows one political party and they don't speak to each other. So it was just discovered that 167 Iraqis were imprisoned in the ministry buildings, and each political party in the interim government is accusing the other, because they don't even know who's arresting and who's torturing. This process doesn't just apply in terms of imprisonment or the militias, but is also having an impact on the population in terms of applying for jobs. To be appointed to the ministry of defence, for example, or the ministry of social affairs or any other ministry, you have to follow the criteria of the minister—what party he or she represents. If he is in the PUK [Patriotic Union of Kurdistan], you have to be a member of the PUK, otherwise forget it. It has nothing to do with your qualifications.

And it becomes almost part of the constitution. In fact it has been shown that the committee to write the constitution [in Iraq] was divided into sectarian and ethnic categories. Even that didn't work, and the committee has been pushed aside. The Americans have taken over the process because they felt it was taking too long. Their agenda is set by what is needed in America, rather than what is needed in Iraq. So they said, 'No, forget about it. We'll just present you with a copy of the constitution—you just agree or disagree.' But the minor details of it are sectarian division, totally, and it reflects on employing people. Employment is so important.

SR: There is a degree of tolerance in Iraqi society which allowed for the existence of a lot of sects, a lot of religions and nationalities. And that translated socially in terms of mixed marriages, mixed communities. There are more Kurds in Baghdad than in any city in Kurdistan, and so on. There are Shia communities all over Iraq. A quarter of the population of Basra is Sunni. These are all indications of the general mix in the country, which they tried actively to break, to discourage.

The Western media say many Shias support the occupation and many Sunnis oppose it.
SR: I wouldn't describe it as most of the Shia community supporting the government. I think there are obviously Shia mass organisations like the SCIRI or the Da'wah Party, who are part of the government, and they do have strength within the southern cities and parts of Baghdad. But by no means—in my own assessment—do they represent the majority of people in those areas. The Sadr movement, for example, is quite popular, but it is very anti-government and anti-occupation.

Muqtada al-Sadr is playing quite a complex political role, whereby on the one hand he is maintaining a very hostile stand towards the occupation and government policies while, on the other hand, he is allowing his supporters to stand in these elections. But his latest decision to actually let some of his supporters join the official Iraqi National Coalition list has created a lot of debate among the ranks of his own supporters—some being completely against it, some saying, 'If we're to join in the elections we might as well go it alone, or at least unite with other anti-occupation groups which might be inclined to take part in the elections.'

Are the occupying forces trying to break the country up?
SR: I don't think that they came in to stir up civil war. They came to exploit Iraq and its oil and turn it into a strategic base within a global context. But because of the level of opposition to their presence in the country, and the swift rise of armed resistance across Iraq (except in Kurdistan), their policy of dividing people along sectarian and ethnic lines was developed into a full-scale scheme of inciting communal strife and violence. This is the only way that a colonial power—or any power—dominating another society would deal with this situation, even in a spontaneous way. If you have an enemy you try to divide them, and overwhelmingly the Iraqi people have proven to be anti-occupation to varying degrees. And the occupation's response was to try and entrench or play on differences, and to start to encourage or turn a blind eye to organisations which preach sectarianism and practice sectarian and ethnic violence.

HZ: I think it is divide and rule. The colonial powers experimented with this previously, during the British occupation. They didn't succeed. It was a complete failure for them during the 1920 revolution, which was followed by many other uprisings. Also the 1958 revolution itself, a major event in our modern history, really was a slap in the face for the colonial powers, to indicate that Iraq is far beyond these sectarian divides.

SR: I am on thin ground in terms of material evidence, but I am more in favour of what the popular street says in Iraq, and that is that the US is either behind, or encouraging, or turning a blind eye to organisations like Zarqawi's—even though they think that Zarqawi is a mythical figure now, but let's use him as an allegorical figure, or a symbol of a sectarian voice. This type of sectarianism and killings are strongly believed in the country to be the work of the occupation. However, there is enough evidence now, some of it emanating for the US itself, that the US forces run active American and Iraqi death squads engaged in assassinations and other murderous activities.

Nobody has come up with a logical reason as to why any anti-occupation resistance force which wants to free Iraq from the occupation would go around blowing up innocent workers or worshippers in mosques or churches. Even if it is a nakedly sectarian force, as Zarqawi's statements indicate, the path it is following does not make sense, even within its own compass. Just to say that they are after creating chaos does not wash, because if they are clashing with the majority of the population in Iraq then obviously they have no chance in hell of evicting any occupier. To instantly make enemies of the overwhelming majority of the Iraqi people and of their friends across the world does not make sense at all. These terrorist acts so very obviously serve the occupation.

There have been a lot of incidents where there have been indications that these were not suicide bombers, but carefully timed devices in lorries and cars. There was an incident of children being killed a few months ago in Baghdad, and people throughout that area and in that street testified to the presence of American forces coming in and pretending to check a car which was booby-trapped but they then declared safe. Two minutes after they left, the car exploded. Before the car exploded they were actually distributing chocolates and toys to children, so many children gathered near that explosion site. Parents of the children were accusing the Americans of planting the bomb. There are even victims of a lot of these bombs in mosques and so on who say, 'The Americans are doing this so that we will fight each other.' So this anti-sectarian feeling is quite deeply ingrained.

HZ: If you ask any Iraqi in the street, 'Do you want Sunni or Shia to rule you?' the answer will come, 'Let the devil rule, as long as he is first an Iraqi, and second he brings us safety and security, and thirdly we can lead what is more or less a normal life—we don't give a damn.' Even when Talabani was being chosen as the president, I didn't hear an Iraqi saying, 'This Talabani is Kurdish, and we don't want him because he is Kurdish.' They can sit down and give you a list of why they hate Talabani: he is corrupt, to start with; he is responsible for killing many Kurds; sometimes it was almost a competition between himself and Saddam Hussein, how many Kurds he killed. So it is about economics and politics.

That's completely opposite to the picture that's presented here in the media, because the common view is that Iraq is divided between the Kurds in the north, the Sunnis in the 'Sunni Triangle' and the Shia in the South, and so on. Is this a false picture?

SR: Absolutely. And this picture unfortunately has struck roots, because it was repeated so many times that it has been taken for granted. The power of the modern media is such that this kind of myth becomes virtual reality in the minds of people outside Iraq. Within Iraq it has an impact in intellectual circles, and among certain political organisations. But down at the level of the street it's not that deep, and so far it has failed among the communities.

But something is happening around the militias and the armed groups?

HZ: This is the surface of things happening, and the surface says that there are militias—for example, Ahmad Chalabi's militia is still powerful. We have the Badr Brigade of SCIRI, which is notorious—and anyway we know they were established in Iran and they moved with the party itself to Iraq without having any roots in Iraqi society. We have the peshmerga [Kurdish militia] who have been used by the occupying forces in Najaf and Fallujah.

If we are talking about political parties, it is there, it does exist. But when we are talking about the people, on the contrary. For example, when the stampede happened on Jisr al-Imma' bridge in Baghdad and hundreds were killed, people hurried to help everyone. During the siege of Fallujah, people were donating and giving blood and sending cars to help with food and so on, from various parts of Iraq. So there is real solid unity, and I believe this is the heart of Iraq. But how long will that unity survive under this daily hammering by politicians, the media—whether inside Iraq or outside?

SR: Obviously the past is important to look at, though there is no logical reason why the past and historical continuity could not be broken and new events take shape. There is a threat, the longer the occupation stays, the more these divisions will become antagonistic. The occupation is no longer an external factor to Iraqi society. It is within Iraqi society. It is building armed forces and security forces. It is colonising the state. It is dealing with political forces that are fairly well organised. It has spread its tentacles within every organisation in society. It has tens of thousands of foreign mercenaries and tens of thousands of 'secret' private armies roaming the country.

So obviously it is important to point to history, to point to the way the masses do not have this massive wall between them in terms of religions and nationalities and sects. But the longer the occupation stays, I think there are threats to this cohesion among communities in Iraq. In fact, one should reverse the slogan about the threat of civil war in Iraq, to say that the longer the occupation lasts, the more likely it is that conflict will occur. The sooner they withdraw, the more likely it is that Iraq will revert back to the relative cohesion that existed between the various communities. Your politics were always more important than your religion or nationality in Iraq.

In terms of organisations which could cut across the trajectory towards sectarianism—for example, genuine workers' organisations—do they exist at the moment, and if so what's their attitude to the occupation?

SR: This is probably one of the saddest aspects of Iraq today. Although historically the left was strong in Iraq, 35 years of fascism and Saddam's regime have meant that the organised secular left has been weakened beyond recognition. Saddam compromised with all political forces in Iraq, except the secular left. He would not tolerate a secular anti-regime left in Iraq. The Communist Party's leadership joined Saddam's regime in the early 1970s and up to 1978, and this further weakened the secular left. Its support for the Governing Council after the occupation dealt it yet another blow.

Secular and left wing ideas are still strong, but there is no organisational expression today which is strong enough to mobilise the people along a political platform which could mobilise the working classes and people in Iraq to defeat the occupation, and bring about genuine democracy in the country. So that is a crisis that Iraq faces. Despite the ruthless occupation and despite all that's happening in terms of the inadequacy of the religious forces and so on, there is as yet no secular left wing political force which is strong enough to mobilise across Iraq. And all the political forces are aware that they are addressing a population which is generally sympathetic to left wing and secular ideas, so they don't tolerate organisations which might grow that way.

There are good, healthy signs as well, in terms of workers organising in trade unions, in terms of the unemployed being active. There are signs that the student movement can be quite enlightened, and so are some professional organisations, like teachers, lawyers, and so on. There are sections within the various communities which give hope for the future, but as of today there isn't a strong, left wing secular force to unite the Iraqi people.

There isn't one unified trade union movement either, and the picture became quite complex because the various political parties that cooperated with the occupation tried to take over the old trade unions, the Saddam federation. They were all after the federation because it had buildings all over Iraq, its assets were enormous, and it had exclusive rights to organise in all Iraq's establishments and factories. So all these pro-occupation political organisations were forming their own federations, including the IFTU federation. But there is independent trade union activity as well, especially among the oil workers in the South and in Basra. There is a strong trade union that organises oil workers, but a unified trade union movement across Iraq is lacking—despite the big-sounding names of the various federations that claim to be representing all workers in Iraq.

HZ: Look at the journalists' unions—we have five or six of them. Teachers, it is the same thing. A couple of months ago I think there were elections for the teachers to choose their new union representatives. And when they didn't manage to get the people they wanted, who would really represent the line of the government—the sectarian line—they abolished the union, saying, 'This isn't really representative.' There are something like three writers' unions—each one of them claiming to be the legitimate union, and each one of them accusing the others of malpractice. So we don't know who is representing who or what. There are students' unions, and again there are a couple of them. It seems as if union elections are taking place more or less locally rather than to represent the whole country.

None of them can claim that they represent all writers, or teachers, or journalists, or doctors, or university academics. Regarding the oil, this is a big thing. Also there is IFTU which claims to represent all the unions. And there is the Basra Oil Workers Union. They issued a statement last month saying that they are trying to unify their work with other branches of the unions in Nasiriyyah, Al-Amarah area, and they are hoping to do something in Kirkuk. I think that this would be a fantastic way of working together if they can achieve that, although it will be very difficult—especially as all the programmes of the political parties are tending to divide it, as they are looking to who is taking control of this part of the oil industry.

SR: Unemployment is still very high. A lot of the industries have been crushed. It wasn't just that they shut down the ministry of defence or the armed forces or they closed the ministry of information, but they actually mothballed hundreds of factories and establishments across Iraq. The Coalition Provisional Authority had a website detailing hundreds of factories and establishments in Iraq, and within neat columns they would put what sort of assets each factory had, which one is suitable for closure, which one is suitable for mothballing and selling off. The upshot is the total closure of all these working class areas and centres of work. So unemployment rose enormously—some estimated up to 70 percent of the labour force becoming unemployed literally overnight.

The factories that have reopened are a minority. Work is intermittent because of the power cuts and lack of raw materials, and the security situation. So people do other jobs—sell things in the streets, do decorating work, building work. Casualisation of labour is very extensive now. So this has hit the working class very badly. One incident that showed how callous the terrorists can be in Iraq, and how the working class is so badly hit, is the explosion in Kadhimiyya (in Baghdad) in September 2005 that killed 114 workers and injured 156. They were casual workers, building workers gathered early in the morning. A van approached and somebody left the van, and they all thought that this was somebody asking for workers. Hundreds of them surrounded that single van which then exploded and killed so many of them. The desperation to do 'an honest day's work', as they say, is so powerful. Patrick Cockburn of the *Independent* saw the dying and injured in hospital. Most told him that the occupation was behind the explosion, so that they make them blame and fight the Sunnis.

What about women's rights? One of the arguments advanced by people who are reluctant to call for the withdrawal of the occupation is that if the occupying forces leave then Iraqi women will be left at the mercy of the religious parties and anti-women bigots.

SR: This is parallel to the argument that if the occupying forces withdraw from Iraq there will be civil war. It sounds very appealing, sounds very logical, just like the civil war scenario—if they withdraw then all Iraqis will cut each other's throats and launch communal civil war tomorrow. I think this is a myth.

The conditions of women in Iraq have deteriorated sharply since the occupation, so if we want to assess whether there'll be civil war or whether women will be worse off one has to look at what is happening today rather than try to extrapolate into the future on the basis of logical arguments.

The facts on the ground are that women have suffered enormously, more than the men in many instances. For example, when there is no electricity, think of all the babies and children in poor working class areas, or across Iraq—no electricity means that the women have to struggle to look after the babies, give them clean water, try to warm up the place or cool it down in the heat of the summer. Think of the lack of fuel—the place will freeze up in the cold winter nights or will boil in summer. How are children and babies coping with that? How are their mums managing?

Water-borne diseases are hitting children and babies enormously, and traditionally who looks after them? The women. Who takes them to the hospitals? The women. And the hospitals have been run down—the health service is literally crumbling. So the burden on women is across the board, from the moment they wake up until the moment they sleep. Burdens of life have enormously increased, not to mention the security threats to women, their fear of going out—even in daylight hours women are frightened to go out. The kidnapping of women, the hurt that is being imposed on women, is across the board. Unemployment hit women probably proportionately more than men, as is usual in these circumstances—when there is a crisis women are hit first. So across the board women are suffering. Their situation is deteriorating. And I haven't even mentioned being bombed from the skies, or attacked by white phosphorous, or raided in the middle of the night by the US Marines, or the newborn babies affected by DU. But the women of Iraq, like most of the men, are fighting back in a variety of ways.

So to talk about an imaginary situation where if these 'enlightened occupiers' withdraw, Iraqis will turn against the women of Iraq is ridiculous. It doesn't bear close examination at all.

HZ: Iraqi women have never been victims, and they have never been weak. In fact, they are very well known in the Middle East for being quite powerful characters. They have been active politically and economically in building the country, in the legal system. They were equally responsible for building the new Iraq, from the 1920 revolution until now. So Iraqi women are not passive victims who are at the mercy of men, whether politically or otherwise. Of course, repression under Saddam's regime targeted everybody, so there was no difference. It wasn't based on sectarianism, or on ethnicity, or on gender—it was political, purely political.

So women are quite capable of deciding for themselves what they do, and examining what the US and British forces promised when they came to Iraq—and there is little room for optimism here, or that Iraqi women themselves can look forward to something different. They would rather deal with their problems organically and by themselves. Maybe some women were deceived to start with, by these ideas of democracy and women's rights. There were millions of dollars spent on it by the US government.

I did research on the women's organisations that came from the States with the invasion. They are facing daily failure in Iraq. Women themselves dismiss them as representatives of women, though they claim that they have women leaders of this and that. But they are only an attachment of the sectarian or ethnic parties. So it doesn't really make a difference whether you are male or female, in a sense, if you are there to spout the same rhetoric of your political party, which is echoing US policy in Iraq. It has nothing to do with Iraqi women or establishing their rights

Look, for example, at the Women's Alliance for a Democratic Iraq. One of its biggest projects was about writing an essay, 'I love Iraq', and giving $100 to the family whose son or daughter won. The second project was to get women to draw on the old murals that Saddam put up. I mean, if you think that women hardly venture into the streets of Iraqi, can you imagine an Iraqi woman, with all the dangers, risking her life to walk in the street and stand in front of a huge mural, to draw a new mural. This is farcical. Its main project is to buy sewing machines, and they go on and on about the little details—how much it cost them, how they sent this delegation to negotiate the prices and so on. In the end, they got 15 sewing machines and they had photo opportunities and delegations to go and visit the families. The whole project was really just a photo opportunity for the media.

So it's more about a public relations exercise for the Western media than helping Iraqi women?
HZ: They used to tour the military camps in America to encourage the soldiers by saying thank you—thank you for what? For killing Iraqi people? All this was happening while Iraqi cities were under continuous bombardment, while women and children were being killed all the time, whether by direct bombardment or by using unconventional weapons, cluster bombs, white phosphorous, DU [depleted uranium], or by the effect of the conflict, of the war itself, on Iraqi health, education. So they are completely detached from Iraqi reality, and in particular the reality of Iraqi women.

And we can see, if we are talking about human rights in general, the occupation has nothing to do with human rights. In the end women's rights are part of human rights. Without the struggle for national liberation, which Iraqi women have been part of throughout all the history of modern Iraq, I can't see how they can really achieve anything.

China's economy and Europe's crisis

Chris Harman

The message is repeated over and over again: 'Europe has to change because of the rise of China and India.' To question it, as the majority of French people did in last year's referendum and millions of Germans in the general election, is supposed to be like saying the Earth is flat. Growing industrial and agricultural output in one part of the world, it seems, necessarily means reduced consumption, longer working hours and worse pensions in another part. All the politicians who have told us for the last decade and a half that there is no alternative to capitalism now tell us that capitalism means European states cannot afford the welfare provisions granted when they were all producing much less in the 1950s, 1960s and early 1970s.

The message has an ideological purpose—to make people believe they have no alternative than to accept ever more draconian neo-liberal 'remedies' that cut into living standards, welfare benefits and working conditions in the West. But its impact relies on pointing to dramatic changes that are taking place in what were previously assumed to be 'backward' economies of little significance to the world system.

Where do these changes come from? What is their real extent? What impact are they having on the established advanced capitalisms of Western Europe and the US? And how do they affect the ups and downs of the system as a whole? These are some of the issues this article tries to address.

The reality of rapid growth

There can be no argument about the massive industrial growth of China. It is something we have recognised repeatedly in this journal in the past.[1] Since 1978 China's growth rate per year has been 9.5 percent.[2] Last year it became the world's third biggest exporter, with 6 percent of the world total, and has also become the world's biggest single recipient of fixed direct investment. It is 'the leading producer in terms of output in more than 100 kinds of manufactured goods. China now makes more than 50 percent of the world's cameras, 30 percent of the world's air conditioners and televisions, 25 percent of washing machines and 20 percent of refrigerators. Some 85 percent of bicycles and 80 percent of shoes sold in the US are made in China'.[3]

Chinese cities like Beijing, Shanghai, Guangzhou or even Xian no longer bear much resemblance to Third World stereotypes. The forests of skyscrapers in Beijing or Shanghai make London's much vaunted Docklands development look like Toytown, while the vast industrial developments around Shanghai have few comparisons in Western Europe, let alone Britain. And for the moment there seems no end in sight to the expansion of industry and cities. Some 40 percent of output flows back into investment, with cranes towering over new construction sites every 300 or 400 metres in the cities.

The Chinese economy is currently about 19 percent of the size of the US's, measured in terms of current currency exchange rates. Some estimates suggest a figure of 60 percent measured according to 'purchasing power parity', which is based on domestic buying power.[4] The first measure considerably underestimates the level of resources available for consumption by China's population (since domestic prices of basic foodstuffs like rice and basic services like urban transport fares cost a quarter or less than in the West), while the second overstates the value of the Chinese economy in terms of internationally traded capital goods, raw materials and consumer durables (which cost more or less the same inside China as in the West).[5] But whichever measure is taken, it is not fantasy to conceive of China's overall output overtaking the US's in the not so distant future if expansion continues at its present level—by the middle of the present century according to the Chinese government. On the other hand, it would be folly to ignore the strong possibility of economic crisis halting China's ascent, just as it did Japan's in the early 1990s.

In either case, China's rise is producing a major shift in the balance of economic weight in the world system, and will inevitably have an enormous impact in the years ahead.

Simply bracketing India with China—as is done routinely in the media and in politicians' speeches is, however, carrying the hype too far. India's economy has grown more or less continually since independence 58 years ago, demolishing the claims of various dependency theorists that economic development of any sort is impossible under capitalism.[6] India's manufacturing output today is 12 times that of 1951. Agricultural output is four times bigger, keeping ahead of population growth, so that continued malnutrition in wide areas of the countryside is a result of the impact of class on food distribution, not of underproduction. It is nonsense to say there is not development. But it is capitalist development. It is not the sort of all-round development, with everyone becoming better off, of neoliberal ideology. There are enormous differences between what happens to rich and poor, and between geographical regions. It is environmentally destructive and leaves hundreds of millions in poverty. That is what capitalist development is.

But the growth has been slower than China, varying enormously from year to year. Since 1978 it has varied only between 4 and 7 percent, barely touching the last figure in the last two years, despite hype from the World Bank which implies that 'market reforms' have made it the norm. The proportion of output going to investment in India has only in the last couple of decades reached the relatively high figure of 25 percent, and that is still way below the Chinese level. As a result, India's output in purchasing power terms is only half that of China's, and less than one tenth that of the US or of the combined EU countries. India remains 31st among the world's exporters, with only 0.7 percent of the total (with roughly the same population, China is nine times more important for the world system), and India barely appears on the list of the world's recipients of foreign direct investment (see graph 1).

India has some much-hyped advantages in computer and software services, back office processing tasks and call centres. Here the existence of millions of fluent English speakers puts it in a better position than China when it comes to providing for the needs of Western multinationals. But the scale of India's impact on the world market for these things is vastly overstated in much media coverage. So the call centre

Graph 1

India-China GDP (Annual Growth Rate) 1991-2004

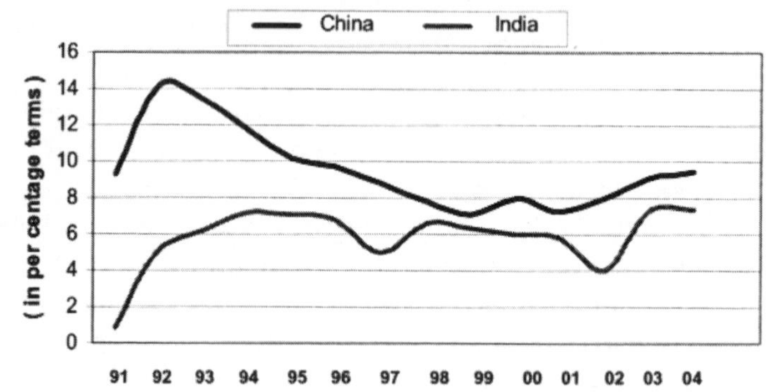
China
India
16
14
12
10
8
6
4
2
0
(in per centage terms)
91 92 93 94 95 96 97 98 99 00 01 02 03 04

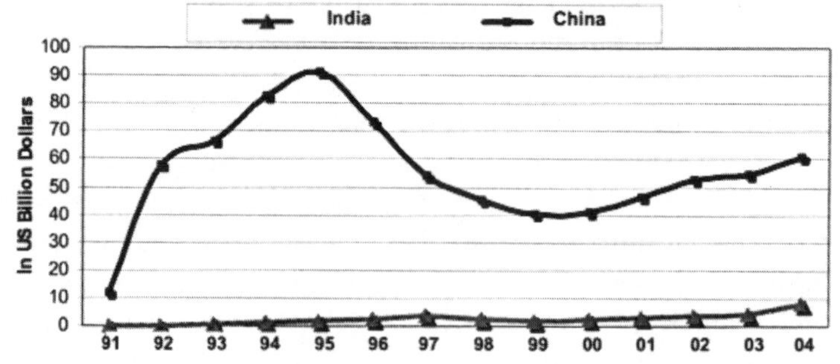
China India FDI (Trends between 1991-2004)
India
China
100
90
80
70
60
50
40
30
20
10
0
In US Billion Dollars
91 92 93 94 95 96 97 98 99 00 01 02 03 04

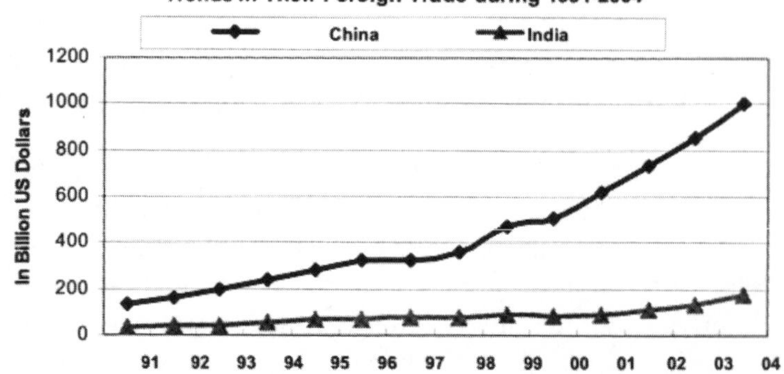
Trends in Their Foreign Trade during 1991-2004
China
India
1200
1000
800
600
400
200
0
In Billion US Dollars
91 92 93 94 95 96 97 98 99 00 01 02 03 04

industry in Britain is expected to employ four times more people than in India next year.[7] The growth of India's software industries is constrained both by a growing shortage of skilled personnel (which has pushed up salaries) and infrastructural deficiencies when it comes to providing a secure environment for high-tech industry—something revealed vividly this year by the damaging impact of floods in the 'high-tech capital' of Bangalore. There are niches in which these industries are growing rapidly. But niches are not enough to lift a whole economy into the world's big league. At present, even the most optimistic estimates suggest that such industries only provide employment for about 0.01 percent of India's adult population.

The stages of Chinese growth

Chinese economic growth since the victory of the People's Liberation Army in 1949 has gone through a number of stages:

(1) *The early 1950s:* The first, short, stage was that of reconstruction after 20 years of civil war and Japanese invasion. There was an improvement in the lives of the mass of people as communication routes were restored, industry began to function, and land reform reduced rents and redistributed land from landowners and bigger peasants to the middle and poor peasants. But power did not lie with the peasants, still less with the workers of the cities. Rather it lay with the radicalised middle classes who commanded the People's Liberation Army—and they had a programme, like that of the members of the new middle classes who took power in the same period of the post-war decades right across the Third World, of wanting to turn their country into a modern industrial state, into a great power like any other.

(2) *The 1950s and 1960s:* The key was seen (again, as in many other Third World countries) to lie in following the apparently successful Russian approach, with the imposition of 'plans' which diverted resources towards new heavy industries—steel, cement, electricity. But doing so in a very poor, overwhelmingly agricultural country like the China of the early 1950s meant squeezing the living standards of the mass of the population. What the middle and poor peasants had gained through land reform, they lost through a rigorously enforced taxation of their output. When this was not enough to provide the resources for industrial accumulation and a

growing arms budget, the Mao group within the regime turned to the ultimately disastrous attempt at collectivisation through so-called People's Communes, in an attempt to bring about a 'Great Leap Forward'. The leap failed miserably to build viable industries and actually cut total agricultural output, leading to famine in vast areas of the countryside and some 30 million deaths through starvation. In its aftermath, the ambition of total control over the peasants' lives was abandoned. But the enormously high rate of exploitation of a heavily repressed peasantry persisted, and in the decades that followed an enormous proportion of total output was towards accumulation—some 30 or 40 percent. And this did, in the medium term, build up the heavy industry and arms (notably nuclear weapons) deemed necessary by those who wanted to rule a 'great power'.

The new industry was, however, far from efficient. Again, as in many other Third World countries, a growth of heavy industry out of all proportion to what was happening to the rest of the economy led to acute shortages of inputs needed to keep plants running, and to the production of other goods which had no immediate use. There were massive swings between spells of fast industrial expansion and spells of near stagnation, and many of the grandiose new giant plants were only able to work at a fraction of their potential capacity.

By the mid-1970s a quarter of a century of what Marx called primitive accumulation had built up some of the bases of modern industry—but it was industry that was no match in terms of efficiency for that in many other parts of the world system.

The sheer scale of exploitation of the mass of the population led to all sorts of pressures building up from below and to repeated crises within the ruling group, which culminated in the massive upheavals of 1967-75 (from the 'Cultural Revolution' to the rise and fall of the 'Gang of Four'), as Charlie Hore explains elsewhere in this journal. These were only finally resolved after Mao Zedong's death in 1976 and the rise to power of Deng Xiaoping.

(3) *From 1977 to 1989:* A series of reforms pushed through in 1978-81 began with relief for peasants through a raising of the purchasing price paid by the state for their produce. The peasants were now to decide for themselves how to use some of the surplus left after (just about) feeding themselves. There was a huge rise in agricultural production, and the

increased incomes provided a market for some of the under-utilised industrial capacity. A loosening of state controls allowed it to satisfy this demand, and overall output soared ahead.

Increasing social differentiation within the peasantry led some to accumulate a surplus, and then to use the new freedoms from state control to invest in establishing locally based 'village industries'. Formally owned by village governments, in practice these provided a means of self-enrichment by those with connections to the local party apparatus. A new market capitalism grew up in the south east of the country alongside the old state capitalism centred mainly in the north of the country, and the regime allowed the new industries to link up with overseas Chinese capitalist interests in Hong Kong and elsewhere.

Despite the reforms, the surplus passing from the peasantry into the hands of three groups of capitalists (state, 'village' and overseas) was still massive, and low peasant incomes meant a ready supply of workers for the new industries, which did not even have to provide the guaranteed minimum living standards and social protection (the so-called 'iron rice bowl') of the old state-run heavy industries.

In effect, there was a new model of capitalist accumulation, combining the high level of exploitation and repression of the old state capitalism with a turn towards catering for markets—and the markets came from exporting to the rest of the world system, and from providing for the increasingly conspicuous consumption of the old state bureaucracy on the one hand and its children as they took over privatised industries on the other.

The new hybrid economy has contradictions of its own, with the ups and downs of a market capitalism superimposed on the ups and downs of the old state capitalist, primitive accumulation model. These contradictions led to a crisis in the late 1980s and the shock to the regime of the Tiananmen Square protests of 1989.

(4) *1992 to the present:* The regime found a way out of the crisis by pushing village governments to privatise the new industries, which were encouraged to link up with foreign (and no longer just overseas Chinese) capitalists, as were the managers of the great state-owned enterprises. There has been a massive rationalisation of old industries, with perhaps 30 million workers losing their jobs. These measures have been acclaimed as 'progressive' by

pro-capitalist economists right across the world. What they mean for workers has been portrayed graphically in the recent Chinese film *Blind Shaft*, about how the degrading conditions under which the miners work lead two of them to murder a co-worker in an attempt to blackmail corrupt managers. The closeness of reality to the fiction was shown in a mining disaster in Guangdong (supposedly China's most 'advanced' province) last summer. As more than 100 miners suffocated underground, the owner fled when it was revealed he had paid out millions of dollars in bribes to take over the previously shut down state-owned mine, and at the same time to buy himself a senior position in the local police force. In this way he had been able to ignore all safety precautions while parading himself as an exemplary 'entrepreneur' for his role in supplying coal to satisfy the energy needs of a booming economy.[8]

Alongside the attack on the old working class has been a renewed upping of the level of exploitation of the peasantry, who still make up two thirds of the population. Average peasant incomes have probably declined in recent years. One (banned) Chinese study tells of a fall of 6 percent in peasants' per capita farming incomes since 1997, and 'given the rising costs of health and education, their real purchasing power has probably fallen still further'.[9] But the average does not tell the whole story. Class differentiation in the peasantry has proceeded apace, with the local officials using their powers to grab money (in the form of local taxes) and land off other peasants with the aim of enriching themselves as petty agrarian capitalists—the cause of many recent local near-uprisings. The World Bank admits that 204 million people, or one in six of the population, still live on less than $1 a day. Other estimates suggest that 'the vast majority of the 800 million peasants' have incomes at this level.[10] Some 100 million peasants pour into the cities each year seeking any sort of casual work they can get in competition with 30 million urban unemployed.

China-India contrasts

The pattern in India since independence in 1947 parallels that in China in some ways. The early years saw recovery from the (much less serious) dislocation caused by the Second World War. Then came the push to industrialise on the bases of five-year plans, inspired in part by the Russian model (but never going as far as China either in overriding the old private industrialists or in subordinating consumer goods to accumulation). Middle and poor peasants and workers paid the price for this in terms of stagnating living standards and, in many cases, permanent malnutrition (but without the sudden lunge into horrific starvation of the Great Leap Forward period). Finally, there were attempts from the late 1970s onwards to overcome a crisis in that model of accumulation by a series of market reforms and an opening up to the world market.

India started off with more industry than China, but accumulation in the 1950s to the 1970s never reached Chinese levels—it is only in the last decade or so that India's rate of accumulation occasionally exceeded 25 percent. Partly this was because the relatively peaceful way the post-independence regime came to power in 1947 meant it never had the machine to confront old exploiting classes in the countryside. It bought them off rather than launching an all-out assault on them and diverting their incomes into accumulation. But it was also because it never had the strength simply to trample on the mass of middle peasants or the workers. Its governments relied on elections, but could not win elections without some concessions to the masses. And the one attempt at non-parliamentary rule—Indira Gandhi's emergency in the mid-1970s—failed miserably. Hundreds of millions of peasants have suffered long-term malnutrition and some appalling caste oppression, but there has been nothing comparable to the famine of the Great Leap Forward years.

As a result India's rulers achieved less than China's during the phase of primitive accumulation, so find themselves less able to benefit from a turn to the world market today—exporting less and remaining much less attractive to foreign capital than their Chinese competitors.

Contradictions in China's growth

Capitalism is a dynamic system. Those who have said capitalist development is not possible in parts of the Third World have failed to grasp this. But the other side of its dynamism is the contradiction that arises from expansion of production for the sake of production, from the 'self-expansion of capital' (sometimes rendered using the French term *valorisation*).

It has two inevitable results:

- Investment grows much more rapidly than the number of workers employed and exploited—the source of surplus value. This produces a tendency for investment to grow more rapidly than profits, and for the ratio of profit to investment (the rate of profit) to fall.

•Expansion produces goods that cannot be bought by a working population whose living standards are held down in an effort to sustain profit rates ('overproduction', sometimes seen as 'underconsumption'). The only outlet for the increased production is then through investment in the expansion of means of production. This then leads eventually to further downward pressure on profit rates. Both factors are visible in China.

As we have seen, expansion has been based upon huge levels of extraction of a surplus from the peasants and workers, ie upon the poverty of a huge chunk of the Chinese population. The Chinese National Bureau of Statistics calculates that only 5 percent of the population are in the middle class that can afford the luxury consumer goods that industry is turning out.[11] This 5 percent amounts to some 60 million people, and can look very big when it crowds into the shopping districts of the major cities. But it is not big enough to absorb the burgeoning output of Chinese industry profitably. Growth is therefore dependent on massive sales outside China. Exports accounted for 74 percent of Chinese growth in 2002.[12]

But there is enormous competition in export markets—not just with goods produced abroad, but with other goods produced in China itself. In many lines of business, different Chinese firms are now competing with each other—or, more accurately, are tied into competing international networks through the multinationals that are competing with each other: 'The percentage of exports produced by foreign-based corporations grew from 17.4 percent in 1990 to 50.8 percent in 2001'.[13]

In many industries, firms (or, more often, foreign firms operating in China) are importing components from elsewhere in east and south east Asia, assembling them into final products in China and then exporting them to the US, Japan and elsewhere. But this does not stop competition leading to overproduction. The National Statistics Bureau has reported that 'of all Chinese manufactured products, 90 percent are in oversupply'.[14] The pressure to sell these goods leads to massive price cutting on world markets: 'Among Chinese companies the price war is particularly intense because competitors often chase market share rather than trying to increase short-term profitability'.[15] The relentless downward pressure on the price of manufactured exports can be seen by the fall of prices in Western shops for Chinese-produced products like DVD players and recorders, breadmaking machines, cameras and air conditioners: 'Relentless competition among local suppliers keeps profit margins almost invisible for many firms'.[16]

At the same time, 'investment in many sectors—including property, cement, steel, cars and aluminium—is being overdone', according to Chinese government officials.[17] Partly this is because the political apparatus has been constructed around the goal of accumulation for the sake of accumulation. Top managers measure their success by the speed at which their firms grow—and the government-run banks reward those that grow fastest by allowing them to accumulate debts.

The pressure also comes from the logic of competing in a capitalist world system where success does not only depend on cheap labour, but also on keeping up with rivals when it comes to new, capital intensive investment. There has been a decline in the number of new workers needed for each percentage increase in output.[18] Despite the cheapness of labour, China has lost a large number of manufacturing jobs in recent years—according to one estimate 15 percent, or 15 million, disappeared between 1995 and 2002, with falls in employment in 26 of 38 Chinese industries.[19] China is experiencing a rising capital-labour ratio (Marx's organic composition) at the same time as a continual tendency to overproduction that can be relieved if ever-increasing exports are sold for declining prices.

Stephen Roach of Morgan Stanley points out:

> With private consumption having fallen to a record low of just 42 percent of GDP in 2004 and likely to have declined further in 2005...China's growth dynamic has become increasingly reliant on exports and on the investment in infrastructure and factories required to build a state of the art export platform on a scale the world has never seen. Collectively, exports and fixed investment, which now account for over 80 percent of Chinese GDP, are still surging at close to a 30 percent annual rate.[20]

The result is a relatively low rate of profit which is compensated for by the willingness of the banks to lend to enterprises at low rates of interest—and by a parallel willingness not to push loss-making enterprises into bankruptcy, so that the banking system is owed vast, probably unrepayable debts. The official estimate for the 'non-performing loans' of the banks is 20 percent of all loans—an unofficial estimate suggests 45 percent of GDP.[21]

As with any capitalist boom, there is a burgeoning of all sorts of speculation. Everywhere in China's major cities there is the apparently endless building and rebuilding of luxury apartment blocks, relatively expensive (by Chinese standards) fast food outlets, high class hotels, and shopping malls dedicated to selling designer products (even though such stores often seem virtually empty of shoppers).

The big question is the degree to which continued rapid economic growth is dependent on a speculative bubble which is bound sooner or later to burst. Capitalist booms can last longer than anyone really expects (apart from the most glib of pro-capitalist economists), but they can also collapse suddenly with little warning. So the *Economist*, for instance, has issued periodic warnings over the Chinese economy for at least the last decade (partly because the state plays too large a part in the economy for its neo-liberal fundamentalism) and has been proved wrong. Yet it is impossible for a capitalist economy to keep growing indefinitely if the real fundamentals in capitalist terms—the rates of profit of major sections of industry—are so weak. And this is an issue not just for the Chinese economy, but for the world system as a whole.

The US-China tango

It is precisely its interconnections with the world system which have enabled China to maintain its massive level of accumulation and to overcome past symptoms of crisis. Particularly important has been the ability of the US to absorb Chinese exports.

But the US has only been able to do this because of its ability to borrow ever-increasing amounts from the rest of the world. The country's current deficit mushroomed from zero at the beginning of the 1990s to $400 billion in 2000 to close to $750 billion by the end of 2004. The gap has been filled by a continual inflow of foreign funds, coming mostly from east Asia, with China playing a very important role (although Japan still holds over three times as much US Treasury debt as China).[22] The Chinese banks take the surplus made on the country's trade and use it to buy US treasury bonds, ie in effect they lend it to the US government which in turn passes some on to US banks to lend to firms and consumers. Or, to put it another way, China 'saves' about 50 percent of its national product as firms and the government extract profits, taxes and rents from the country's workers and peasants—and then about 40 percent of GDP goes into domestic investment, and the rest (10 percent) is lent to the US via the Treasury bonds route. The final twist is that some of this flows back into China as investment by multinationals.

So the US economy holds the Chinese economy up by buying its excess production as imports, and the Chinese economy holds the US economy up by providing its firms and consumers with the cash to maintain their present level of consumption.

The US end of the arrangement is, like the Chinese end, a result of the contradictions built into capitalism. Various studies have shown that since the 1960s US firms have built up an ever-greater ratio of capital to labour—from 0.5 for manufacturing in 1982-90 to 2.2 in 1992-2000, according to a calculation by Robert Brenner.[23] There has been a downward pressure on the rate of profit which can only be overcome by increased exploitation of US workers, with real wages falling by nearly a sixth from their peak in the mid-1970s through to the mid-1990s, while working hours lengthened.[24] And the fall in real wages has made consumption increasingly dependent on borrowing. The American dream is increasingly one paid for on tick.

The recession of 2001-02 hit some US companies hard, and millions of industrial workers lost their jobs, never to regain them. But the recession did not have the positive effect for capitalism that crises have usually had in the past, of restructuring the economy so as to clear the way for a new period of sustained expansion. Instead recovery has depended on a deepening of one imbalance from the past, the ever increasing inflow of funds from abroad, especially east Asia, and the addition of a new imbalance, the excess of government spending over government revenues that results from the Bush administration increasing military spending while cutting taxes for the rich. There is now considerable fear in some capitalist circles that the economic recovery cannot last long, as poor profits threaten a giant like General Motors, high levels of middle class consumption depend increasingly on a bubble in house prices, and oil prices are raised to very high levels by the Chinese boom and the continual shutdown of most Iraqi supplies.[25]

What happens to the US and China is decisive for the rest of the world economy, since they are the only major parts of the system to experience strong growth in recent years. So China has played an important role in the recovery of the east Asian economies from the crisis of the late 1980s. It is the destination for around half the export growth of Japan, Malaysia, South Korea and Australia, and 30 percent of the total exports of the whole region.[26] In effect, the US is sucking in imports from China, and

China is sucking in imports from the rest of east Asia. A related process has been taking place with Latin America. The Chinese boom has provided a massive market for raw materials and agricultural produce from the previously recession-hit economies of Brazil and Argentina, as well as for oil from Venezuela, reducing their dependence on the US and the European Union (each of which have imports of about $14 billion a year from Brazil). As the *Financial Times* said two years ago, 'China was Argentina's biggest export market in June and July, and Brazil's exports to China jumped 136 percent'.[27]

If the interdependent booms in the US and China turn out to be no more than a double bubble that bursts, the impact on the rest of the system will be immense.

The challenges for European capitalism

The growth of China's economy expresses itself in the growing importance of trade with the European Union countries, particularly when it comes to many basic consumer goods like electrical products and low cost clothing. However, the widely propagated notion that Chinese goods are already displacing European goods on a massive scale in the domestic market does not hold up. Imports from outside the European Union area still only account for about 10 percent of its total goods and services, and only 10 percent of these imports come from China. At the same time, Germany, not China, is the world's biggest exporter for the moment (with $893 billion of exports in 2004, as against $583 billion from China and a mere $69 billion from India). The European Union's combined exports to non-EU countries are nearly twice as big as China's exports.

So the argument that 'Europe must change' does not hold water if by Europe is meant the mass of its people. There is no intrinsic reason why the increased output of China's people should stop Europe's people continuing to produce what they have in the past and to improve their living standards with advances in technology. But the present system is not organised on the basis of the needs of the mass of people. It is organised through capitalist firms, most of which use their national bases to engage in global competition, overriding national boundaries as they seek to expand their scale of production and their markets.

The discourse about 'China and India' is in reality about what the Europe-based firms need to do to expand globally. They want to discipline the workers in Europe who still make up most of their global workforces.

The prime competitors for European firms are not Chinese firms (although, if the present rapid pace of Chinese industry continues, some could be in a few years' time). Particularly important are US firms; these have ratcheted up the level of exploitation of their domestic workforces over the last two decades.

This is most vividly shown by the hours worked in different countries. The US is the only advanced country where average hours worked per worker have risen in recent years. US, Japanese, Korean and Chinese workers all work 2,000 hours or more a year. In France and Germany the figure is around 1,500 hours.[28] In other words, workers in the core economies of mainland Europe work 10 or 12 weeks a year less than US and East Asian workers. This means that even when European bosses have invested in new technologies in advance of the US, and achieved higher hourly productivity rates, they lag behind in annual output per worker. (As I have pointed out before in this journal, while capital per worker and hourly productivity is higher in France and Germany than in the US, annual productivity is lower.[29])

The 'China-India challenge' talk is part of the response to this. It goes along with the threat, especially in Germany, to move production to cheaper labour sites in Eastern Europe if workers do not agree to work 'more flexibly' for longer hours.

Of course, there has also long been in operation a second response—that of physically moving production overseas. But this takes time with most sorts of industrial production (fully equipped factories are rarely easy to move, and even when they are there is then the question of energy supplies, transport facilities, a secure political environment, and so on). So it is that after 30 years of restructuring and factory closures, with a halving of the workforce, the output of manufacturing in Britain has not declined. Even when considering a long-term moving of production, in the interim the giant European firms still depend on finding some way to increase the exploitation of their local workforces. In practice few firms envisage, for the moment, moving all their production abroad, and this makes the need to raise the exploitation of the domestic workforce paramount.

Here, however, there is a political problem in what George Bush calls 'Old Europe'. Capital and the state sought to legitimise themselves in the long boom after the Second World War through the ideology of national consensus while collaborating to various degrees with the trade union bureaucracy. This applied not only to social democracy in Germany and France, but also to the Christian Democrat and Gaullist variants of conservative politics. And there seemed no reason to disturb society by overturning this approach so long as economies seemed to be advancing in comparison with their major competitors—which they did, even into the 1980s.[30] But once this advance faltered there was a growing feeling among ruling class circles and their conservative and social democrat hangers-on that something drastic had to be done. Otherwise the only way to stop economic growth leading to pressure of wages on profits was to follow monetary and budgetary policies (encapsulated in the behaviour of the German national bank, the Bundesbank, and then in the rules of the European central bank) aimed at restricting economic growth the moment it gave any hint of being 'inflationary'. The outcome has been a paradoxical situation in which Germany has a big trade surplus and German capital has good profits, but it suffers at the same time as slow growth reduces the share of world investment and production in its hands.

Hence also the Schröder government's attempts in 2003-05 to push through its Agenda 2010 and Hartz IV counter-reforms. Hence too the repeated attempts in France from 1995 onwards to implement welfare cuts and neo-liberal policies (see Jim Wolfreys' article in this journal).

There are some parallels between the dilemmas facing the French and German ruling classes and that facing Britain's rulers from the mid-1960s onwards. Until then all mainstream parties had been agreed on the programme of social consensus, partnership with unions and Keynesian economics embodied in 'Butskellism' (a term coined by merging the names of the economics spokesmen of the two main parties). But as Japan and West Germany began to challenge British domination of export markets, establishment intellectuals began to bemoan 'the Stagnant Society' and 'the suicide of Britain', while City speculators made periodic raids on the currency. So began a long campaign by governments and employers to break the shopfloor strength constituted by the networks of rank and file trade union activists that had grown up over the previous 30 years. The first great manifesto of this campaign was the *Donovan Commission Report into*

Industrial Relations of 1968. It was followed by the Labour government's *In Place of Strife* (1969), the Tory government's *Fair Deal and Work* (1970), and many subsequent proclamations. But it was not until the defeat of the year-long strikes of miners and print workers under Margaret Thatcher's government in the mid-1980s that the battle was finally won for the ruling class—and in the interim three governments had been broken by their inability to impose capital's will on the workforce.

The parallel points to the scale of the problems facing the French and German ruling classes. Even if they can find some politician with the political legitimacy to wage the battle as Thatcher did (and the French attempt with the referendum and Merkel's approach in the German election seriously backfired), they can still find themselves stirring up opposition forces capable of beating them back—it is worth remembering what a 'close run thing' Thatcher's victory in 1984-85 was. In the meantime, their attempts to go onto the offensive can destabilise the politics of the two most important states in mainland Europe.

The pattern so far is of them going on the offensive, stirring up resistance against themselves—and then losing the initiative (and their nerve) and having to undertake the sort of partial retreat that gives increased confidence to sections of the resistance.

Tony Blair has attempted to benefit politically from the problems of the French and German political establishments, trying to present himself as a man of destiny for capitalism across the whole of Europe. So he tried to thrust himself to the fore with the Lisbon declaration pushed by the BBA trio (Blair, Berlusconi and Aznar) three years ago, and then tried to go centre-stage after the French and German votes, looking to a new alliance with Merkel in Germany and Sarkozy, who he hopes will be president of France after next year's election.

The British government has the advantage over the European ones of having inherited the defeats inflicted on organised labour by Thatcher. This did not just involve a humbling of the union leaders and an immense weakening of shopfloor resistance. It also involved cuts in expenditure on social housing and public transport, the abolition of wage-related unemployment benefits, the pioneering use of market testing to hit the conditions of civil servants, the use of contracting-out to hit the worst paid sectors in the health service, and driving down the real value of the state pension.

Yet for all the Blairite-Brownite boasts about the advantages in terms of the 'flexibility' of the British economy, the record in capitalist terms is not all that brilliant. Productivity lags 10 or 15 percent behind the US, and working hours are still shorter than in the US, even if longer (by about an hour a week) than in France and Germany. And the 'flexible labour market' has not been enough to bring about the fall in real wages that has occurred in the US.[31] This may be connected with the fact that the official unemployment figures conceal the way in which very large numbers of people who are out of work have been moved onto invalidity benefit—a device used to massage the unemployment figures which also serves to reduce the pressure on the 'reserve army' of the employed section of the working class. (Tellingly, the proportion of GDP absorbed by public sector expenditure remains at around 40 percent.[32])

So it is that, at the same time as taking the neo-liberal moral high ground against 'Old Europe', Blair and Brown feel compelled to try to push through still more measures of a neo-liberal sort at home—and with them measures like city academies and attacks on civil liberties that give right wing ideological signals even if they can hardly do much directly to solve British capitalism's competitive weaknesses. But theirs is a government weakened by following Bush into the morass of Iraq and which can, like the European states, find itself compelled to back off, at least partially, in the face of real resistance. This was shown by the way Blair did not, at the end of the day, want to take on the risks involved in trying to impose an across the board increase of the pensionable age to 65 for the whole public sector. It was only the pessimism and cowardice of the trade union leaders that allowed the government to get away with raising the pensionable age for newly employed workers. And even then Blair had to endure attacks from his friends in the right wing press on his 'weakness' and his 'surrender to union power'.

Emerging faultlines

There is a tendency for people to ask of any analysis of the world economy, 'What follows next—boom or slump?' or, even more bluntly if they are on the left, 'When will the bubble burst?'

I have no doubt that at some point the double bubble will burst. But no one can predict when—the sheer complexity of a world system involving the interaction of a score of major states, a thousand major multinationals and tens of thousands of medium-sized firms makes any scientific judgement as to the timing and amplitude of its ups and downs impossible.

For the moment, however, we can see some of the necessary political impact of what has been happening. This is because any capitalist boom (a bubble or otherwise) brings about enormous material changes to the substructure of the system. Industries expand and output rises—massively in the Chinese case. Some capitalists—and the states they rely on—find themselves strengthened, others weakened. New competitive pressures hit firms and states, and toss some asunder. Political adventurers emerge who promise to bring about a new stability by pursuing aggressive policies abroad or by tearing up the old compromises with exploited classes at home. Such political effects are bound to be especially strong when boom in two parts of the world is accompanied by stagnation elsewhere.

It is this interaction of economics and politics which explains the three current faultlines in the world system:

- *The morass in which the US finds itself in Iraq:* There is only one coherent explanation of the Bush-Rumsfeld adventure in invading Iraq and then trying to occupy it with a mere 130,000 troops—the feeling of major sections of the US ruling class that an opportunity existed to use the sheer weight and technical superiority of US weaponry to assure US hegemony in the face of potential challenges in the decades ahead.[33]

There have been and will continue to be divergent interests between European capital and US capital. The fact that European multinationals operate inside the US, and US multinationals inside Europe, does not alter the reliance of each on states to fight for the international interests—hence the hard bargaining between them in the World Trade Organisation. And the growing interaction in terms of markets between China and the US does not prevent US capital from wanting its state to have the power to dictate the terms on which this interaction takes place (as in the pressure on China to revalue its currency still more). Hence the debate within the US political establishment over whether China is to be treated as a welcome 'strategic competitor' or a potentially hostile 'strategic rival' which might have a bigger economy than the US in a couple of decades time.

Seizing physical control of the heart of the world's biggest oil producing region seemed an easy way of warding off such threats to hegemony—especially since Europe, Japan and China are more dependent on Middle East oil than is the US. But, by the same token, the failure to crush resistance in Iraq and establish a stable puppet regime now means US global hegemony is much weakened, with increasing divisions inside the US ruling class over how to deal with a crisis in many ways worse for it than that created by the Vietnam War in the early 1970s.

● *The rising insurgency in Latin America:* The overthrow of governments by popular uprisings in Argentina, Ecuador and Bolivia grew out of spontaneous eruptions of anger by the popular classes at the effects of economic crisis and neo-liberal policies. So has the upsurge of struggle from below that has defeated the three attempts to remove Chavez in Venezuela. The weakening of US hegemony caused by the Iraq morass now makes it difficult for it to intervene to restore capitalist stability in what it has always regarded as its backyard. At the same time the major South American governments are now taking advantage of this weakening, of their increased economic links with China, and of divergences between the US and Europe to buy off popular discontent with nationalist rhetoric and increase the leverage of certain national capitalist interests within the world system. The beef and sugar barons of Brazil have joined with their fellow capitalists in insisting that Lula follows a neo-liberal domestic agenda, but they have no problem with him taking advantage of the weakening of US hegemony in the fight to gain greater access to US markets. Hence talk at the time of the Summit of the Americas in Argentina of the US 'losing the plot' in Latin America.

● *The crisis of the European governments:* Three years ago, resistance to the neo-liberal policies being pushed through by governments expressed itself in one-day general strikes or public sector strikes in Spain, Italy and Portugal. Now the French European constitution referendum and the German election results have brought political instability to the heart of Europe. We are in for a long period of social and political turmoil as Europe's capitalists attempt to cope with increased global competition by taking away from the working classes what they conceded to them to buy class peace in the past.

The China-US syndrome also points to the possible emergence of yet another faultline. If the double bubble were to burst it would have profound political effects inside both countries. It would shake still further a Bush administration already in deep trouble because of Iraq. And it would profoundly weaken the ability of the Chinese ruling class to contain the growing, but still fragmented, struggles within the peasantry and the working class, and make possible a new—but bigger and more explosive—Tiananmen Square.

But even short of this, those who run the world system are in for a rough ride. They will respond, as they always have in the past, with a mixture of fine words and the most barbaric practices. All sorts of opportunities are opening up for those of us who are battling against the system—but the most terrible dangers if we do not take advantages of those opportunities.

NOTES

1: See C Harman, 'Where is Capitalism Going? Part Two', *International Socialism* 60 (Autumn 1993); C Hore, 'China's Century?', *International Socialism* 103 (Summer 2004).

2: Figures given in M Hart Landsberg and P Burkett, 'China and the Dynamics of Transnational Accumulation', paper given at conference on 'The Korean Economy: Marxist Perspectives', Gyeongsang National University, Jinju, South Korea, 20 May 2005.

3: Ching Kwan Lee, 'Made in China: Labor as a Political Force?' (University of Montana, 2004), available on www.umsst.edu/mansfield/Ching%20Kwan%20Lee%20paper.pdf

4: See, for instance, the CIA's estimates for different countries at www.indexmundi.com/g/r.aspxc=ee&v=65

5: For a critique of the use of parity purchasing power measurements see, for instance, J Studwell, *The China Dream* (London, 2002), pp160-162.

6: See my criticisms of such theorists in 'Where is Capitalism Going? Part Two', as above, and in 'Analysing Imperialism', *International Socialism* 99 (Summer 2003). For India, see my 'India: A Rough Guide', *International Socialism* 103 (Summer 2004).

7: According to the Department of Trade and Industry in 2004. See S Desai, Reuters report, 6 May 2004, www.ciol.com/content/news/BPO/2004/104050601.asp

8: For the full story see the issues of the *China Daily* (Beijing) for the second week of August 2005.

9: C Guidi and W Chuntao, *Survey of Chinese Peasants*, quoted in Yang Lian, 'Dark Side of the Moon', *New Left Review* 32 (March-April 2005), available on www.newleftreview.net/NLR26606.shtml

10: *South China Post*, quoted in M Hart Landsberg and P Burkett, as above, p24.

11: Figure quoted in M Hart Landsberg and P Burkett, as above.

12: As above, p5.

13: As above.

14: Quoted by J Kynge, *Financial Times*, 23 September 2003.

15: *Financial Times*, 4 February 2003.

16: *Financial Times*, 4 February 2003.

17: Quoted in *Financial Times*, 18 November 2003.

18: According to Li Shuguang of Beijing's Zhengfa University, quoted in *Financial Times*, 23 September 2003.

19: McGuckin and Spiegelman, quoted in M Hart Landsberg and P Burkett, as above, p36.

20: *Asian Times*, 26 October 2005. There seems to me some incompatibility between his figures for the share of consumption in GDP and for exports and investment.

21: Quoted in J Kynge, *Financial Times*, 23 September 2003.

22: From year end 1997 to year end 2004, China's foreign exchange reserves (invested heavily in US Treasury securities) rose from $143 billion to $578 billion, South Korea's from $20 billion to $199 billion and Japan's from $220 billion to $834 billion, according to Robert J Samuelson, *Newsweek*, 21 March 2005.

23: R Brenner, *The Boom and the Bubble* (London, 2002), table 9.2, p235.

24: For sources, see my article, 'Beyond the Boom', *International Socialism* 90 (Spring 2001), pp49 and 51.

25: See for instance, recent pieces by Stephen Roach of Morgan Stanley, 'The Big Squeeze', and *Asian Times*, 26 October 2005.

26: Figures quoted in M Hart Landsberg and P Burkett, as above, p10.

27: *Financial Times*, 26 September 2003.

28: These are figures for full time workers—including part time workers reduces the yearly total for all countries.

29: See C Harman, 'Beyond the Boom', as above, p49. My source was Samuel Brittan of the *Financial Times*. There are various measures of labour productivity and levels of investment. G Duménil and Levy in *Resurgent Capital* (London, 2004) show labour productivity per hour in Europe still slightly behind that in the US, but investment per worker ahead. Andrew Glyn ('Global Balances', *New Left Review* 34, July-August 2005) shows productivity in Europe well behind that in the US. But the differences in calculations do not alter the basic point about hours and exploitation.

30: Duménil and Levy show the Europeans catching up with the US in terms of productivity, but losing their advantage in terms of growth rates from the mid-1970s onwards. See Duménil and Levy, *Resurgent Capital*, as above, graphs on pp31, 40 and 56.

31: For an excellent summary of what has happened in US, see M D Yates, 'A Statistical Portrait of the US Working Class' (a review of *State of Working America*), written by economists at the Economic Policy Institute in Washington, DC) in *Monthly Review*, April 2005.

32: See, for instance, Martin Wolff, *Financial Times*, 4 November 2005.

33: There was a sense within the US political establishment right through the 1990s, as expressed in the utterances of Kissinger and Brzezinsky, that they lacked a clear strategy for maintaining their hegemony—for some details see my article 'Analysing Imperialism', as above.

Anti-capitalism, social forums and the return of politics

Chris Nineham

Six years after its coming out party at Seattle, the anti-capitalist movement faces its biggest challenges yet.

The movement has made huge advances. Its basic critiques have become mainstream. Walk in to virtually any bookshop in the world and you will find a shelf of popular books putting the case against corporate power and the neo-conservative warmongers. Few now believe that privatisation delivers better services, that the international financial institutions like the WTO and the IMF are there to help the people of developing countries, or that the occupation in Iraq has anything to do with liberation.

Huge mobilisations against the neo-liberals continue. Some 100,000 marched against the G8 at Geneva and Annemasse in 2003, 300,000 protested at last year's G8 summit in Scotland, up to 5,000 attended the Southern African Social Forum in Harare in October 2005, and a month later George Bush was greeted by tens of thousands of protesters when he flew in to the Summit of the Americas at Mar del Plata in Argentina. The protests helped block the implementation of the Free Trade Area of the Americas. Meanwhile, the first electoral successes for the radical left in generations show how far the aspiration for another world is gaining ground.

On the other hand, political issues are arising that challenge some of the movement's basic assumptions. Some of its characteristic methods are faltering. In Britain and elsewhere the anarchist or autonomist inspired street actions peaked early and have virtually disappeared.[1] The protests at economic summits continue to inspire but appear to be changing. Whereas the early protests at Nice, Gothenburg, Genoa and Cancun were multinational, recent summit protests have been more local affairs. The great demonstration in Edinburgh at last year's G8 was the biggest ever in Scotland, and comparable in size to the Genoa G8 protest of 2001. But unlike Genoa or Geneva in 2002, this was basically a national rather than an international protest. It was a testament to the depth of anti-capitalist feeling in Scotland and England, but also maybe a sign that summit-hopping is losing its appeal.

The other big difference with past protests was the politics. In Scotland for the first time a mainstream political party made a play to co-opt a global justice protest. Through its influence on the NGOs, New Labour helped define the protest's agenda and publicly claimed the marchers' aims as it own.[2] This made the protests highly contested. In line with government thinking, the big NGOs in the Make Poverty History coalition fought hard to keep the main demonstration single issue. They excluded Britain's main anti-war organisation, the Stop the War Coalition, from their alliance, and tried to keep the left away.[3] This approach was a depressing betrayal of the promise of unity in diversity on display at Seattle, Genoa and the other great mobilisations.

The attempt to limit the protest largely failed because it contradicted the protesters' mood. Most of the marchers took it for granted that war and poverty are linked, and that it makes sense to protest at the two together. Up and down the great 2 July demonstration, anti-war placards, T-shirts and slogans mixed comfortably with calls for debt cancellation and trade justice.

The attempt at co-option by the Blairites is just one example of the way in which politics is becoming inescapable. In many European countries new left parties or coalitions have suddenly started winning mass electoral support. In Latin America the left's one-time hero, Lula, has capitulated to the globalisers in office in the birthplace of the World Social Forum, but Chavez has become an electrifying symbol of more serious opposition. A series of insurgent movements have shaken the regimes in Argentina, Bolivia and Ecuador. In Bolivia last year the insurgency swept away two presidents and became so threatening in June that the government couldn't meet in the capital, La Paz, to choose a new candidate. The central demand of the mass movement was the renationalisation of hydrocarbon reserves. Up to now the anti-capitalist movement has downplayed politics in general and avoided the issue of state power in particular. It now needs to reconsider.

The origins of a movement

Seattle was the outcome of 20 years of struggles against neo-liberalism. Throughout the 1980s workers and the poor, North and South, fought IMF and World Bank programmes, but most of the struggles in this first round were defeated. The experience of defeat led to demoralisation and retreat into identity politics. Through the 1990s the impact of the neo-liberal programme became clear to more and more people and new struggles broke out from South Korea to Bolivia displaying a new spirit of militancy.

Most of these were single-issue campaigns and remained isolated. There were two significant exceptions. French public sector strikes in 1995 received huge popular support, became politicised and challenged the authority of the government. On 1 January 1994, on the day of the implementation of one of the most aggressive free trade agreements of the decade, a mysterious army of peasants emerged from the Chiapas Forest in south eastern Mexico. They called themselves the EZLN (Zapatista Army of National Liberation, Zapatistas for short). They were carrying guns, demanding autonomy and declaiming poetic slogans. 'They are trying to turn Mexico into a shopping mall,' they said. 'We thought we were up against the state of Mexico, but in reality we were up against the great financial powers'.[4] Images of the indigenous uprising that followed were beamed round the world, and lifted the spirits of millions hurting from the globalisers' shock therapy.

By the late 1990s millions had rediscovered that what was good news for the corporations was bad for workers and the poor. Free market triumphalism had raised expectations that never came through, and at the same time advertised the scale of the globalisers' superprofits. Even when there were no struggles, people were searching for ways to express their discontent. In 1998 in France the founders of the anti currency speculation ATTAC network were overwhelmed at the response to their tentative launch letter:

> The appeal was launched like a bottle in to the sea, without any idea of what the reaction might be. But no sooner had the article appeared than we were deluged by phone calls and letters. I have never seen any article generate such a response. Normally, a piece of paper will generate half a dozen letters...

> This time we were filling boxes with them day after day… I was astonished by the speed with which the different organisations decided financial commitment that accompanied it to take part, including trade union committees not usually quick off the mark.[5]

Seattle and the summits

It was the new visibility of the financial summits, particularly the WTO, which really focused the international movement. The 1999 Seattle protests against the WTO were the turning point. They had a huge impact because they took place at the heart of the beast and in the home of Microsoft, and because they so visibly encapsulated a new alliance between trade unionists and young activists. A series of protests followed that brought hundreds of thousands of activists together at summits in Prague, Stockholm, Brussels, Bangkok, Washington, Barcelona and Genoa.

The summits conveniently embodied the connections between ecological devastation, sweatshop labour, privatisation of the public realm and corporate greed. They illustrated the global ambitions of the big corporations, so underlining the possibility of North-South alliances. The summit protests generated widespread support and helped put the anti-capitalist critique on the map. The *Economist* was expressing alarm back in 2000:

> The protesters are right to say that the most urgent political moral and economic question of our time is Third World poverty. They are also right to say that wave of globalisation, however powerful it may be, can be turned back. It is the fact that these two things are true which makes the protesters, and crucially the current of opinion that sympathises with them, so terribly dangerous.[6]

The protests had an electrifying effect on activists. Genoa rejuvenated the Italian left and helped inspire a run of monster demonstrations in Spain and elsewhere. In fact it is probably the movement's very success that has made international summit protests less of an activist priority over time. They fitted the movement when it first emerged. They offered a convergence that gave fledgling movements and networks the confidence of numbers and suggested a whole range of possible new alliances. As the movements have grown in social weight, activists have focused more on the domestic agenda.

Also, it has become obvious that action on the streets against the summits on its own cannot stop the neo-liberal juggernaut. The ambush at

Seattle shook the WTO. The recent protests at the Summit of the Americas in Argentina have graphically underlined Bush's isolation in the world. It is humiliating that the G8 have been literally driven out of the cities into the hills. But at the same time WTO and G8 leaders have learnt how to deal with protests and continue to meet. And the summits themselves are not make or break for the neo-liberal order. The G8 is a discussion forum with no joint staff or institutional memory. The WTO is a much more important forum for pushing the Western globalisers' agenda and attempting to resolve trade disputes. But WTO negotiations are currently two years behind, and the world trading system continues to function. Even when a combination of protests and deadlock between rival blocs disrupted the Cancun WTO in 2003, the terms of trade were not radically overhauled. Business continued either on the basis of the status quo or through new bilateral agreements.

International mobilising is here to stay. It hardly needs saying that the struggle against the war in Iraq has been hugely strengthened by international coordination. The same is likely to be true for climate change campaigning. Domestic European opposition to the neo-liberal EU constitution and the Bolkestein directive was boosted by the fact that tens of thousands marched against them in Brussels in March 2004. This incredibly resourceful movement will no doubt invent new forms of international solidarity and networking. But it remains the case that neo-liberal policies are mainly implemented at the level of the nation-state. If we are to stop them there is no getting round the fact we have to be able to stop them at home.

The international social forums

The idea that the new movement should have its own gatherings flowed from the same logic as the summit protests. Bernard Cassen, who had helped found the Attac network in France, was one of the prime movers of the World Social Forum. For him the purpose of such gatherings was 'to give a global visibility to struggles that are atomised and aren't even aware of each other. It also exposes what they have in common...we will analyse but we will also outline propositions for action over the coming months and years'.[7] Travelling across countries or continents was a step towards the kind of global movement which was felt necessary to challenge the globalisers. Like the summit protests, it was a chance to escape the frustrations or relative isolation of your own country or community.

The WSF has spawned regional forums that have galvanised the movement in many parts of the world. The Florence European Social Forum in 2002 was an important moment in European politics, ending as it did with a million-strong demonstration against an attack on Iraq and a call for anti-war demonstrations across Europe on 15 February 2003. The Asian Social Forum in Hyderabad in 2003 helped kickstart a new dialogue on the left in South Asia, leading to the coalition of the left and the NGOs that hosted the massive 2004 Mumbai World Social Forum and a new optimism in the movements in India.

The World Social Forum continues to be an inspirational gathering for tens of thousands of activists. At its best it brings together activists from different countries, backgrounds and campaigns in a creative maelstrom of debate and discussion. But there is a worrying lobby in the movement for decentralisation. This year a 'polycentric' WSF is taking place in three locations. It is too early to tell what impact this will have, but the tendency towards fragmentation at the events themselves is undoubtedly damaging. Organisers at last year's WSF at Porto Alegre built sectionalism into the event by assigning different areas of the huge site to single issues. Such segregation deadened and depoliticised the event.

The WSF has fitted a need of the movement, but it was initiated and organised from above by a small group of activists from Brazil and France. This has had important consequences for internal democracy. The ruling International Council was self-appointed at the start and remains unelected to this day. Initially decisions were taken by a handful of people—the decision, for example, about where to hold the second WSF was taken in a restaurant in Porto Alegre.[8]

This lack of democracy remains. There are still no democratic decision-making bodies or meetings at the WSF at all. In fact the WSF is constitutionally unable to make decisions, and political parties are banned from participating, despite the fact that a huge number of the activists involved are members of left wing parties. This is no accident. The given reason was that the only way to persuade moderate organisations to enter the political ring with thousands of radical activists was to promise there would be no conclusions, no decisions they had to respect. The underlying truth is that adherence to these rules allows moderate, reformist forces to dominate unchallenged.

Some regional forums have had a big impact. The European Social Forum has been an important gathering for the movement since its inception in 2002. The recent Southern African Social Forum was a success but drew people overwhelmingly from the host country, Zimbabwe. But the picture is mixed—the Mediterranean Social Forum has never reached out beyond a hardcore of activists.

The international forums mainly continue to thrive because they have a specific purpose—to provide a chance for activists to meet at regional or global level. However, their continued success shouldn't hide important limitations in the way they are conceived and the way they work.

Local social forums

Some predicted that social forums would become the cornerstones of the anti-capitalist movement in every locality. By and large this has not happened. Italy is the one country that came near. In the year after the great Genoa demonstration forums sprung up across the country. In October 2001, 2,000 delegates met in Genoa from 92 local forums and announced the formation of the Italian Social Forum.[9] At the movement's peak 18 months later there were perhaps 170 forums around the country meeting with various degrees of regularity. The forums were able to mount significant mobilisations in different parts of the country.[10] But today, just three years later, the forums have collapsed and activists have moved on. Elsewhere citywide or national social forums are sometimes successful as annual gatherings for the movement, but they hardly ever meet more regularly. Many appear to have fizzled out or become refuges for one or other strand of the movement.[11] Unlike the international forums, the local forums could easily become one more meeting for activists who were in contact anyway through campaigns. They could work when focused around a particular mobilisation. At other times they were in danger of becoming talking shops. Bernard Cassen's vision of 'a thousand forums' spreading across the globe never materialised.

The NGOs

NGOs are among the biggest and best funded, and therefore most influential, participants in the international movement. They gave the movement an important early boost. The formation of the NGO coalition Jubilee 2000 in Britain in 1996 led to an 80,000-strong mobilisation at the Birmingham G8 in 1998, an important prototype for later summit protests. The rise of the NGOs was a product of the privatisation of aid. Between 1975 and 1985 the amount of aid transferred from developed to developing countries nations via NGOs shot up 1,400 percent.[12]

On the one hand neo-liberalism has radicalised the NGOs. The international business meetings were a legitimate lobbying target for them, and they had the resources and the infrastructure to coordinate internationally. At the same time there has been an active programme by neo-liberal governments and international agencies to shape NGOs to their own ends. Given the tendency of neo-liberalism to undermine democracy and create popular resistance, the guardians of the New World Order have turned to NGOs as agents of 'local development' and controlled participation to offset the emergence of real popular mass movements.

As early as 1994, the World Bank had identified both the unique ability of NGOs 'to reach poor communities and remote areas, promote local particiapation, and operate at a low cost, identify local needs and build on local resources', but also the drawback of the direct democracy some NGOs promoted with 'its limited replicability, self-sustainability, managerial...capacity, narrow context for programmes and politicisation'.[13] Funding bodies have spent a huge amount of energy trying to pressure NGOs to accept a narrow and apolitical approach to working with the poor, and to limit local participation to small-scale local projects that raise no questions about broader social priorities.

A study of Latin America explains how 'the micro-reforms and NGOs promoted a pacific or "civil" [non-confrontational] form of politics, turning the rural poor away from the social movements into local self-help "projects" funded [and designed] from above and the outside. It also created the conditions for an adjustment to the discipline of globalisation and its governance requirements'.[14]

In the worst cases NGOs are directly manipulated—and sometimes even created—by governments to help open up the public sector to private capital. This appears to be the recent experience in Singapore, for example.[15] Most NGOs have more distance from politicians, but they are at least partially dependant on governments. So though many NGO workers and activists, North and South, support the general aspiration for global justice, they are often wary of mass movements. The experience of Make Poverty History shows how this instinct can lead to efforts to gag sections of the movement and to attempted hijack by neo-liberals. The spate of Live 8 concerts that accompanied the MPH campaign reflected popular concern about global poverty but ended up promoting Blair's pro-market initiatives for Africa.

Of course there are important dissident voices coming from many NGOs, and the most mainstream NGOs often express frustration with politicians. After the event many British NGOs criticised the deals over debt, aid and climate change made at the G8, for example. But this cycle of lobbying and disappointment only illustrates the problem. NGOs cannot tackle the deep structural problems of neo-liberal capitalism head-on. Even the most radical NGO activists who reject the state tend to adopt autonomist politics that ignore it rather than finding ways to change it or confront it.

For all these reasons NGOs tend to push for a movement structured around single issues. They try to keep radical political parties at arm's length and avoid opening themselves up to the democracy of the movements.

Autonomism

As Stathis Kouvélakis has pointed out, one of the reasons neo-liberalism created a crisis of legitimacy for the capitalists was that it depended on abandoning Keynesian social compromises.[16] The hollowing out of social democracy helps explain why the anti-capitalist movement emerged in such explosive and unexpected ways. It also helps to explain the kind of ideas that flourished early on.

The movement developed at a time when most of the left was in some disarray. On the one hand social democrats everywhere were embracing the market. On the other hand much of the socialist left was still demoralised and confused by the collapse of the Soviet Union. Meanwhile workers were only slowly regaining the confidence to fight. Whereas in the late 1960s in many places a militant working class was present at the birth of the movement, in the late 1990s that was a minority experience.

So the ideas that dominated early on reflected growing resistance to and rejection of neo-liberalism but also a feeling that traditional left strategies had failed. Zapatista spokesperson Subcomandante Marcos expressed this combination crudely but clearly in his parody of 'old left' practice: 'There is an oppressor power which decides on behalf of society from above, and a group of visionaries which decides to lead the country on the correct path and ousts the other group from power, seizes power, and then also decides on behalf of society.'

It is really left nationalism he is critiquing here, but his attack is aimed at the left as a whole. His conclusion is that all leadership is a problem:

> We could not and should not try to lead the struggles encountered on our journey, or fly the flag for them... We had imagined that those below would not be slow to show themselves, with so many injustices, so many complaints, so many wounds... In our minds we had formed the image that our march would be a kind of plough, turning the soil so that all this could rise from the ground.[17]

These sentiments were taken up by many of the movement's most popular writers. They gave a new lease of life to the tradition of 'autonomist Marxism' that had seemed buried in the rubble of the Italian left in the late 1970s. Though there are different strands of autonomist ideas, they share the belief that capitalism creates the conditions for its own transcendence through spontaneous action by individuals or networks. 'Old left' concepts of organised confrontation are useless or worse because they deal in notions of power and class that inevitably lead to new hierarchies. The stress is on the paradoxical notion of spontaneous, decentralised organisation. For the most influential autonomist writers, Tony Negri and Michael Hardt, 'each local struggle functions as a node that communicates with all the other nodes without any hub or centre of intelligence'.[18]

For John Holloway, author of *Change the World Without Taking Power*, any attempt to understand or describe the nature of the system that we face is suspect: 'There is nothing fixed to which we can cling for reassurance: not class, not Marx, not revolution, nothing but the moving negation of untruth'.[19] All the autonomists are wary of any politics that addresses the issue of the state, as if even admitting the possibility of a concentration of power in society will lead to betrayal: 'Power is not possessed by any particular person or institution. Power lies rather in the fragmentation of social relations... The state is not the locus of power that it appears to be'.[20]

Politics returns

Though these ideas have had an influence way beyond autonomist circles proper their hold has been progressively weakened. Violent state repression at the Gothenburg and Genoa summits threw the idea of 'non-confrontational confrontation' into question. Events post-9/11 have dramatically confirmed the importance of state power in shaping world politics. While initially most writers influenced by autonomist ideas played down the importance of the war on terror, many have now recognised the geopolitical importance of the war and have therefore had to amend their approach.[21]

The seriousness of the left electoral alternatives challenges the idea that politics can be ignored. The Italian Disobedienti, largest and most influential of the European autonomist groups, is split over whether to support the electoral alliance between Rifondazione Comunista and the centre-left in next year's presidential election.

The mass struggles in Latin America have put further strain on autonomism. It is hard to ignore the issue of power in Chavez's Venezuala when the elites have tried to remove Chavez from office three times. In Ecuador, Bolivia and elsewhere organised workers have played a vital role alongside peasants and indigenous peoples in struggles which have had to confront state power head-on. In situations like these the movement has to discuss how to respond collectively.

The December 2001 uprising in Argentina which removed the De la Rua government was marked by a high degree of spontaneity. It led to months of permanent mobilisation and the creation of popular neighbourhood committees in many urban areas that rightly celebrated their autonomy from old clientist political structures. Commentators on both left and right talked of a pre-revolutionary situation. But in the course of just two years the movement for democracy from below petered out, and the Kirchner government has managed to organise a return to 'normal capitalism'.

The basic problem was that the spontaneous and autonomous nature of the uprising—originally a strength—became a strategic weakness. No national leadership emerged that could unite the diverse elements of the movement behind a coherent programme aimed at taking state power. There was no systematic effort to challenge the union leaders' attempt to insulate organised workers from the movement. After a while the insurgency fragmented into a series of smaller movements, each dominated by a leader or a small left party. After a period of panic and confusion the ruling class was able to restore order by dividing, isolating and co-opting the movement.[22]

Despite all this, autonomist ideas still have an influence.[23] Many of the movement's writers are reluctant to discuss strategy, still less to talk about it in terms of class.[24] There is still hostility to left parties in some circles. Partly this is because the radicalisation in society has yet to be matched by breakthrough class struggles in most parts of the world. Partly it reflects the heavy involvement of NGOs in the movement. NGO intellectuals naturally tend to privilege new, non-class based social movements and identity politics. They lose sight of the state in a fuzzy discourse of 'civil society'. There is an identifiable continuum from autonomist language proper right through to the official developmental rhetoric of 'self-help', 'participation' and 'empowerment'.[25] But autonomist prejudices against party politics and centralised organisation are also built into some of the practices of the movement because they benefit the more moderate forces involved.

Limits of the forums

The ban on political parties and the lack of decision-making in the forums is important for the NGOs. But paradoxically it is highly convenient for any moderate political parties trying to relate to the movement. The Brazilian Workers Party gained a lot of credit from hosting the first WSF in Porto Alegre. Despite its drift towards neo-liberalism it could happily associate itself with the forum, because its leaders knew the forum could not become a centre of practical opposition. Deliberately or otherwise, the growing fragmentation of the forums makes them safer from the point of view of the social liberals.

One of the Brazilian pioneers of the World Social Forum, Chico Whittaker, compares the forum to 'a square without an owner':

> If the square has an owner other than the collectivity it fails to be a square and becomes private property. Like the public square, the forum is an open but not neutral space. The forum opens from time to time in different parts of the world with one specific objective: to allow as many individuals, organisations and movements as possible that oppose neo-liberalism to get together freely, listen to each other, learn from the experiences and struggles of others and discuss proposals of action; to become linked in new nets and organisations aiming at overcoming the present process of globalisation dominated by large international corporations and their financial interests.[26]

To take him literally for a moment, Chico must know that under capitalism no space is altogether open. Even so-called public spaces have administering powers. The organisers of every world and regional social forum have had to negotiate with local authorities who have had certain concerns and requirements. The presence of politicians at or around all the forums shows that, despite the nominal ban on political parties, the space of the forum is in fact affected by the balance of power in the real world. At last year's WSF in Porto Alegre the speakers at the biggest venue, the 20,000-seat Gigantino stadium, were Lula at the start of the event and Chavez at the end. These were fascinating events, but the fact is these men represent the two dominant strands of politics in Latin America today. There was no debate at the events. Trade unionists and socialists who opposed Lula's neo-liberal reforms were reduced to heckling during his speech

The notion that the social forums operate independent of party politics was always a myth, but it is becoming harder and harder to sustain. One of the 'polycentric' forums this year is taking place in Caracas, Venezuela. It is difficult to see how the forum can ignore the struggle between Chavez and his supporters and most of Venezuela's capitalist class. The movement in Italy has actually demanded that this year's European Social Forum be postponed so that it does not interfere with the Italian elections! And the organisers of the 'polycentric' World Social Forum in Karachi, Pakistan, can hardly feel like they are operating in a political vacuum.

But in this model of a structureless open space there is nowhere to collectively discuss the big questions about how to tackle neo-liberalism. Some participants see this lack of formal politics as a plus: 'Like the jazz of Charlie Parker and Miles Davis, the forum is experimenting with a politics that can cope with uncertainty and is not constantly straining for formal harmony (in political terms, political unity)'.[28] In reality such lack of definition suits the reformists more than anyone. In fact autonomist language often barely disguises a defence of gradualism: 'The WSF privileges rebellion and non-conformity at the expense of revolution. There is no unique theory to guide the movements, because the aim is not so much to seize power but rather to change the many faces of power as they present themselves in the institutions and sociabilities'.[28]

Just as crucial for the reformists, the autonomist conception of the forum rules out collective strategic thinking on more immediate issues as well. As Chico says, 'Nobody in the forum has the right or the power to say that one action or proposal is more important than another'.[29]. In fact the forums have no capacity to make any proposals for action at all. Activists within the forum have invented the Assembly of the Social Movements to try to overcome this problem by producing a list of upcoming campaigns for the movement. The assembly has done some important work, and was crucial to launching the 15 February global day of action in 2003. But while it is action-orientated, it runs by consensus as opposed to democracy and it has no elected leadership. Deciding priorities without voting is virtually impossible. In so far as there are decisions, they are taken at interminable and dwindling pre-meetings. The assembly itself is experienced by many as the presentation of a list predecided by unknown persons somewhere else.

Consensus decision-making is not just slow and unwieldy—it builds in a veto that can be used by any group, however unrepresentative. Despite massive support for the initiative, some French groups tried to use a veto to stop the launch of the global day of action against war on 15 February 2003 at the Florence ESF. More recently the European Preparatory Assembly was blocked from sending a message of support to the campaign against the EU constitution in France on the grounds that the assembly was not allowed to take political positions!

Social forums are partly shaped by what is going on around them. The Florence ESF was so dynamic because the Italian movement was on the rise after Genoa and because opposition to the war on Iraq was coming to boiling point. In that situation many of the limitations of the forum model were swept aside. Whatever the technicalities, people will remember the forum for its call for action against the war. At other times even the great World Social Forums can feel like tamed incarnations of the movement. They collect the movement's energy without giving it direction. They bring together tens of thousands of activists in discussions without conclusions. They are the foremost gatherings of a movement that demands people power but are themselves undemocratic, and therefore open to co-option and manipulation by mainstream political forces. Of course the WSFs continue to be useful gatherings for activists who would otherwise have no global meeting point—they fit our need for international contact, and exchange of ideas, information and perspectives. They have a huge inspirational charge. But some of their weaknesses will surely have to be addressed if they are to have a useful future as strategic centres for the movements.

Shaping up to the future

It is not possible for the movement to progress without drawing millions more into action and that means tackling political questions head-on. But it is not enough simply to preach. One of the problems with the forums is that they aspire to mass participation on the basis of generalised opposition to neo-liberal capitalism. Despite the rhetoric of openness and inclusivity they are not designed to attract people just getting active. Officially the

WSF is open only to 'groups and movements of civil society that are opposed to neo-liberalism and to domination of the world by capital and any form of imperialism'.[30] It is a mark of the depth of radicalisation that they have thrived at all on that basis. But the reality is, whatever their general view of the world, most people actually get involved in political activity first round some specific issue and develop their politics as they go. Single-issue coalitions or united fronts round the most pressing issues of the day are therefore crucial to maximising involvement.

That was the nature of the victorious French campaign against the European constitution and the German coalition against Schröder's welfare reforms that shook the government in 2004. It was the basis for the anti-war mobilisations that took the movement to a new level at the beginning of 2003 and continue to destablise Bush and Blair. Such campaigns have drawn millions of people into action for the first time. They bring together existing activists with what the British media have called 'virgin protesters' in a mutual learning curve. Though this kind of encounter generates fantastic debate, its strength depends on staying practical and keeping demands as simple as possible.

In this context setting priorities is crucial. It is not true that all campaigns should have an equal importance. Serious opposition to the neo-liberal project means prioritising the campaigns that can mobilise the maximum numbers and inflict maximum damage. These kinds of judgments involve a political analysis. Those that wanted to downplay the anti-war movement delinked war and neo-liberalism. Even after the attack on Iraq Bernard Cassen argued, 'War or peace, the problems of globalisation remained essentially the same on 10 September and 12 September—hunger, debt, inequality, AIDS'.[31] The revolutionary left and others argued that, on the contrary, imperialist war is wired in to the logic of modern day neo-liberalism. Because it is the most extreme expression of a system that puts profits before people, war is deeply destabilising. Because it is such a central priority for the US ruling class, a defeat in Iraq would be a disaster for neo-liberalism generally. As the *Economist* warns about Iraq, 'A loss of nerve and a humiliating retreat might turn America into a shadow of itself, with consequences that would be felt well beyond the Middle East'.[32]

It is hard to see how we can build the broadest, most powerful movement possible if we duck these strategic debates and the exchange of political analyses that go with them. It is equally difficult to conceive of a successful movement in the 21st century that ignores the fight against imperialism. More than that, the prejudice that lingers in parts of the movement against politics with a capital 'P' is disarming. Despite growing cynicism towards mainstream politics, the social democratic parties still have strong influence and contain many strands of opinion. They particularly have close links with the leaderships of the trade unions, who use these links as a rationale for accepting austerity measures and not 'rocking the boat'. It is all too clear from the recent series of false starts and missed opportunities in the British labour movement that these arguments can demoralise militants unless an alternative set of ideas is widely available. Struggle is never purely spontaneous—the ideas in peoples heads always effect how they try to solve problems.

In country after country the movements are now being forced to take up political arguments and try to find ways to challenge the social liberals. The nature of the arguments varies according to the state of the struggle. In Britain the war and the anti-war movement generated a demand for an electoral alternative to New Labour that is anti war and anti-neoliberal. Sections of the movement have set up Respect as a response. For many people politics is elections. Electoral campaigning in turn gives activists the possibility of systematically relating to millions of people. In Germany the mass movement against the 'Agenda 2010' welfare cuts helped to split the SPD and create a the new Left Party. In Brazil P-SOL is attracting many new members with a more clearly anti-capitalist programme. In Bolivia and Venezuela the issue of revolutionary politics is on the agenda. The movements cannot be reduced to the new political formations, but it would be suicide for activists to ignore the possibilities they open up.

We started out just a few years ago full of excitement, travelling to international protests tens of thousands strong. Now there are monster demonstrations wherever George Bush's Air Force One touches down. In almost every country on the globe including the US, polls show a majority against the war in Iraq and the whole range of policies Bush stands for. The rejection of the EU constitution in France and the Netherlands shows that national majorities can be mobilised against neo-liberalism in the teeth of a united ruling class propaganda offensive. We have to continue to put our case in every forum available, but it's time to leave suspicion of politics and strategising behind us.

NOTES

1: For example, the high profile series of May Day actions in Britain that started in 1999 has petered out.

2: For detail of the relationship between Make Poverty History and New Labour see K Quarmby, 'Why Oxfam is Failing Africa', *New Statesman*, 30 May 2005; and S Hodgkinson, 'Make the G8 History', *Red Pepper* 132, July 2005.

3: See S Hodgkinson, as above, p20.

4: A Starr, *Global Revolt: A Guide to the Movements Against Globalisation* (London, 2005), p24.

5: B Cassen, 'Inventing ATTAC', in Tom Mertes (ed), *A Movement of Movements: Is Another World Really Possible?* (London, 2004), p152.

6: *Economist*, 23 September 2000.

7: B Cassen, *Tout a commencé a Porto Alegre* (France, 2003), p78.

8: As above, p62.

9: *Il Manifesto*, 21 October 2001.

10: See T Behan, *Italy: The Politics That Came in From the Cold* (Verso, forthcoming)

11: In the absence of any published overview this summary is based on participants' accounts from Italy, Germany, France, the US, Switzerland, Zimbabwe, Spain, Greece and some recent personal experience in Britain and Australia.

12: J Bunyarutanasuntorn, 'The Dynamics of Thai NGOs' in N Petprasert (ed), *NGOs 2000: Political Economy (For the Community)* no 11, p74. Quoted in J G Ungpakorn, 'NGOs: Enemies or Allies?', *International Socialism* 104 (Autumn 2004), p49.

13: Quoted in S Kamat, 'NGO's and the New Democracy: The False Saviours of International Development', *Harvard International Review*, Spring 2003, p66.

14: J Petras and H Veltmeyer, *Social Movements and State Power Argentina, Brazil, Bolivia, Ecuador* (Pluto, 2005), p229.

15: See J G Ungpakorn, as above.

16: See S Kouvélakis, 'France: The Triumph of the Political', *International Socialism* 108 (Autumn 2005), p8.

17: Subcomandante Marcos, 'The Hourglass of the Zapatistas' in Tom Mertes (ed), as above, p5.

18: M Hardt and A Negri, *Multitude* (London, 2005), p217.

19: J Holloway, *Change the World Without Taking Power* (London, 2002), p99.

20: As above, pp72-73.

21: Naomi Klein, for example, argued up until mid-2003 that the war was not the central issue for the movement and that it could be a diversion for the movement against neo-liberalism. By early 2004 she was emphasising the links between the war on terror and corporate globalisation and writing extensively about the occupation of Iraq.

22: See J Petras and H Veltmeyer, as above pp40-42.

23: See, for example, Naomi Klein in the *Guardian*, 5 November 2005. Here she argues that the indigenous struggles in Latin America provide the template for a new politics of autonomy.

24: It has been noticeable from the start that many leading figures including Klein, Chomsky and Monbiot as well as Hardt, Negri, Holloway, etc, are very reluctant to debate movement strategy. Sometimes this can be put down to the understandable wariness of the intellectual to prescribe to the movement. On closer inspection it is often down to a more thoroughgoing attachment to spontaneity. See, for example, Chomsky's comments on strategy in 'Movement Organising' in P Mitchell and J Schoeffel, *Understanding Power, The Indispensible Chomsky* (New York, 2003), p339.

25: See J Petras and H Veltmeyer, as above, p23.

26: C Whitaker, 'The WSF as Open Space' in *World Social Forum: Challenging Empires* (New Delhi, 2004), p113.

27: H Wainwright, 'The Forum as Jazz' in *World Social Forum: Challenging Empires*, as above, pxx.

28: B de Sousa Santos, 'The World Social Forum: Toward a Counter-Hegemonic Globalization (part 1)', in *World Social Forum: Challenging Empires*, as above, p243.

29: C Whitaker, as above, p114.

30: World Social Forum Charter of Principles, www.wsf-fsm.org

31: B Cassen, 'Inventing ATTAC', as above, p165.

32: *Economist*, 15 September 2005, p24.

Gramsci and revolution: a necessary clarification[a]

Roberto Robaina

The name of Antonio Gramsci is regularly invoked internationally by people looking for a version of Marxism that avoids references to revolution. Roberto Robaina challenges this approach, criticising fellow Brazilians who use it.

Brazil was one of the first countries in Latin America to rediscover Antonio Gramsci. This was important in itself, but it was also attended by the theoretical distortions of a left that, although it was breaking with Stalinism, still resisted the alternative of a revolutionary perspective.

The first disseminators of Gramsci's thought, particularly Carlos Nelson Coutinho, extended the discussion about the state to include questions of hegemony, the accumulation of forces and the necessity or otherwise of insurrection. And it was precisely on these questions that Gramsci has been most misused within the Brazilian Workers Party (PT), where his work has been represented as reformist. Concepts like hegemony and historic bloc, for example, have been consistently distorted. Some leaders of the PT, indeed, are still using these concepts to defend a politics of class collaboration with the bourgeoisie, or at least sections of it.

The concept of the historic bloc, for example, has nothing to do with alliances with the bourgeoisie, nor can hegemony be transformed into a justification for concessions to the exploiting classes or a search for consensus with them—at least not in the name of Gramsci. When he led the Italian

---

a: This is a slightly edited version of a chapter from Robaina's book, *Una vision desde la izquierda: La Socialdemocracia, el Estado y el PT*. The translation is by Mike Gonzalez.

Communist Party, before he was imprisoned, Gramsci left no room for doubt as to the necessity for the movements of industrial and agricultural workers to build alliances with the peasants of the south and the islands.[1] He affirmed the decisive role of intellectuals in the formation of these alliances, arguing that they played a key role in binding the peasantry to the big landowners, and arguing the urgent need to break that link by building a left current among the intellectuals. Gramsci certainly pointed to the need for consensus among the broad peasant masses as a prior condition for mobilising them against capitalism—a consensus among the peasants, be it noted, rather than with the capitalists, with the purpose of breaking the links with the landowning class. This was the historic bloc that would have a determining role in social change—it has nothing to do with collaboration between workers and capitalists, nor between their parties, be they populist, liberal or anything else.

Gramsci also made a clear distinction between hegemony and domination, affirming that domination was not enough, but that the object was hegemony—that is, a real capacity to lead, employing a complex network of relationships not based on coercion. The essence of his concept of hegemony is that it responds to the proletariat's need to raise itself into a class capable of leading its class allies in the struggle against capitalism:

> Mass action is not possible while the masses remain unconvinced of the purposes it is pursuing or the means to achieve them. If it is to become a governing class, the proletariat must rid itself of all the residue of corporatism, of every syndicalist prejudice. What does this mean? It means that not only must the divisions between different jobs be overcome, but that to achieve consensus and to win the trust of the peasants and some of the semi-proletarian urban masses some prejudices have to be addressed as well as elements of egotism which still persist among workers even when they have left behind craft particularisms. The metal worker, the carpenter, the building worker will need to learn to see themselves as members of a class that will lead the peasants and the intellectuals, a class that can only win and build socialism if it is supported and followed by the majority of society. If it does not achieve that, and the proletariat does not become the leading class and those sectors, who are still the majority in Italy, remain under bourgeois control, it will give the state the possibility of crushing the rising tide of workers' struggles and breaking the movement.[2]

Gramsci was against the state. That could hardly be clearer. The strategy of seeking democratic changes in the bourgeois state or seeking consensus with sectors of business or with public opinion in general appears nowhere in Gramsci's work.

The discussion of the war of movement[b] and the war of position[c] adds a rich new dimension to the discussion of revolutionary strategy. Gramsci took these concepts from discussions about the art of war: 'In the East, the state was everything, and civil society was primitive and sticky. In the West, there was an appropriate relationship between state and civil society, and when the state was in turmoil, the robust structures of civil society became evident.' The state was a frontline fortress 'behind which sheltered a robust system of inner keeps and walls'. From that Gramsci deduces that in the East the war of manoeuvre is more appropriate while in the West it is the war of position, with much greater emphasis on the accumulation of forces within the institutions and civil society.

Vladimir Pomar set out to synthesise these two concepts—the war of movement or manoeuvre would be the participation of the social movements, of all the struggles which produce tensions in the domination of capital, even the most reformist and localised: 'The principal effort should be directed towards unifying these movements on an increasingly broad base—regional, provincial and national—so they converge in a social movement capable of achieving social transformation.' The war of position, in this sense, would be the participation in and contestation of the apparatus of civil society and the political system 'through trade unions, parliaments, governments, with the central purpose of interacting with the working class...mobilising them and working to resist their fragmentation and division'.

Some scholars, like the Argentinian sociologist Atilio Boron, define Gramsci's position as giving priority to the war of position in returning to the arguments presented by Engels in his introduction to *The Class Struggles in France*,[3] and more specifically to an approximation to the arguments of social democracy for wearing down the state. Given that Gramsci elaborated most of his ideas in the wake of the defeat of many of the revolutionary

b: 'War of manoeuvre' or 'war of movement' refers to wars based upon rapid movements of troops over considerable distance aiming to win quick victories, like the rapid Prussian advance on Paris in 1870 or the German Blitzkrieg of the Second World War.

c: 'War of position' refers to wars of attrition in which the two sides face each other in lines that move very slowly, as with sieges or the trench warfare of the First World War.

movements inspired by the Russian Revolution of 1917, it is possible that the Italian communists did take some inspiration from those ideas, although this is never explicit. The most probable explanation is that they derived them directly from discussions within the Third International concerning the workers' united front.

The differences between the Russian Revolution and those in Europe had been forcefully argued by Lenin in 1918. Lenin, it should be remembered, never opposed the tactic of wearing down the state, but understood it is as a tactic and not as a strategy, in the way that Bernstein[d] had argued it. His words at the Seventh Extraordinary Congress of the CPSU could not have been clearer:

> The revolution will not come as quickly as we had hoped. History has spoken, and we have to know how to recognise the reality, we have to recognise that in the advanced countries the socialist revolution will not begin as easily as it did in Russia, the country of Rasputin and Tsar Nicholas, and where for a majority of the population it was a matter of indifference what kind of people lived on the periphery or what was happening there. In countries like these, starting a revolution is as easy as lifting a feather. But in a country where capitalism has developed and produced a democratic culture and organisations that involve every last person, it is absurd to imagine that the revolution can begin without proper preparation. If we fail to do that, we will destroy the socialist revolution before it begins. That is the reality.[4]

So Gramsci had learned from Lenin and was trying to develop his ideas. It is possible that Kautsky[e] also had some influence, but not the renegade Kautsky, still less the so-called legalistic and pacifist Engels, who exists only in revisionist falsifications. Yet Gramsci was to fall victim to the same falsifications, confirming once again the anxiety of reformists to find in the arguments of Marxists a justification for their abandonment of revolutionary theory.

---

d: Eduard Bernstein, who first argued for reformism within the German Social Democratic Party.

e: Karl Kautsky (1854-1938), leading intellectual in the German Social Democratic Party from the 1880s to his death. Until 1914 seen as a revolutionary theorist, but increasingly moved toward reformism, refused to oppose the First World War and was vehemently against the Russian Revolution.

A useful contribution to the discussion about the war of position has been transformed by reformist intellectuals into a negation of insurrection at the key moment of revolution and thus into the negation of revolution itself. Taking Gramsci as their starting point, intellectuals like Carlos Nelson Coutinho have argued that a country as complex as Brazil should be considered 'Western' (which we agree with), in order to legitimise a conclusion we find unacceptable—namely, that the war of position should define the political activity of the workers, while abandoning the perspective of insurrection. As we shall see, nothing in Gramsci justifies such a conclusion.

Two confusions

Gramsci's writings certainly do leave some room for confusion and reformist reinterpretation. There is room for debate about his view of the capacity of the workers to achieve cultural hegemony before they have conquered state power, for example. The confusion arises from the analogy he draws between bourgeois and proletarian revolutions, without making it clear that the proletariat cannot achieve cultural hegemony in a bourgeois society precisely because of the nature of bourgeois hegemony and its domination of the most powerful ideological apparatuses—a very different situation from that of the bourgeoisie in its battle against feudalism.

According to reformist logic, then, the task would be the accumulation of forces until that hegemony was achieved. Elections would be the barometer of progress in this regard, and successive elections alone would provide the proof or otherwise of the level of consciousness of the citizens. This one-dimensional vision overemphasises the significance of elections and suggests the possibility of conquering hegemony over the whole of society, but without mentioning its class character, the very reason why the working class cannot achieve a position of leadership over the dominant classes and the upper middle classes, given that their interests are neither the same, nor even similar.

A more careful reading shows that Gramsci lays great store by the achievement of cultural hegemony by socialists, not over the whole of society but over the classes exploited in one way or another under capitalism, with whom the workers and their organisations must build links and seek the strategies that will win them leadership. This is a very different position, even if it still leaves much room for question insofar as the struggle for cultural hegemony involves major areas like values, ethics and world view. It requires a very high level of class consciousness and maturity in a context in which even the best organised workers are not particularly well educated and in which political power has yet to be won.

And even if it were possible to exercise cultural hegemony prior to taking political power, the reformist conclusion that this would eliminate the need for an act of force to change the social relations of domination is plainly wrong. Even the bourgeoisie, whose cultural hegemony as a class over its allies enabled it to become the dominant class, was not able to take power by democratic or peaceful means, but had first to destroy the political apparatus of the feudal monarchy. This lack of clarity in Gramsci's thought regarding cultural hegemony takes nothing away from the sharpness of his opposition to the illusion that the working class could lead or represent the interests of the whole of society prior to taking power. And it does not negate the need to incorporate Lenin's key notion of the struggle for the hegemony of revolutionary strategy. The conquest of political hegemony refers to the capacity of the working class to lead political alliances and win its slogans and proposals for the intermediate classes (the peasantry and the impoverished middle class in particular)—that is a precondition for victory.

There is a second basis for confusion in Gramsci's writings, revealing either a prejudice against or an ignorance of Trotsky's theory of permanent revolution. In formulating his theory of the war of movement and of position the Italian directly attacks Trotsky's theory. These attacks were repeatedly used by reformists subsequently, as if permanent revolution referred to a continuous frontal assault on the bourgeois state. To place this discussion in context, we should return to the last debates in the Third International before Lenin's death.

As is well known, in the early 1920s Lenin proposed the united front tactic in opposition to the theory of the revolutionary offensive,[f] which argued that the permanent task of the mass movements in Western Europe was to prepare for the insurrection. The united front tactic, by contrast, proposed the unity of working class parties, the unity of Third International revolutionaries with the European Mensheviks, a politics of the accumulation of forces which would allow the majority of the working class to be won over before an insurrection. The so-called 'offensivists' accused Lenin

---

f: Theory put forward by Bukharin, Radek, Bela Kun, Thalheimer and others early in 1921, particularly associated with the abortive 'March Action' of that year. Opposed by Lenin and Trotsky. For details, see Chris Harman, *The Lost Revolution* (London, 1997), pp 201-209.

of giving up on the very strategy the Bolsheviks had pursued in Russia, without stopping to consider the downturn the revolutionary movement had undergone since then—which Trotsky emphasised in his contribution to the debate.

The caricatures of Trotsky's position fabricated by the Stalinist apparatus tried to suggest that the theory of permanent revolution and the revolutionary offensive were one and the same. And Gramsci repeated the accusation when it was clear that the founder and leader of the Red Army always defended the need for the accumulation of forces rather than the suggestion of a frontal assault on the state. Gramsci's misunderstanding is exposed when he points to the united front as the classic expression of the war of position and then argues that Trotsky is only concerned with the war of manoeuvre. Yet Gramsci must have known that it was Trotsky who presented the concept at the Congress of the International, and that he was always its most fervent defender. In fact, his most serious disagreement with the Soviet leadership came on this very issue. The refusal of the German Communist Party to build a united front against Nazism was the direct cause of his final break with a now wholly Stalinised Third International.

Trotsky defended the united front in all the debates in the International, in his writings about the German situation in 1923, his articles of 1933 and his analysis of France between 1934 and 1936. Throughout his life he fought the parliamentary cretinism that refused to use bourgeois parliaments, proposing instead a combination of Gramsci's war of manoeuvre and war of position according to the correlation of forces. If Gramsci argued that the united front was an illustration of the war of position, and Trotsky was one its principal defenders, how could Gramsci attack Trotsky?

Stalinist propaganda played its part. The debates about permanent revolution began in 1923. In 1926 Stalin elaborated his theory of socialism in one country, but the bureaucracy had already launched its attacks on so-called Trotskyism well before that, describing Trotsky's politics as adventurist and irresponsible, claiming he was proposing an immediate international revolution when the conditions did not exist for it. In this period Gramsci wrote to the Executive Committee of the International criticising the opposition led by Trotsky. There is nothing to indicate that he did not understand the reactionary nature of the theory of socialism in one country or that he might even have identified that theory with the war of position. In the same letter he expressed doubts about both Bukharin and Stalin's methods, indicating his independence from the Stalinist bureaucracy. It was sufficient reason for Togliatti, the Italian Communist Party representative at the Third International, not to deliver the letter—it was the source of the split between the two men, and the origin of Gramsci's relative isolation within the PCI leadership. It is worth adding that at this stage Stalinism had not yet revealed its true horrors—and future Trotskyists like James Cannon[g] and Andres Nin[h] were at this stage still supporting Stalin against Trotsky.

It is also well known that Gramsci, in contrast to Trotsky, paid little attention to the art of insurrection. On the other hand, we cannot forget the conditions under which Gramsci was writing—under the eye of the Fascist censors. Jailed in 1926, he was virtually excluded from the debates in the International from then on. And after Trotsky's expulsion from the Soviet Union in 1929 Gramsci had no access to Trotsky's writings, even though he repeatedly asked to see them.

Against this background, it cannot be argued either that Gramsci defended reformist positions, or that he was identified with Stalinism. There were certainly people who used Gramsci to deny the need for insurrection or the struggle against bourgeois power—there were sectors who wrote in conditions which would have enabled them to face reality, but they did not. So the discussion is not simply about Trotsky's positions. It is Lenin himself and the strategy of the Russian Revolution that are called into question when the different characteristics of the revolution in East and West are emphasised to the point where they deny the very idea of revolution and of insurrection as its decisive moment, as if this contradicted the idea of hegemony and the accumulation of forces.

There is a new attempt to confuse Marxism with Blanquism.[i] Carlos Nelson Coutinho says that 'Marx and Engels defended the Jacobin paradigm put forward by Auguste Blanqui—that is, of revolution as the product of the actions of a small battle-hardened and courageous vanguard... To consider the revolutionary strategy proposed in *The Communist Manifesto* as

---

g: 1896-1974, a leader of the US Communist Party in the 1920s and then of the American Trotskyist movement.

h: 1892-1937, Catalan revolutionary, leading figure in CNT, then Red International of Labour Unions and finally POUM. Murdered by Stalin's agents.

i: Method of August Blanqui (1805-1881), heroic French revolutionary who attempted to overthrow the state through secretly organised armed uprisings from early 1830s through to 1871.

valid today is clearly an anachronism.' An anachronism?! The writer is not only abandoning Marxism altogether—he is slandering Marx and Engels. How can Coutinho still call himself a Marxist? And his calumnies are not even original—he is simply repeating Bernstein's allegations of nearly a century ago. Lenin said, 'Bernstein, the leader of the reformists, has won a sad notoriety by accusing Marxism of Blanquism'.[5]

How did Lenin respond to Coutinho's progenitor, Bernstein?

> First, a successful insurrection must rest not on a trick, nor even on a party, but on an advanced class. Secondly, insurrection can only be based on the revolutionary rise of the people. And thirdly, it must arise at that turning point in the history of the growth of the revolutionary movement when the activity of the vanguard of the people is at its highest point, when the ruling class is at its most divided, and the weak supporters of revolution are at their most indecisive. These are the three conditions for determining when and where the insurrection shall take place—and which distinguish Marxism from the ideas of the Blanquists.[6]

For Marxism, revolution can only be the act of the masses, not of a small minority, and insurrection is the culminating point of the process, a qualitative leap organised as art. And to win the masses, to convince them of the socialist revolution, an arduous day to day activity will be necessary, wearing down the bourgeois political regime and accumulating forces within the working class. Engels devoted his whole political life to arguing this—in fact he was accused not of Blanquism, but of yielding to reformism towards the end of his life, an accusation as unfounded as the first. When he wrote his often quoted introduction to a new edition of Marx's *The Class Struggles in France*, Engels analysed the German SPD at length and offered some important reflections on the revolutionary struggle. He showed that universal suffrage had been an important victory for the working class, and was an essential tool in the struggle. He argued that the struggle on the barricades would become less important in the future, but he never for a moment denied the necessity of revolution, the preparation for which must start with an understanding that the workers cannot be sent into the streets just like that—because defeat would be inevitable.

Extracts from this introduction were later republished to give the impression that Engels was a defender of the peaceful legal road. Engels himself, however, wrote to Kautsky protesting at the cuts made in his text and demanding its publication in full 'to dissipate any possible misunderstandings'. His demands were ignored.

The defence of the socialist revolution, of the necessity for revolutionary violence to destroy the bourgeois state and establish the workers' state, does not imply, however, any defence of ultra-left adventures that take the working class into the street only to be defeated. A revolutionary organisation has to know how to distinguish between the time for accumulating forces and the time to employ these forces in revolutionary actions. The terrible error of social democracy was to transform the need to accumulate forces into a permanent strategy, in which standing for elections became a strategy for taking power rather than a tactical instrument for accumulating forces, making propaganda for the party and convincing workers of the need to destroy capitalism, fighting ceaselessly for its immediate demands against whichever government was in power.

When we assert the actuality of revolution, this does not mean that we consider the victory of the working class to be an easy thing to achieve. The destructive capacity of the US military state was never as great as it is today, for example. If Engels emphasised the importance of accumulating forces before launching decisive offensive actions, and foresaw great difficulties for the insurrection given modern armaments, modern technology and even the new urban architecture which replaced the narrow streets of Paris with wide avenues which made it more difficult for workers' insurrections, how much greater those difficulties are today. The whole 20th century has been devoted to developing new military technologies—the internet itself arose out of those experiments. In the 1990s pilotless planes were used for the first time in Iraq, Bosnia and Kosovo. There have been great advances in computer technology, in the use of sensors, to the extent that the Pentagon's strategy is to generalise remote control warfare.

That is why today more than ever mass mobilisations and a growing consciousness of the working class and the people of Europe and the US in particular are critical. No military response to imperial aggression can be determined centrally, yet preparation in these areas is crucial. The defeat of imperialism must be political, seeking above all to undermine internal support for its external interventions. Internationalism and the solidarity of peoples in struggle have become a matter of life and death.

Marxists are always aware of the need to accumulate forces. Lenin more than anyone was always concerned with the issue of hegemony, with the party's ability to lead. That is why the Bolsheviks did not take power in July 1917 when 500,000 workers were demonstrating in the streets of Petrograd, many of them with arms in hand. They did not take power because they did not have the forces to maintain it, and that July the Bolshevik line had the full support of Trotsky.

The prejudice against the Bolsheviks led to caricaturing the position of the revolutionaries as if their only concern was leading an assault on the Winter Palace. That is absurd. The assault on the palace was certainly a decisive moment, carefully and deliberately chosen. That was Lenin's genius, knowing the exact moment when there was the greatest support for turning the country around, and breaking down the power of the bourgeoisie—a genius that Daniel Bensaid underlines in his essay 'Lenin and the Politics of Time'. Such was Lenin's achievement that there was minimal violence. The power of the bourgeoisie was broken with a minimum number of casualties, so mature and appropriate were the conditions for the 'assault on heaven'.

This strategy will only be questioned if the objective is the conquest of hegemony over sectors of the bourgeosie. And that is incompatible with Lenin and with Gramsci. Here Gramsci shows that he is a revolutionary Marxist. In an article called 'Revolutionaries and Elections' he responds to the question of what revolutionaries, workers and peasants expect from parliamentary elections:

> They certainly do not expect half plus one of the seats in a parliament characterised by dozens of laws whose purpose is to blunt the sharp angles and facilitate cooperation between the classes—between the exploiters and the exploited. On the other hand, they do expect working class electoral activity to carry into parliament a good number of Socialist Party militants who will stand in the way of every move the bourgeoisie try to make, make it impossible to establish a strong and stable government, in a word force the bourgeoisie out of the democratic compromise, abandoning bourgeois legality and making possible a rising of the whole working class against the oligarchy of the exploiters.[7]

The caricature of Lenin, therefore, is also a caricature of Gramsci. But it is an expression of those who do not want to break the existing machine but want only reforms of the state. In this case, insurrection is irrelevant and the strategy becomes the search for 50 percent plus one of the parliamentary seats—the opposite of the strategy argued by Gramsci.

None of this means that we should deny the differences between East and West, nor ignore the differences between more and less developed countries, nor fail to recognise that the instruments of cultural hegemony, as well as coercion and control, have become increasingly sophisticated. In that sense the bourgeois state is stronger than it was at the beginning of the 20th century, and thus more difficult to destroy.

Gramsci foresaw a problem which we in Latin America have come to know well, since the majority of military regimes were overthrown and replaced by bourgeois democratic governments which have continued the super-exploitation of the working class, yet they have survived for years without the working class articulating any kind of alternative institutional order. Gramsci did offer a not altogether happy solution to the problem of how to fight such states with his formulation of the war of movement and the war of position, without showing more precisely the necessity and manner of their articulation. That allowed others to take his ideas to places where they did not belong.

Bourgeois democracy and dictatorship

The discussion of the difference between East and West was one of Gramsci's important contributions. Apart from the differences in economic structures and in the levels of industrial, technological and cultural development, the point can be developed to make clear the differences between dictatorial and bourgeois democratic regimes—and this has important implications for the different mass struggles as they confront a dominant bourgeois class.

In democracies, the weight of the ideological apparatus, of the mass media, of common sense, of the illusions of the masses and the capacity of the ruling class to achieve hegemony, are fundamental. Dictatorial states, on the other hand, rest more on the use of force, on coercion and domination, yet even they need some level of consent and shared illusion, one expression of which is fear.

In bourgeois democracies there are many institutions, and so the capacity to convince, hegemony, has a greater weight. But this does not change the nature of the state—it is still bourgeois. And when consensus is not achieved, it strips the bourgeois state of the ability to be what it also is, a dictatorship of capital, so that the repression of the masses is then lived out equally in both regimes, albeit in different forms and with different intensity—although in bourgeois democratic regimes violence is widely and systematically used when the mechanisms of consensus and hegemony fail to function.

In confronting these situations there must be a response from trade unions and mass organisations. That much is obvious. But the question is what the purpose of that activity is. The issue is not whether or not we fight for spaces of struggle against hegemony, but rather what interests we intervene to support, and over which classes we wish and are able to establish hegemony, whether we seek class conciliation or 'the rising of the widest layers of workers against the oligarchy of the exploiters'.

In dictatorships the struggle for the machinery of civil society is much more difficult, and these apparatuses are often less important in defining the correlation of class forces. This is because it is rigidly controlled by the regime, or because it is simply absent—in dictatorships even the institutions of parliament often do not exist. Yet there are always spaces, mechanisms which can be contested. In regimes of this kind the process of defeating them develops through a slow, clandestine accumulation of forces until they erupt in influential sectors, be it the student movement, in emerging organisations (as was the case of UNE, the Brazilian student union), in trade union or popular movements. It is not important which sector initiates the movement. In general, it takes on the character of a mass mobilisation after a long period of underground preparation driven by democratic demands—'Down with the dictatorship', 'Down with the government'—which eventually alter the correlation of forces, finally undermining the dictatorial regime.

At first sight this appears to be a war of movement but, as always, it takes a combination to bring about an explosion—the rise of great struggles, the deepening of social contradictions. The social and political subjects of change win spaces, recover institutions and rebuild them, accumulate forces and thus stimulate in one way or another offensive actions. Although the possibilities are fewer, it is also a matter of occupying spaces to demonstrate, with examples, propaganda and actions, the incompatibility between the interests of the working classes, the poor and the repressive regime.

These mass mobilisations in dictatorial regimes are usually multiclass in character, and even include sectors of the bourgeoisie. Yet the bourgeoisie as a class is inconsistent even in the struggle for democratic demands—it does not want any kind of revolution at any price for fear that the masses might go on to demand more than merely changes in the forms of domination. Despite this fear, sections of the bourgeoisie do participate at points during the struggle for democracy, generally when those struggles are approaching their high point, and in order to keep them within the framework of the capitalist mode of production. In the democratic revolutions, therefore, the bourgeoisie can use its economic and social power to manoeuvre and divert the revolution, freezing it in its democratic stage. This understanding was one of the Trotskyist leader Nahuel Moreno's[j] important contributions to the strategic analysis.

To unleash a revolutionary offensive of this sort—that is, a democratic revolution—it does not matter whether or not a revolutionary party has an influence among the masses, let alone leads it, although history suggests that in practice that influence has always been key to the achievement of democratic demands. Nor is it necessary that there should exist at that stage organs of workers' power like workers' and peasants' councils, centralised or not.

And that is the qualitative difference in comparison with revolution in bourgeois democratic countries, where going beyond bourgeois democracy implies a completely different movement. Here the construction of organs of workers' power is definitive, even when the bourgeois regime is exhausted and its hegemony in crisis. Marx always argued that the revolution would begin in France, England or Germany, yet it began in Russia, and no successful socialist revolution has occurred thereafter in any bourgeois democracy. This should not make us sceptical of the project. There have been rehearsals—May 1968 in France, the Portuguese Revolution of 1974—and today we are witnessing deepening contradictions at the heart of the system.

The fact that insurrections in bourgeois democratic regimes have not succeeded, however, should lead us to reflect on the preconditions for their success. It is particularly worthwhile to look at the Latin American experience of bourgeois democratic regimes from the 1980s onwards, and to clarify the differences between them and the experience of Russia. This raises an important issue regarding the institutions—because only in the Russian Revolution of 1917 was an insurrection able to overcome a recently established bourgeois democracy. The first revolution which brought down Tsarism had at its disposal a revolutionary party and organs of mass mobilisation and self-determination, workers', soldiers' and peasants' councils.

---

j: Nahuel Moreno (1924-1987), leader of the Argentinian PST and then MAS.

What was peculiar about Russia was that a workers' party was contesting the leadership of the revolutionary democratic struggle against Tsarism. Later, after February, it was able to assume the leadership of the whole process and drive forward a second revolution in the space of a single year. It was unique because the soviets already existed (having been created in 1905) and re-emerged at this time, and because there existed a revolutionary party with influence among the masses. So the victory of the democratic revolution, against a Tsarist regime which rested on the army and repression, could not be diverted by the liberal bourgeoisie in a direction that enabled them to build their own castles to replace the old ones. The soviets were already the main institutions, and the evolution of the internal struggle was decisive in shaping the new type of state.

The Russian experience was not repeated in the course of the collapse of the Latin American military regimes. In Brazil in 1984, for example, revolutionary pressure from below was combined with a self-reform from above which produced a negotiated transition and guarantees of civilian bourgeois domination. The repressive machinery of the previous regime was not even dismantled, though its role was much attenuated by the new constitution of 1988 which established a new legal order incorporating the popular democratic demands of the time. There were no mass organisations of any weight in the society, and the working class did not have an independent role, dissolving into the more general democratic movement. The bourgeoisie was able to set up its 'new democracy' and create an electoral process that was able to persuade the people that it was they who were determining the economic and political direction of the country.

A revolution began in Argentina in 1982. The military were literally driven out of power, which also explains why the military were unable to intervene in the crisis of December 2001. The fall of the military was not accompanied by the rise of soviet-type organisations, that is, organs of dual power. Nor did there exist any party with mass influence, although Argentinian Trotskyism was very influential among the vanguard. So the Argentinian democratic revolution of 1982,[k] the Argentinian February we might call it, did not become the Argentinian October, when the workers eliminated the bourgeois state. The sector of the bourgeoisie that took power was then able to create its own machinery of control and its own means of deluding the masses.

---

k: The collapse of the military junta of 1976-82 in the aftermath of defeat in the Falklands/Malvinas War.

The Argentinian example is in no sense unique. The whole of Latin America experienced similar processes—the fall of the dictatorships in the absence of alternative organs of power, and a ruling class that was ready to use the institutions of bourgeois democracy to divert the mass movement and freeze the revolutionary process at its democratic stage.

The exception, many years earlier, had been the Cuban Revolution of 1959 and, to a lesser degree, the Nicaraguan Revolution 20 years later. In neither case did there exist any organs of mass self-determination, yet in both cases there did exist a situation of dual power in which a guerrilla army confronted a dictatorship. In both cases there was a democratic revolution with the participation of the mass movement and, albeit reluctantly, some bourgeois sectors too. The bourgeois regimes were dismantled, and so too was the army and with it the bourgeois state, leaving room for the creation of a new type of state. This is what happened in Cuba. The US would not accept even minimal capitalist development, which drove the Castro regime to expropriate the bourgeoisie. In this way a new state was created, although one without mass democratic organisations. The deformations of Castro's Cuba arise from this limitation as well as the criminal US economic blockade and the no less criminal Soviet foreign policy, which gave aid to Cuba in exchange for its moderation on the Latin American and world scene. In Nicaragua, of course, it was a different story. The Sandinistas did not expropriate the bourgeoisie, and the bourgeois state was rebuilt, albeit in a state of continuing crisis in which it remains today.

These were the experiences of struggle that began with democratic demands and revolutions against dictatorial regimes. In general there were no organisms of dual power and, when there were, they were not mass democratic organisations but guerrilla armies. Yet there were mass mobilisations against dictatorships and they were victorious because the mass democratic movement proved superior to a state based on a regime of fear and repression.

In bourgeois democratic regimes, however, the barricades and fortresses, to use Gramsci's phrase, are much more powerful—bourgeois hegemony and domination are surrounded by a network of defences. To overcome electoralism and the illusion among the masses that parliament is the only means through which to express their political will, even when bourgeois democratic institutions themselves are falling apart, the decisive thing is to build alternative organs of power in the mass movement. Without them it becomes difficult, if not impossible, to overcome bourgeois domination even against the background of a hegemonic crisis of the bourgeois state. This largely explains the long period of bourgeois democracy that we have had in Latin America, although many of these regimes are now entering a period of crisis.

The process is a slow one. The bases of a different type of state are to be found in workers' self-organisation, the factory committees, the organisations of the peasant movement like Brazil's Landless Workers Movement (MST), the popular mass organisations like the MNLM[1] in Brazil, which fights for the right to housing and against homelessness, in sum in the structures and superstructures of the movements of those at the bottom of the social scale. In Ecuador we have recently seen clear embryos of dual power with the emergence of the People's Parliament, and similar developments in Bolivia, with the Cochabamba Coordinadora de Agua (Coordinating Committee against Water Privatisation), and in Argentina in the local popular assemblies.

The fact that the traditional leaders of the mass movement are often unhappy with these developments and often work to dismantle them is certainly one obstacle to the radical transformation of society, which is why the urgent task is to build a revolutionary party that does share those strategies. There is no need to fetishise any one form; they might be soviets or councils, cordones industrials like those which arose in Chile in 1972-73, Ecuadorean-style People's Parliaments or Popular Assemblies like those that emerged in Peru, or indeed any of the new forms that the revolution itself will throw up.

What is decisive is that revolutionaries work within the workers' movement, among the youth, in the popular and peasant organisations, on the basis of this permanent strategy—to organise from below, to work for unity among them all, and to patiently explain the need to build a new kind of order based on the continuing mobilisation of the masses and on their self-organisation.

1: The national housing movement.

NOTES

1: See A Gramsci and P Togliatti, 'The Italian Situation and the Tasks of the PCI' (Lyons Theses), in A Gramsci, *Selections from the Political Writings, 1921-26* (London, 1979), pp464-513.

2: The translation differs slightly from that in A Gramsci and P Togliatti, as above, p605.

3: Available on www.marxists.org/archive/ marx/works/1895/03/06.htm

4: Again the translation varies slightly from that available on www.marxists.org/archive/lenin/works/1918/7thcong/01.htm

5: Available in a slightly different translation on amadlandawonye.wikispaces.com/1917,+Lenin,+Marxism+and+Insurrection

6: As above.

7: A Gramsci, *Selections from Political Writings, 1910-20* (London, 1977), p188.

Crusade and jihad in the medieval Middle East

Neil Faulkner

Bush explains he is engaged in a 'crusade' for freedom. Osama bin Laden calls for a 'jihad' against the new crusaders. Saddam Hussein portrayed himself as a latter-day Saladin. Maybe Blair thinks he is Richard the Lionheart.

The debate about the Iraq war echoes with references to the conflict eight centuries ago between Christian Crusaders from Western Europe and the Islamic people of the Middle East. These echoes raise questions for socialists. How accurate is the traditional image of the Crusaders as chivalrous knights inspired by piety? Is there something inevitable and eternal about conflict between 'the West' and 'the Orient'? To what degree can the conflicts of the medieval past inform our understanding of the present and provide a guide to action for the future?

Our answers must depend on an analysis of Western feudalism, the Early Islamic states, and the dynamics of the conflict between the two in the 11th to 13th centuries. We must start, though, by clearing away some of the confusion caused by the concept of 'imperialism' when making comparisons between capitalist and pre-capitalist societies.

Imperialism past and present

The classic Marxist accounts of capitalist imperialism are, of course, Lenin's *Imperialism: The Highest Stage of Capitalism* and Bukharin's *Imperialism and World Economy*. Central to their argument is the idea that modern imperialism grows out of the competitive accumulation of capital. Competition leads to the centralisation and concentration of capital—big corporations and giant factories come to dominate the economy. The increasing scale of production transfers competition onto an international stage. Continuing profitability and accumulation now depend on global sourcing and sales, and the state acquires a central role in capitalist competition, its arms spending and wars designed to advance the interests of its own capitalists at the expense of rivals. Economic competition between blocs of capital and geopolitical competition between states fuse, producing such titanic confrontations as the First World War, the Second World War and the Cold War.[1]

None of this applies to ancient or medieval 'imperialism'. If I continue to use the word, I do so only because it is too well embedded in the literature to be ditched—and there is, in any case, no obvious alternative. But we must be clear that the term 'imperialism' in pre-capitalist societies implies nothing more than the use of military force by strong states to dominate weaker ones and exploit their resources. The dynamics of this process are radically different from those of capitalist imperialism.

In contrast to the dynamism of capitalist economic development, the normal condition of the pre-capitalist economy was technological 'stagnation'. Change was the exception, not the rule. Occasional bursts of innovation (spread over decades or centuries) would be followed by much longer periods of stability (lasting for centuries or millennia). For example, a new agrarian system based on the heavy plough, animal manure, large open fields and water mills developed in the 'champion' landscapes of central England in the Late Anglo-Saxon period (c AD 850 to 1066) lasted for about 500 years—only with the 'enclosures' of the 16th century and later was it substantially altered.[2] The medieval economy, in short, was essentially stable and self-reproducing,[3] and the agrarian system centred on the medieval village achieved a finely balanced equilibrium, where the regulation and conservatism of rural life were a matter, therefore, not of 'backwardness' but of survival.[4]

Change was not driven by the normal working of the system—not, that is, by direct economic competition rooted in the very circumstances of production. It was driven by occasional crises, by exceptional events, by something untoward disrupting traditional cycles of agrarian production and commercial exchange. Economic change ('progress') was abnormal. Economically driven accumulation, as opposed to simple reproduction, was minimal or non-existent. People were often no more productive than their ancestors centuries before.

Yet pre-capitalist societies *were* driven by competition. The ancient and medieval worlds were divided into rival polities that were frequently at war. No pre-capitalist ruling class could afford to be complacent about military preparedness if it wished to hold onto its property and power. Indeed, in the *absence* of increases in the productivity of labour, the principal mechanism available to any ruling class wishing to increase surplus appropriation—and therefore military capacity—was warfare.

The extent of their territories and conquests, and the numbers and quality of armed men these could support, underlay the power of rival states. Because of this, states were involved in a fiercely contested geopolitical struggle to accumulate military capacity.[5] And if war was the principal method for increasing surplus appropriation, the state was necessarily the principal agent of this process. Through the state, rival ruling classes grew rich and increased their power at one another's expense. A stable global economy with fixed output made the struggle for surplus a zero-sum game—one ruler's gain was necessarily another's loss. Thus the history of pre-capitalist class societies was dominated by the state, war-making and an eternal geopolitical struggle for empire.

I have attempted elsewhere to apply these ideas to the analysis of the Roman Empire.[6] Rome represents an extreme example of what I have called 'ancient military imperialism'—a system of robbery with violence, in which war, by yielding great hauls of booty (not least slaves), transferred surplus from defeated enemies into the hands of the Roman imperial elite, increasing their war-making capacity yet further, thereby creating the basis for further aggressive wars. What follows here is, in essence, an attempt to understand Western feudalism, the Early Islamic states and the Crusades in a similar way.

The dynamic of Western feudalism

The 9th and 10th centuries AD were a period of particular geopolitical instability in Europe, the Mediterranean and the Middle East. Kings were overthrown and civil wars raged. Towns disappeared. Long-distance trade declined. Viking, Magyar and Saracen raiders plagued the coasts. The most effective response to the crisis emerged in Western Europe, perhaps because, as Chris Harman has suggested, 'the very backwardness of Europe allowed it to leapfrog over the great empires'.[7] Without the dead weight of powerful vested interests and a great state superstructure, the way was open to forge a radically new social, political and military order. Medieval rulers took control of the land and parcelled it out to their supporters in return for military service so as to crush domestic rebels, defend borders against raiders and beat back the armies of rival kings. They created a hierarchy of greater and lesser lords, of barons and knights, bound together by personal ties of homage and fealty. In essence, they created an immensely strong body of armed men by rooting the state in private landlordism.

The Duchy of Normandy, a state created by 10th century Viking settlers, was an extreme example of the new feudal order.[8] Power was highly centralised. The ruler was the legal owner of all land, and it was his appointees, often his kinsmen, who held the great estates. These men remained his vassals, his tenants in chief, liable to be cast down as easily as they had been raised up if they earned their master's disfavour. Under them, land was further subdivided into fiefs able to support a knight, each fief being an estate with income sufficient to free a man from the need to labour, to allow him to devote himself full time to war and training for war, and to provide him with the horses, chain-mail armour and weaponry of a heavy cavalryman. Here was the core of the Norman state—several thousand armoured horseman, organised in lordly retinues, bound by ties of personal loyalty and dependence, and rooted in the control and wealth of landed estates.

By linking landholding and military service, feudalism forged a tight bond between the state and the ruling class. It also ensured that the agrarian base of the system was carefully tended, since the maintenance of rank came to depend partly on the good management of estates.

But there were dangers. The system was inherently unstable. State power was directly related to the numbers of fiefs and knights controlled by the ruler, intensifying the struggle between rival polities for control over land. Moreover, to avoid fiefs being subdivided and becoming non-viable (ie unable to support a knight), the rule of primogeniture prevailed, whereby the eldest son inherited the entire estate. Younger sons therefore had to fight for their place in the world. Denied an inheritance and threatened with loss of rank, they had to survive through mercenary service or by winning a new fiefdom for themselves. This was true of knights, nobles and princes—all ranks of the feudal aristocracy produced younger sons able to maintain rank only through the application of military force.

Opportunities were numerous. Civil and foreign wars were frequent. Competition for land and power kept the feudal aristocracy divided. On the one hand, the princes needed more land, fiefs and knights to pursue their struggles with rival states. On the other, the younger sons of the warrior caste sought pay, booty and estates to maintain themselves. The dynamic of feudal imperialism was therefore double-edged. To prevent the feudal elite from tearing itself apart in fratricidal slaughter, the princes tried to export the violence inherent in the system, and at the same time turn it to their own advantage in wars of foreign conquest. It was this bloody logic that powered the Crusades. When Pope Urban II launched the First Crusade at the Council of Clermont on 27 November 1095, he was clear about the military anarchy threatening Western Christendom:

> Let those...who are accustomed to wantonly wage private war against the faithful march upon the infidels in a war which should be begun now and be finished in victory. Let those who have long been robbers now be soldiers of Christ. Let those who once fought against brothers and relatives now rightfully fight against the barbarians. Let those who have been hirelings for a few pieces of silver now attain an eternal reward.[9]

The consolidation of Western feudalism in its heartlands came to depend on massacre and mayhem abroad. The feudal host was not a weapon that could be sheathed. Violence was inherent in the system—something for which the peoples of medieval Europe and the Middle East paid a heavy price.

By the mid-11th century the Norman state, having achieved a high degree of unity and coherence, became aggressively expansionist.[10] Under Duke William (later William the Conqueror), the colonisation of Lower Normandy was completed, several territories were seized on the southern frontier, and overlordship was sought over neighbouring states. Meantime, freelance Norman adventurers had seized control of Southern Italy (1053) and Sicily (1072) after arriving in the early 11th century to take service as mercenaries. Before these conquests were complete, Anglo-Saxon England had fallen to another force of Norman adventurers, this one led by Duke William himself (1066-70). It was followed by attacks on Ireland, Wales and

Scotland and, in England, by the wholesale dispossession of the Anglo-Saxon aristocracy, among whom only five landholders of any substance survived by the time of the famous Domesday survey in 1087.

Feudal violence was contradictory. It was, of course, essential to the survival of the feudal states—the warrior host defended the homeland, conquered new territory and maintained internal order. But the violence had a dynamic of its own and the potential to blow the feudal order apart. Pressure-valves were needed to extrude surplus violence. This was the genesis of the Crusades.

The limits of Early Islamic civilisation

In the century after AD 630 Arab armies swept across the Middle East, North Africa and Spain to create a vast new empire ruled by Umayyad caliphs based in Damascus. They were inspired by Islam, a radical new synthesis of the Judaeo-Christian religious beliefs long established in the Western Arabian mercantile cities of Mecca and Medina. Transcending traditional conflicts, Islam bound together desert tribes and urban merchants in a powerful alliance which erupted out of Arabia after the Prophet Mohammed's death in 632. To the north Egypt, Syria, Iraq and Egypt lay under the control of the Byzantine and Sassanid empires, both gravely weakened by a war raging between them from 603 to 628.

The burden of military accumulation had been eroding the socio-economic foundations of the ancient empires since at least the 3rd century AD. Now it became crippling. The Arabs, widely welcomed by local populations ravaged by taxation, labour service and military insecurity, quickly broke through.

The Arab rulers and their warrior retinues found themselves the inheritors of rich civilisations, not only those of Syria and Iraq, but also those of Egypt, Tunisia, Spain, Sicily and elsewhere. The achievements of these civilisations were eagerly appropriated, and the Arab world soon boasted rich irrigation agriculture, sophisticated urban crafts, a dynamic banking system, and a strong tradition of scholarship, literature and art. The West was, indeed, by comparison, living in 'the Dark Ages'.

At first, the vast area the Arabs had conquered remained, at least formally, a single geopolitical entity under the Umayyad caliphs of Damascus (661-750). But the geography of the new Arab world contained several natural economic units in which separate ruling classes with interests of their own quickly developed.[11] Distance limited the effectiveness of Umayyad rule. How could armies in Damascus expect to control Baghdad, Cairo, Tunis and Fez? Nor was this the only problem. The Umayyads represented the Arab warrior aristocracy who had carried out the first Islamic conquests and then been settled in the ancient imperial cities of Syria. Their rule was increasingly resented by other sections of the population, many of them more recent converts to Islam in the cities of the wider Arab-dominated world. The result, as Chris Harman has explained, was the Abbasid revolution:

> Previously the empire had been run by an exclusively Arab military aristocracy, whose origins lay in war and conquest for tribute. Under the Abbasids, Islam became a genuinely universal religion in which Arab and non-Arab believers were increasingly treated the same and in which ethnic origins were not central.[12]

In the Abbasid revolution, rebels from Iran led by a descendant of the Prophet raised an army, overthrew the Umayyad caliphate, established a new dynasty, and laid down a wider and more secure base for continued Arab rule. But there were limits to the achievement. Society was centred on towns in which power was vested in an elite composed of officials, merchants, and Islamic scholars and clerics. These communities, largely self-sufficient and independent, were preoccupied with agriculture, trade, and the maintenance of peace and good order. A wide gap separated them from the Abbasid caliphs, who were threatened by the secession of outlying parts of their empire, by coups launched by disaffected factions within the ruling class, and by revolt from below, whether of religious sectarians opposed to worldly corruption, or of sections of the exploited rural masses.[13]

The Early Islamic state thus acquired an existence over and above society, becoming a mechanism of military accumulation designed principally to perpetuate the rule of the reigning dynasty. The Umayyads had already separated themselves from civil society by building great palaces and appropriating the luxuries of Byzantine and Sassanid civilisation. The Abbasids took this much further.

The independence of the Abbasid state from civil society was symbolised by the new Islamic palace-city of Samarra, built on the Tigris 120 kilometres upstream from Baghdad during the 9th century.[14] Sprawling along 35 kilometres of riverbank, it was larger than Imperial Rome at its peak, and was dominated by monumental mosques and huge palace complexes. The Abbasid caliph al-Mutasim, founder of Samarra, built himself a palace in 836-42 that was larger than Louis XIV's Versailles. Even so, his Abbasid successors built new ones—al-Mutawakkil a second in about 849-59, and al-Mutamid a third in 878-82.

> In the century between the reign of Harun al-Rashid (786-809) and the accession of al-Mutadid (892), the Abbasid caliphs went from fabulous wealth to bankruptcy...an important one of the ingredients in the recipe for disaster must have been the creation of Samarra, aptly described as 'an act of folly on a vast scale'.[15]

But there was more to Samarra than a ruler's folly. The caliphs may well have been corrupted by 'worldliness'. Greed and self-indulgence are characteristic of ruling classes throughout history. Great monuments are also, however, a way of expressing power—their size and magnificence are designed to impress, to intimidate, to make others feel puny. Samarra was important also in being a new centre of power, distant from Baghdad, thus freeing the Abbasid caliphs from political subordination to the urban elite. Equally, they sought to free themselves from military dependence on the old tribal host, building instead armies of mercenaries, mainly Turks, who were barracked in special quarters at Samarra.

In contrast to Western feudalism, where landholding and military service were inextricably linked, and rulers and nobles were bound together by strong ties of allegiance and dependence, the Islamic states were tributary. The court and the army were sustained by taxes, especially those levied on the non-Muslim subject population. Because of this, the states were weak—despite palaces and mercenaries. The tribes and towns generated strong local identities and ideologies. Islam generated a powerful overarching allegiance throughout the Arab world. But the activities of the central state evoked no comparable feelings, since the power of the caliphs lacked any firm anchors in society. Consequently, the state was unstable—a prey to coups, civil wars and secessionist revolts.

The unity of the Arab world was shattered during the 9th and 10th centuries. The Abbasid caliph of Baghdad faced a rival Fatimid caliph in Cairo, an Umayyad one at Cordoba, and numerous independent and semi-independent minor rulers elsewhere. Conflicts between and within these polities increased the cost of state power, drained national treasuries, and further weakened the rulers. During the 11th century the Abbasid caliphate effectively collapsed. The caliph's Seljuk Turkish mercenaries seized power for themselves. It was a measure of the state's lack of social roots that its political authority could be usurped by its own mercenaries. There was little enthusiasm for any of the ruling regimes among the population at large, hammered by taxes to pay for palaces, mercenaries and dynastic warfare. The region, moreover, remained a mosaic of minorities, so that political stress was easily transformed into resistance based on ethnic and religious difference.[16] When Urban II called forth the First Crusade in 1095, the Middle East was wide open to attack.

The first crisis of the Crusades, 1096-99

The 200-year history of the Crusades[17] hinged on two major crises—one creating the Crusader states, and the other, a century later, breaking their power and condemning them to eventual liquidation.

The first was initiated by Pope Urban's appeal in November 1095. The church was a vast feudal corporation with estates spread across the whole of Western Europe, which it maintained and enlarged in competition with secular feudal princes. Anything, therefore, that enhanced the political clout of the church—such as the wave of religious zeal and activity unleashed by the First Crusade—was an advantage. Also, like other feudal potentates, the bishops were keen to preserve peace at home by exporting the surplus violence of the warrior caste.

But the response to Urban's appeal exceeded all expectations. Four armies quickly formed: in southern France under Raymond of Toulouse; in northern France, Lorraine, and Germany under Godfrey of Bouillon; in the Paris region and Champagne under Hugh of Vermandois; and among the Normans of Southern Italy and Sicily under Bohemond of Taranto. Each host comprised several hundred knights and some thousands of spearmen and archers. They broke into northern Syria late in 1097, captured Antioch in June 1098, and then Jerusalem itself the following year.

Everywhere, even on the evidence of their own historians, there was massacre, destruction and robbery. Men, women and children were put to the sword as they fled in terror through the streets of captured cities.

Prisoners were routinely decapitated. Mosques and synagogues were ransacked. Carts were filled with plunder.

After the capture of Jerusalem many Crusaders, who had joined as warrior-pilgrims in search of adventure and booty, returned home. Others, however, remained, forming the ruling classes of the four small Crusader states that had been won—the County of Edessa, the Principality of Antioch, the County of Tripoli, and the Kingdom of Jerusalem.

It was the weakness of the Islamic empires that had allowed these states to be formed, and they rested on the weakest of foundations. Feudal heavy cavalry gave tactical dominance on the battlefield, but the Crusaders were politically isolated and strategically over-extended. A mere 500 knights defended the Principality of Antioch. The Crusaders built scores of massive castles to compensate. Impregnable to assault, the castles dominated the countryside around them, providing shelter, protection and supplies to small bodies of armed men who would, when necessary, sally forth to assert their power. The Crusaders were a tiny minority in a sea of potentially hostile humanity.

The rate of exploitation was ratcheted up. Muslims now paid the poll tax previously restricted to non-Muslims. There was also heavy taxation on landholdings. Castles were built by conscripted peasants. Rent collection was organised as a military operation. Many of the Crusaders, especially on the frontiers, were true robber-barons, supplementing their incomes by attacking pilgrims, caravans and settlements. Built on conquered land and ruled by small military elites, the Crusader states could survive only through terror and super-exploitation. Only in this way could they obtain the supplies, mercenaries and fortifications essential to their survival.

But the bitterness engendered took time to find focus and organisation. The Islamic world had been taken by surprise. It had been struck suddenly by a blitzkrieg of feudal violence. The Islamic ruling class was paralysed by political disunity and military weakness. Many sought opportunistic alliances with the Crusaders. Others hoped to live and let live. Few risked active resistance. For a full generation, until 1128, the Crusaders retained the upper hand.

The second crisis of the Crusades, 1185-92

Live and let live was not a long-term option for most Islamic rulers. The Crusader states were colonial settlements based on military power. The Crusaders remained aggressive and predatory neighbours, with continuing robbery and annexations. The Crusader threat to Aleppo in northern Syria forced its ruler into alliance with Mosul in northern Iraq, and by 1144 the city of Edessa had been recaptured and the first of the four Crusader states destroyed.

The Second Crusade of 1146-48 was a direct response to this Islamic counter-offensive, but it ended disastrously, shattering the myth of Crusader invincibility and laying the ground for a more powerful upsurge of Islamic resistance. Damascus and southern Syria were united into the new Islamic state, while the Crusader Principality of Antioch was reduced to a small coastal enclave around the capital city. Equally important, the new state's ruler, Nureddin, a pious man, called openly for a jihad against the Crusaders.

Religion was the language in which men and women discussed their world and how to change it in the pre-capitalist, pre-Enlightenment societies of the 12th century. At one level, Nureddin was one of a number of ruling class leaders, Christian and Muslim, engaged in a struggle for power between rival states. But at another level, he was the leader of an anti-imperialist insurgency. Bolder than his rivals and willing to ride the tiger of popular revolt to advance his cause, he raised the slogan of religious war as a means to mobilise the Muslim masses against their foreign overlords. Nureddin was not only building a new Islamic superstate, he was also leading a popular insurrection to drive the invaders into the sea. These two aims were complementary. Both were a response to the problem posed by the Crusader states. Both contributed to its solution:

> Nureddin, who was also a religious zealot, viewed the jihad as both ideology and policy. The ideology emphasised three basic points: the depth of the gulf separating Franks [Crusaders] and Muslims; a protest against the indifference of their contemporaries to that fact; and a call to holy war... Nureddin elaborated the idea of the jihad into a complete theory, sketching out a precise political path, and put in place an extensive apparatus to ensure its spread. He emphasised the special sanctity of Jerusalem and the Holy Land, and the need to re-establish the political unity of the Islamic Near East as the preliminary phase to driving out the Franks... This became the basis of an important popular movement.[18]

The struggle against feudal imperialism in the 12th century Middle East thus followed a logic dictated by the nature of the state, society and ideology in the Early Islamic world.

It was not Nureddin, however, but Saladin who led the jihad to victory, adopting the policy of jihad and taking the offensive against the Crusaders. Building his base among Muslims in this way, he was, by 1183, after Nureddin's death, able to win control of the whole of Syria. The stage was thus set for the climactic confrontation between Crusade and jihad. Saladin's conquests between 1185 and 1189, culminating in the recapture of Jerusalem, changed the map of the Middle East as comprehensively as had the First Crusade 100 years before.

The decisive battle was fought at Hattin in Galilee on 4 July 1187. It symbolised the whole struggle. Saladin had assembled the greatest Muslim army ever to have faced the Crusaders—30,000 men, including heavy cavalry, swarms of light horse archers, and thousands of jihadist volunteers. By falling back before their advance and plaguing their column with mounted archery, Saladin drew the Crusaders, in the ferocious July heat, through a landscape in which the wells had run dry. Only when men and horses were dying of thirst did he engage, blocking the route to the water of Lake Tiberias, and preparing to stand his ground. The dry scrub around the Crusaders was set alight to worsen their agonies. They launched a series of heavy cavalry charges—their traditional tactics—but this time they were too weak, too heavily outnumbered, to break through against confident and determined opponents. At the end of the day, the survivors surrendered. The entire army of the Crusader Kingdom of Jerusalem had been destroyed.

As Crusader fortresses and cities fell, there was nothing to compare with the wholesale massacres at Antioch and Jerusalem during the First Crusade—there was no general massacre. Of the prisoners taken at Hattin, only one notorious robber-baron was executed (by Saladin himself), along with the Templar and Hospitaller knights, warrior-monks who had waged a war of bigotry and genocide. The difference was not due to Saladin's greater sense of 'honour'—though the Middle Eastern ruling classes were undoubtedly in general more civilised than the invaders. It was really the difference between the imperialism of a hated minority and the resistance of a popular movement.

The Crusaders never recovered. The Third Crusade of 1189-92 was mounted in response to Hattin and the fall of Jerusalem. But under King

Richard I of England—a boorish and brutal man under whose leadership the usual carnage and pillage prevailed—the campaign eventually reached stalemate. Carefully marshalled, the feudal host retained its tactical supremacy, and Saladin kept his more lightly equipped forces at a distance. But the Crusaders' strategic weakness remained, and Richard, convinced Jerusalem could not be held, abandoned the attempt to recapture it. Imperialism may pack a harder punch, but against a national insurgency it cannot make its conquests secure, and ultimately defends only the ground on which its soldiers stand.

Even so, the Crusaders clung to a strip of territory along the coast, where they remained ensconced in fortresses which could be supplied and reinforced by sea. Indeed, hemmed in by hostility, these Crusader toeholds were unable to endure without external support, and their existence, and dependence, helped keep alive Crusader ideology in Western Europe through much of the 13th century. Later Crusades, however, were often diverted by easy pickings and commercial advantages elsewhere. The Fourth Crusade (1202-04), for example, ended with massacre and pillage in the streets of Christian Constantinople. (There were another four, but they proved increasingly ineffective in bringing succour to the remnants of Crusader power on the Levantine coast.)

If it took a century to reduce all the Crusader fortresses (the last fell only in 1291), we must explain this in terms of Islamic weakness. Saladin's revolution had been a limited one. His empire had collapsed after his death in 1193. His dynasty, and with it the union of Syria and Egypt, endured until the mid-13th century. But this Ayyubid regime was undermined by the perennial problems of Early Islamic states, their lack of firm rooting in civil society and consequent instability, and preoccupation with domestic security and survival. The Ayyubid response was to create armies of Mamluk slave-soldiers. But these, like the Turkish mercenaries of the Abbasids before them, eventually revolted against their masters and ruled in their own right. It was an Egyptian-based Mamluk regime that successfully defended the Muslim Middle East against Mongol invaders from Central Asia in 1260, and then, when the Mongols threatened again and the Crusaders, desperate as ever, sought an alliance with them, liquidated the last of the Crusader strongholds on the coast.

Some conclusions

(1) In pre-capitalist societies, long periods of stability in technology and the productivity of labour meant that the use of state power in aggressive war was an essential mechanism by which the more successful ruling classes seized surpluses at the expense of their rivals. The intensity of geopolitical competition required such surpluses to be used mainly for military accumulation.

(2) The relative independence of the state in relation to civil society meant, however, that ruling regimes often lacked strong roots. Instability was a notable feature of Early Islamic states, in which rulers elevated themselves above the tribes and the towns which were the key elements in the new Arab-dominated social order, and invested surpluses in palaces, monumental architecture, mercenaries, and dynastic warfare.

(3) Western feudalism was a partial exception to this general rule. By linking landholding and military service (in contrast to the Early Islamic system of tribute and mercenaries), the state and the ruling class formed a cohesive bloc. Princes, nobles and knights were tightly bound together by ties of allegiance and dependence based on shared interests. A specific and highly effective military system was embedded within this social order—one based on small elite groups of armoured shock cavalry able to dominate battlefields, and a landscape dotted with heavily defensible castles able to dominate territory.

(4) The limits of Western feudalism were exposed in the Crusades. Knights and castles were expensive. Super-exploitation was therefore necessary to sustain them. The bitterness this caused could be contained by fear of feudal violence as long as opposition remained fragmented. Norman feudalism survived in England after the conquest of 1066-70 because no general resistance movement developed. The Middle Eastern jihad, on the other hand, enabled Zengi, Nureddin and Saladin to build an Islamic superstate, mobilise the Muslim masses, and begin the destruction of the Crusader states. It was limited, however, by the class outlook and factional conflicts of the Islamic leaders—such that it took 150 years to complete the liquidation of the Crusader states.

(5) Altogether the Crusades lasted for almost exactly 200 years. In that time the Crusader states had contributed nothing—their rulers were simply brutal exploiters who ruled by force and fear. In this they reflected the inherently violent and restless character of Western feudalism. The rulers of the West, in effect, exported the surplus violence generated by the feudal system to the Middle East, in order to stabilise the political order at home. The closing of this pressure-valve led to a marked increase in feudal warfare inside Europe.[19]

NOTES

1: A good summary and defence of the classic Marxist theory is provided by C Harman, 'Analysing Imperialism', *International Socialism* 99 (Summer 2003), pp3-25.

2: The British evidence for the medieval agrarian economy has been much studied and discussed. Important recent contributions are C Lewis, P Mitchell-Fox and C Dyer, *Village, Hamlet and Field: Changing Medieval Settlements in Central England* (Macclesfield, 2001), and T Williamson, *Shaping Medieval Landscapes: Settlement, Society and Environment* (Macclesfield, 2003).

3: The term 'stable' is better than 'stagnant'. The latter implies something deficient and abnormal. Worse, it implies a teleological and determinist view of history, in which technological progress and a raising of the productivity of labour are regarded as the norm. I think Chris Harman sometimes makes this mistake when discussing pre-capitalist societies in his *A People's History of the World* (London, 1999).

4: This point is made by Chris Dyer of Leicester University: C Dyer, *Making a Living in the Middle Ages: the People of Britain, 850-1520* (London, 2003), pp23-24.

5: The terms 'political accumulation' and 'political capital' have been widely used by Marxists writing about pre-capitalist societies. These terms are a trifle abstract. The truth is always concrete. Political power depends upon military capacity. It was really the means of making war that were being accumulated.

6: N Faulkner, *The Decline and Fall of Roman Britain* (Stroud, 2000), and *Empire of the Eagles: The Rise and Fall of Ancient Rome, 753 BC to AD 476* (forthcoming).

7: C Harman, *A People's History of the World* (London, 1999), p141.

8: R Allen Brown, *The Normans* (London, 1984), pp19-48.

9: Quoted in G Tate, *The Crusades and the Holy Land* (London, 1991), p131.

10: R Allen Brown, as above.

11: A Hourani, *A History of the Arab Peoples* (London, 1991), pp81-97.

12: C Harman, *A People's History*, as above, p129.

13: A Hourani, as above, pp32-43.

14: R Hodges and D Whitehouse, *Mohammed, Charlemagne and the Origins of Europe* (London, 1983), pp151-157.

15: As above, p156.

16: A Hourani, as above, pp96-97, 172-188.

17: The classic narrative of the Crusades is S Runciman, *A History of the Crusades* (3 vols, London, 1965). In the tradition of much British historiography, it is a solid account of events but weak on analysis.

18: G Tate, as above, pp88-89.

19: The English monarchy, for example, was almost continually at war—at home, against the Welsh and the Scots, and against the French—from 1263 until 1485. War was a normal condition for a feudal polity.

Empire built on shifting sand

Joseph Choonara

The last few years have not been kind to Antonio Negri. *Empire*,[1] his most famous book, produced in collaboration with Michael Hardt, heralded the death of imperialism. The authors claimed that the old logic of warring nation-states had been replaced by a de-territorialised Empire, functioning according to a new global logic of rule. The ink had barely dried before the events of 11 September 2001 and the beginning of a new cycle of imperialist wars. By the time their second major collaboration, *Multitude*,[2] was published in 2004 the authors were forced to find a place for the invasions of Afghanistan and Iraq within their theory.

However, their attitude towards these wars has been contradictory. On some occasions they have seen them as an imperialist 'coup against Empire'. This view led Negri to support a yes vote in the May 2005 referendum in France on the proposed EU constitution. Support for this neo-liberal document would, he argued, heelp create a 'counterweight against US unilateralism'. At other times they have seen US military might as sserving the interests of the emerging Empire, referring to the invasion of Iraq as 'an attempt at transition, not at colonisation'.

Hardt and Negri welcome the emergence of Empire, seeing it as the terrain for the struggles of a radical new counterpower, the multitude, which both sustains and can potentially overcome the new order. They attack any nostalgia for previous movements and forms of struggle—seeing them as irrelevant in today's 'postmodern' world. The multitude has been widely identified with the forces that took to the streets against the World Trade Organisation meeting in Seattle in 1999 and at countless other anti-capitalist mobilisations since. But Negri has recently identified other, more curious, allies. A 2004 interview saw him heap praise on Luiz Inacio Lula da Silva and Nestor Kirchner, the presidents of Brazil and Argentina, who have both provoked anger in their own countries by continuing to drive through the neo-liberal attacks of their predecessors.[3]

Despite his political contortions Negri remains an influential figure, attracting considerable interest from both the left and the right. Many of Negri's earlier writings have now been republished. *Time for Revolution* brings together two essays by Negri, the first written in 1981 and the second at roughly the same time as *Empire*.[4] The essays trace the development of Negri's thought over the last 20 years. Like many of his writings, they are almost impenetrably dense and difficult works.

The Politics of Subversion, originally written in the late 1980s, is by contrast one of Negri's most accessible works.[5] It takes up many of the themes that reappear in *Empire* and *Multitude*, but in a far clearer form. A collection of Negri's key pamphlets from the 1970s has been republished under the title *Books for Burning*.[6]

Alongside these early writings by Negri come several articles and collections attempting to grapple with his work. *The Philosophy of Antonio Negri*[7] contains essays tracing the history of Negri's thought from 1968 onwards and some responses to his contemporary work. The essays range enormously in quality. Those by Kathi Weeks, Nick Dyer-Witheford and Kenneth Surin, all of whom are broadly sympathetic to Negri, make some interesting comments and criticisms. Steve Wright's essay on the debates within the 'Autonomist Marxist' current that Negri helped establish in Italy in the 1970s is well worth reading. Wright has also written a very useful book on the history of Italian Autonomist Marxism entitled *Storming Heaven*.[8]

Debating Empire, a more critical collection of responses to *Empire*, brings together several thoughtful contributions from left wing writers including Ellen Meiksins Wood, Giovanni Arrighi and Leo Panitch.[9] It also reprints Alex Callinicos's 'Toni Negri in Perspective', which first appeared in this journal.[10] In a similar spirit of criticism is an essay in the journal *Capital and Class* by Paul Thompson, entitled 'Foundation and Empire'.[11] Slavoj Zizek, who was enthusiastic about the publication of *Empire*, has produced a short essay, available online, critical of the strategic weaknesses of Hardt and Negri's theory.[12] One of the most withering attacks on *Empire* comes from Argentina-based Marxist Atilio Boron. His book, *Empire and Imperialism*, is at times rather shrill in tone, but Boron does deal with many of the key problems in *Empire*.[13]

The wealth of new and republished work by and about Negri makes it possible to trace the development of his thought. In particular it helps explain why Negri has got it wrong on several key questions for the movement. His errors stem both from the trajectory of the Italian movement amid which his politics were shaped and from the strange and eclectic sources of inspiration he has selected in recent years. Lenin famously argued that Marx's ideas were drawn from all that was best of the 19th century—a synthesis of 'German philosophy, English political economy and French socialism'. But today, according to Negri's collaborator Michael Hardt, 'the orientations have changed and revolutionary thought is guided by French philosophy, North American economic science and Italian politics'.[14] As Boron writes, 'Hardt is right, as long as he is referring to the orientation that guided his own work and not to the sources that inspire revolutionary thought. In fact, both French philosophy and the economic theories that are taught in most business schools throughout the United States play a predominant role in *Empire*'.[15]

Italian politics

Negri first came to prominence as a leading theorist of *operaismo* (workerism), a current of Marxist thought developed in Italy and influential in the explosion of struggles that shook the country from 1969 through to the late 1970s. *Operaismo* focused on the conflict between capital and labour in the workplace, tracing the emergence and struggles of the 'mass worker' inside Italy's major factories. This emphasis was a refreshing response to the determinist version of Marxism that dominated the world Communist movement at the time. But it came at the cost of downplaying the relationship between workers' struggles and the objective economic and social context. In particular the strategies adopted by capital were seen simply as a response to these struggles, rather than the result of competition between individual, or groups of, capitalists. This feature of *operaismo* is preserved in Negri's contemporary work, in which Empire is a similarly homogenous entity, called into being by workers' struggles.

In 1969, the year of Italy's 'Hot Autumn', which saw unprecedented levels of industrial struggle, Negri helped to found the Potere Operaio (Workers Power) group. Like many far left groups in Italy, Potere Operaio sought to build a presence among factory workers. What distinguished Potere Operaio 'was its conception of insurrection as a pressing, imminent necessity...if the "party of the insurrection" was not built, it argued, the only possible outcome would be "the general defeat of the movement".'[16] Potere Operaio dissolved in 1973 amid raging disagreements on the meaning of the 'insurrectionary party', its relationship to the factory workers and the relationship of these workers to social movements beyond the factory walls. Some of those involved in Potere Operaio would later resurface in armed and clandestine organisations such as the Red Brigades. Others were absorbed within the Italian Communist Party. Some, including Negri, were to form a series of local groups—each with its own history and body of theory—known collectively as Autonomia Operaia.

The high-water mark of influence for these groups was reached in 1977 with a new explosion of student struggles. But by then the tide of workers' struggles had already ebbed away, replaced by increasingly violent confrontations between Autonomia groups and the Italian state. Ultimately the Italian movement was defeated because the revolutionary left was unable to displace the Italian Communist Party from its dominant position among the working class. The Communist Party was able to act as a floodgate, holding back the struggle, and then striking a deal with the ruling Christian Democrats to stabilise Italian capitalism.

Negri drew rather different conclusions. Increasingly he looked to other social forces outside the working class. For him the whole concept of the working class had 'gone into crisis', and production now took place not in the factories, but across the 'entire social terrain'. As the working class suffered rising unemployment and a series of crushing defeats, Autonomia became 'a percolating radical synthesis of various marginalised sectors: students, unemployed and precarious workers, feminist movements and other new social subjects'.[17] Negri theorised this shift in emphasis. He developed the idea of the 'socialised worker', a working class spread across the whole of society, mirroring the spread of capital out of the factory and into every niche of life. His more recent concept, the multitude, is rooted in the theory of the socialised worker.

The theoretical tools of *operaismo* helped to shape his response to the defeat. Negri carried *operaismo*'s subjectivist Marxism to its extreme with his development of the idea of 'constituent power'. According to this theory, each new cycle of struggle from below forces the restructuring of production so that the ruling power can attempt to once more capture and harness the creative energies of the masses. Each social formation is seen as a response to a previous struggle. For example, the emergence of the mass worker was, for Negri, a response to the struggles of an elite of 'skilled workers', whose organisation reached its acme in Lenin's Bolshevik Party.

Negri claims that the struggles of 1968 marked an even more fundamental break with the past. Rather than seeking to understand the causes of the defeat of the Italian movement, Negri sought to identify a completely new economic system created in response to the struggles of the mass worker. He took his inspiration from an unusual source.

American economics

Already with his concept of the socialised worker, Negri had rejected the central pillar of Marx's economics—the relationship between value and labour. As the whole of society becomes a social factory, so the duration of labour becomes unquantifiable and it becomes impossible to reduce specific forms of labour into abstract socially necessary labour. As the 1980s and 1990s unfolded Negri underpinned his new politics with reference to two fashionable right wing theories—the idea of a 'weightless economy' developing out of a high tech 'third industrial revolution' and, more recently, extreme versions of globalisation theory depicting the death of the nation-state. Today Negri claims that 'immaterial labour' has taken the place of industrial labour as the hegemonic form of production that other forms of labour tend towards. Negri's descriptions of contemporary production will seem unfamiliar to most workers: 'A gigantic cultural revolution is under way. Free expression and the joy of bodies, the autonomy, hybridisation and the reconstruction of languages, the creation of new singular mobile modes of production—all this emerges, everywhere and continually'.[18]

> [Global corporations are anxious to include] difference within their realm and thus aim to maximise creativity, free play and diversity in the corporate workplace. People of all different races, sexes and sexual orientations should potentially be included in the corporation; the daily routine of the workplace

should be rejuvenated with unexpected changes and an atmosphere of fun. Break down the old boundaries and let 100 flowers bloom![19]

Exploitation, in the Marxist sense of the pumping of unpaid surplus labour out of workers, has ended. Exploitation today means capturing the creative energies of a joyous, cooperating multitude—who may be inside or outside of the workplace. The domination of dead labour, such as machinery or computers, over living is finished because living (for Negri, intellectual) labour is now dominant. The tool of production is now the brain. Paul Thompson explains how Negri's thinking parallels right wing accounts of the economic changes since the 1970s:

> This appears to be remarkably similar to knowledge economy arguments, which we might briefly summarise in the following way. In the information age, capital and labour are said to have been displaced by the centrality of knowledge; brawn by brain; and the production of goods by services and manipulation of symbols. As a commodity, knowledge is too complex, intensive and esoteric to be managed through command and control. The archetypal worker in the new economy makes his or her living from judgement, service and analysis... As none of this is calculable or easily measured, it is the inherent property of the producer... This shifts the power balance to the employee, an increasing proportion of whom fall into the category of mobile, self-reliant and demanding 'free workers'.[20]

Thompson goes on to provide a detailed critique of the idea of immaterial labour. Even at the most immaterial end of the labour market, intellectual property regimes allow the commodification of knowledge. And such workers are still subject to exploitation and control centred upon the workplace. Thompson also points to evidence that only 10 to 15 percent of jobs in the US and Britain centre on problem-solving and manipulation of symbols. Indeed, most growth areas involve the creation of large numbers of low skilled, poorly paid jobs. Kenneth Surin points out:

> The US Department of Labour's projections for the occupations that will provide the most jobs for the period between 1994 and 2005 indicate that the ten occupations with the greatest number of new jobs will be cashiers, janitors and cleaners, retail salespersons, waiters and waitresses, registered nurses,

general managers and top executives, system analysts, home health aides, guards, and nurses' aides, orderlies and attendants. Only 24 percent of these can be said to constitute middle class and owner or management occupations.[21]

Far from the workplace ceasing to be the centre of capital accumulation for the ruling class, it plays an increasingly important role in a world of labour intensification and tightening managerial control. The workplace is still the point at which fixed capital necessary for the production of most goods and services is centralised. And it is still the site where surplus value is extracted from workers—the central obsession of capitalists and states—and thus the point at which those opposed to the rule of capital should concentrate their efforts.

Just like his vision of the weightless economy, Negri's account of globalisation is almost entirely unsupported by empirical evidence. He writes that: 'large transnational corporations have effectively surpassed the jurisdiction and authority of nation-states...the state has been defeated and corporations now rule the earth!'[22] Boron proposes an alternative relationship between nation-states and the corporations. Looking at the 200 mega-corporations that between them register combined sales greater than the gross national product of all but nine of the richest countries in the world, he notes:

> The neo-liberal globalisation ideologists' rhetoric is not enough to disguise the fact that 96 percent of those 200 global and transnational companies have their headquarters in only eight countries, are legally registered as incorporated companies of eight countries; and their boards of directors sit in eight countries of metropolitan capitalism. Less than 2 percent of their boards of directors' members are non-nationals, while more than 85 percent of all their technological developments have originated within their 'national frontiers'. Their reach is global, but their property and their owners have a clear national base.[23]

French philosophy

Negri's politics are shaped by the defeat of the movement of the 1960s and 1970s. His borrowed economic theory was shaped by the triumphalism following the restructuring of US capitalism in the 1980s and the collapse of the Stalinist regimes. Having created a Marxism gutted of its central emphasis on the working class, he filled this empty shell with the poststructuralist philosophy developed by a generation of disappointed post-1968 French intellectuals.

Boron argues that Hardt and Negri's increasing reliance on post-structuralist philosophers flows from a shared backdrop of trying to come to terms with working class defeat and capitalist hubris. Faced with a system that appears, for the time being, unbeatable:

> ...a series of theoretical and practical consequences emerge that...are neatly reflected in the postmodern agenda. On the one hand, an almost obsessive interest in the examination of the social forms that grow in the margins or in the interstices of the system; on the other hand, the search for those social forces that at least for now could commit some sort of transgression against the system, or could promote some type of limited and ephemeral subversion against it.[24]

This concern with subversion and transgression is indeed characteristic of many of the autonomist movements with which Negri is associated. But for Negri, with the rise of post-industrial production and the multitude, the potential for postmodern subversion has spread across the whole social terrain, and across the globe. One might expect Hardt and Negri to explain what such a confrontation would look like. However, what we instead get is a retreat into philosophy and descriptions of the multitude that the authors themselves admit are merely 'poetic'.

Hardt and Negri also borrow from the poststructuralists, especially Deleuze and Guattari, an eclectic form of expression known as 'assemblage'. Timothy Brennan writes:

> It expresses itself as a gathering of substantively incompatible positions. In Empire's assemblage, the juxtaposition of figures whose political views are mutually hostile to one another...is presented as the supersession of earlier divisions in pursuit of a more supple and inclusive combination.[25]

So, in *Empire*, philosophers such as Michel Foucault or Baruch Spinoza and revolutionaries such as Rosa Luxemburg rub shoulders with Bill Gates, former US labour secretary Robert Reich and St Francis of

Assissi. This form of expression evolved as a rejection of attempts at a 'grand narrative' such as Marxism that could hope to explain and help transform the world, or of an agency such as the working class that could carry through such a transformation. For Hardt and Negri this method mirrors the multitude that they describe—a series of heterogeneous, isolated subjects, coming together to fleetingly act in common. Indeed they have gone so far as to say that the struggles of the multitude have become 'incommunicable' and lack a 'common enemy'.

Their assertion would be contested by most of those who have attended the great international gatherings and protests of the anti-capitalist movement since Seattle. Here opposition to neo-liberalism and war have become common themes. The world working class may have been traumatised by the impact of neo-liberalism and the defeat of the movements of the 1960s and 1970s. But, rather than celebrating the much-exaggerated demise of the working class, the challenge today is to re-engage the growing ideological opposition to capitalism with the potential power that workers still hold. Negri is dismissive of such a project, but offers nothing substantial in its place.

His recent faux pas—over neo-liberalism, the EU constitution and the war in Iraq—stem from his failure to come to terms with either the defeats of the past or the nature of contemporary capitalism. Almost every assertion in his recent writings vanishes into thin air once subjected to even a cursory empirical examination. As for strategy, *Multitude* ends:

> We can already recognise that today time is split between a present that is already dead and a future that is already living—and that yawning abyss between them is becoming enormous. In time, an event will thrust us like an arrow into that living future. This will be the real political act of love.[26]

With imperialism rampant in the world, multinationals and states wreaking havoc at home and abroad, and global warming threatening our very survival as a species, waiting for an act of political love to save us sounds like bad advice.

NOTES

1: M Hardt and A Negri, *Empire* (Harvard, 2001).

2: M Hardt and A Negri, *Multitude: War and Democracy in the Age of Empire* (Penguin, 2004).

3: L Duart-Plon, quoted in A Boron, *Empire and Imperialism* (Zed Books, 2005), p20.

4: A Negri, *Time for Revolution* (Continuum, 2003).

5: A Negri, *The Politics of Subversion* (Polity Press, 2005).

6: A Negri, *Books for Burning* (Verso, 2005).

7: T Murphy and A Mustafa (eds), *The Philosophy of Antonio Negri: Resistance in Practice* (Pluto, 2005).

8: S Wright, *Storming Heaven: Class Composition and Struggle in Italian Autonomist Marxism* (Pluto, 2002).

9: G Balakrishnan (ed), *Debating Empire* (Verso, 2003).

10: A Callinicos, 'Toni Negri in Perspective', in *International Socialism* 92 (Autumn 2001), http://pubs.socialistreviewindex.org.uk/isj92/callinicos.htm

11: P Thompson, 'Foundation and Empire: A Critique of Hardt and Negri', in *Capital & Class* 86 (Summer 2005).

12: S Zizek, '*Objet a* as Inherent Limit to Capitalism', www.lacan.com/zizmultitude.htm

13: A Boron, as above.

14: As above, p106.

15: As above.

16: S Wright, as above, p143.

17: N Dyer-Witheford, 'Cyber-Negri: General Intellect and Immaterial Labour', in T Murphy and A Mustafa (eds), as above, p137.

18: A Negri, 'Kairos, Alma Venus, Multitudo', in *Time for Revolution*, as above, p201.

19: M Hardt and A Negri, *Empire*, quoted in A Boron, as above, p48.

20: P Thompson, as above, p80.

21: K Surin, 'Now Everything Must be Reinvented: Negri and Revolution', in T Murphy and A Mustafa (eds), as above, p229.

22: M Hardt and A Negri, *Empire*, quoted in A Boron, as above, p52.

23: A Boron, as above, p46.

24: As above, p102.

25: T Brennan, 'The Italian Ideology', in G Balakrishnan (ed), as above, p111.

26: M Hardt and A Negri, *Multitude*, p358.

North Korea's hidden history

Owen Miller

Recent writing on North Korea from South Korea's internationalist left

North Korea is often in the news these days, albeit relegated to the inside pages of the papers, while English-language books on the country have proliferated in the last few years. But all these tend to approach North Korea from the perspective of the 'Korea problem', international relations theory or even a voyeuristic fascination with the last true Communist dictatorship cum workers' paradise. What about the view from South Korea, where the 'Korea problem' is all the more immediate and potentially disastrous?

In recent times there has been a clear divergence between the interests of the South Korean ruling class and their erstwhile patrons in the US. Although some 36,000 US troops remain on the southern half of the peninsula and the US is still ostensibly protecting the democratic South from Communist aggression, the current government of Roh Moo-hyun has taken a more independent and nationalist stance in its foreign policy and relations with the North, somewhat to the chagrin of the Bush administration. While the US appears to favour the status quo in north east Asia as part of its China containment strategy (actually its room for manoeuvre is severely curtailed by the current disaster in Iraq—hence the recent softening of its stance towards North Korea), the dominant sections of the South Korean ruling class want a 'soft landing' for North Korea. They see the workers of the North as a source of cheap labour to rival Chinese workers, and even harbour ambitions for a future united peninsula that will be a powerful political and economic player in the region—an outcome that China, Japan and Russia all seem rather keen to forestall.

A more nationalist, North-friendly mood has also come to dominate popular attitudes towards North Korea in the South. As opinion of the United States has plummeted, so the old anti-Communist rhetoric towards North Korea has lost its grip, with some 47.6 percent of South Koreans in a recent survey saying they would back the North if the US bombed the country.[1] Although the forces on the Korean left that are still openly pro-North Korean have dwindled, ideas about the history and formation of North Korea that were once the preserve of the pro North left have become more mainstream.

A professor at a leading university in Seoul has recently caused great controversy by making supposedly pro North Korean comments to the effect that the Korean War was started by the North for unification, and that after liberation from Japanese colonial rule in 1945 most Koreans wanted to live in a communist or socialist society. But the controversy has centred as much on the attempt to witch-hunt Professor Kang Jeong-koo using the outdated anti-Communist National Security Law as it has on his actual comments.[2] Professor Kang and others like him appear to represent a tendency to look somewhat nostalgically at the early years of North Korea and to compare the origins of the North very favourably with the US-dominated origins of the South Korean state.

Andrei Lankov, a historian of North Korea who has made extensive use of Soviet archives opened in the 1990s, used a recent article in the *Asia Times* to attack left nationalists like Kang, who he believes have come to dominate South Korean academia, for their romanticised and counter-factual approach to the origins of the North Korean state. He says:

> They [the left intellectuals] chose to believe that the early North Korean state was a complete opposite to the allegedly corrupt and dependent Seoul government of the era. There are hard facts that demonstrate that until 1950 for all practical purposes the North Korean state was a Soviet puppet, but these facts do not fit into their world picture nicely, and hence are not mentioned.
>
> Even a cursory look through now-available historical documents clearly indicates: in 1945-50 the North Korean regime operated under complete control of Soviet supervisors. Who drafted the above-mentioned land reform

law? Soviet advisers. Who edited and, after some deliberation, confirmed the North Korean constitution of 1948? Joseph Stalin himself. Who arrested all major opponents to the emerging Communist regime? The Soviet military police. Where were the dissidents sent to do their time? To Siberia, of course.[3]

But, whether knowingly or not, Lankov disregards recent writing coming from within South Korea's increasingly important internationalist left. Some recent examples of such writing include Han Kyu-han's current series on the modern history of Korea in the socialist newspaper *Ta Hamkke* (*All Together*), published to mark the sixtieth anniversary of liberation, and Kim Ha-yong's important 2002 book *The Korean Peninsula from an Internationalist Perspective*.[4]

A long article within this book, entitled 'The Formation of North Korean State Capitalism', actually goes further than simply mounting a polemic against the nationalist or pro-North left in South Korea. It attempts to understand the origins and subsequent development of North Korean society prior to the Korean War of 1950-53 by making use of the theory of state capitalism. This is a significant development because, although Marxist ideas became very popular in both social movements and academia during South Korea's 'democratic revolution' of the 1980s, Trotskyism and the theory of state capitalism have only had an audience more recently.

'The Formation of North Korean State Capitalism' is divided into four chapters: the occupation of the North by Soviet troops; the emergence of Kim Il-sung as their chosen leader; the consolidation of the country's long-term division into two opposing states; and the economics of its transformation into a 'people's democracy'. Here I will present some parts of Kim Ha-yong's analysis, concentrating on those sections dealing with the Soviet occupation and the subsequent transformation of North Korean society on the model of the Soviet Union's state capitalist economy.

The liberation and division of Korea

Kim begins by looking at how the North Korean state has viewed its own origins, revealing the huge change that occurred in the late 1950s as the North began to assert its independence from Soviet control and develop its Juche ideology[5] as a protection against the upheavals that were besetting the Stalinist countries in the wake of Stalin's death.

In August 1946 Kim Il-sung read aloud a letter of thanks from the Korean people to Stalin:

> Long live the great Generalissimo Stalin, liberator, supporter, benefactor and friend of the Korean people. The people of North Korea recognise that their liberation and development has been achieved only as a result of your affectionate consideration and the assistance of the Red Army, and they offer their greatest respect to you.[6]

As late as 1956 writings praising the 'Great Soviet Army' can be found alongside illustrations depicting their triumphant march into P'yongyang, complete with women throwing flowers and smiling Russian soldiers bouncing Korean children on their hips.[7]

But by the late 1950s things had changed remarkably, and the North Korean state set about eliminating records of the Soviet Union's central role in its own formation, even erasing Soviet officers from a photograph of Kim Il-sung at a rally in October 1945.[8] The official record of Korea's liberation from Japanese colonial rule became very different and aimed primarily at promoting the burgeoning personality cult around the 'Great Leader' Kim, as in this passage from a publication of the 1980s: 'Above all, we should understand that it was not the people of some other country but our leader who restored our fatherland and established in this land our flourishing socialist nation'.[9]

The reality is not only that Soviet troops liberated the northern part of the Korean peninsula from Japanese rule by occupying it in mid-August 1945, but the Soviet Union continued to exercise close control over North Korea for at least the next five years. As Lankov points out, even seemingly small matters such as the staging of a parade in 1948 required approval from Moscow.[10] The North Korean regime was a 'puppet government' of a variety not significantly different from the current regime in occupied Iraq.

As Kim Ha-yong emphasises, the Soviet Union did not simply stumble into this position at the end of the Second World War—it had been aware of the strategic importance of the Korean peninsula for some time, and negotiated with the Allied powers at Potsdam and Yalta with an eye to gaining a strategic foothold in north east Asia and regaining the territory and concessions in the region lost by Tsarist Russia after its defeat in the 1904-05 Russo-Japanese war. For Kim this clearly demonstrates the imperialist nature of the Soviet Union's intentions on the Korean peninsula:

> The basis for Soviet policy towards the Korean peninsula was not revolutionary internationalism but the desire for imperialist expansion. Stalin's ambition was to inherit the old possessions of the Tsar's empire and to restore its former glory.[11]

She also points out the significance of the Soviet acceptance of the US military's 'General Order No 1'. Under this order the US divided east Asia into Soviet and US occupation zones, unilaterally splitting the Korean peninsula at the 38th parallel. In 1945 the Soviets were at pains not to upset the Americans, and dutifully observed the line arbitrarily set down across the peninsula. Both sides must have known that this actually meant the long-term division of the country into two halves, and from early on they began to construct their own systems within their zones of occupation.[12]

The nature of the Soviet occupation

What of the occupation itself then? The nationalist and pro-North left in Korea has been keen to contrast the Soviet occupation of North Korea with the US occupation of the South. They cite the fact that soon after their arrival the Soviets handed over civilian administration to the Committees for the Preparation of Korean Independence—or People's Committees as they later became[13]—formed by Korean nationalists and Communists, whereas in the South these committees were bloodily suppressed. It is not only prominent left nationalist Koreans like Kang Jeong-koo who see this aspect as positive—the American historian Bruce Cumings also argues that:

> The Soviets had pursued a highly cost-effective strategy in creating a regime that was responsive both to their minimum demand—a friendly border state—and to the desires of the mass of Koreans in the liberation era... [This was] quite in contrast to the American occupation.[14]

However, as Kim Ha-yong points out, the Soviets' original decree on administration, issued on 25 August, had called for the continuation of Japanese administrative structures and personnel. She argues that their U-turn a day later when they decided to recognise the Peoples' Committees:

...did not mean a massive change in policy for the Soviets. It meant only that by recognising the People's Committees and controlling them, the Soviets could realise their interests in Korea. This method looked better and offered more stability than using the old Japanese-staffed administrative organs.[15]

Kim Ha-yong also argues that the main task facing the Soviet occupation forces was not the establishment of a society controlled by the Korean people, but actually the suppression of popular demands for democracy, independence and workers' control of production. She writes:

With Korea's liberation on 15 August 1945 the long-suppressed demands of the Korean people began to explode into the open. The Japanese surrender created a power vacuum, and people became excited with the hopes of constructing a new state. All over the country organs of self-government were created. The situation in the northern part of the peninsula was not particularly different to other areas.[16]

The northern part of the peninsula was also the industrial heartland of the country, with an estimated 1 million workers out of a total population of 10 million in 1945. In the early days of liberation many factories in industrial cities like Hamhung and Haeju went over to workers' control once the Japanese managers had been driven out, and in the major port city of Wonsan an organisation called the Korean Labour Union took charge of keeping public order.[17] But this movement was swiftly suppressed by the Soviet army when it arrived on the scene and enforced the 'normal operation' of factories.

Besides this, the Soviet occupation forces were also responsible for shutting down or censoring Korean-language newspapers and banning various organisations that they saw as 'anti-Soviet', such as the Democratic Youth association of Hamhung. Crucially, Kim argues that the big difference in popular resistance to occupation between the Soviet-dominated North and the US-occupied South can be accounted for not by the relative benevolence of the Soviets but by the swiftness of their arrival in the North:

The Soviets nipped in the bud popular movements that might otherwise have broadened further. This provides us with one of the answers to the question of why it was that the mass struggles that erupted so fiercely in the

> South immediately after liberation did not occur in the North. The masses of the North had to face the Soviet occupation army before they had even had a chance to wake up properly. Whereas the US army was not stationed in the South of the peninsula until 8 September, the Soviets had started to advance into the North on 12 August.[18]

Against the claims of nationalist historians that the Soviets guaranteed the autonomy of the People's Committees in the North, Kim shows clearly that the occupiers saw them as more of a safety valve and a means through which they could exercise their control more effectively.[19] Once an overarching administrative bureau was formed to coordinate the People's Committees in November 1945, the Soviets made sure that it followed orders from the Soviet civil administration or army headquarters, and all its proclamations had to be approved by them. As Kim writes:

> The People's Committees suddenly found themselves reduced to mere representatives of the administration, rubber-stamping decisions at the request of the Soviets... In contrast to [Kang Jeong-koo's] evaluation that 'the power of the provincial People's Committees rested upon the popular masses', real power lay with the Soviet army.[20]

Other aspects of the Soviet occupation also made it clear that this was an imperialist occupation. In fact, as with the current US adventure in Iraq, economic interests were not too far behind military and geopolitical ones. Soviet economic plunder of the North took a number of forms: the enforced use of Soviet-issued military certificates as currency; continuous demands to the nascent North Korean government for money for the upkeep of the Soviet military; the removal of large quantities of industrial plant from factories and other facilities in North Korea; aid directed towards industries producing goods for them to be taken back to the Soviet Union; and extremely unequal trade terms.[21]

Resistance to the Soviet occupation

Despite the Soviet anxiety to 'nip in the bud' popular movements for genuine self-government, there was resistance to the Soviet occupation of North Korea. Like the occupying army of any imperialist nation, the Soviet soldiers did not treat the Koreans as their equals, and cases of looting, theft, rape and murder committed by soldiers were common, especially in the early period of the occupation.[22] In late 1945 and early 1946 there was growing antagonism towards the occupying forces and towards the internal security forces, called the *poandae*, commanded by the Soviets' rising protégé, Kim Il-sung. Kim Ha-yong describes how in this context there were two significant uprisings against the occupiers. These, she argues, were genuine expressions of popular anger towards the Soviet occupation and the increasingly arrogant behaviour of their Korean Communist allies, not anti-Communist demonstrations organised by the far right as people on the nationalist left in South Korea have argued.

The first incident occurred in November 1945 at Sinuiju in the north west when hundreds of middle and high school students in the city marched to the courthouse, currently occupied by the local headquarters of the Communist Party, to protest at interference by the party in local schools. The students attempted to occupy the building themselves but were savagely attacked by the *poandae* and Soviet troops, with the loss of between 15 and 24 lives. Although Kim Il-sung is said to have been very worried by the incident and heavily criticised the local Communist Party, the resistance spread to the city of Hamhung in March of 1946. Once again students were at the forefront, but this time the demonstration took on a more explicitly anti-Soviet complexion, with calls for the Soviet troops to go home and stop taking local rice while the Koreans were starving. When the students attempted to attack the local Communist Party offices they were again brutally repulsed by Soviet troops and the *poandae*, and as 1946 went on the jails of North Korea were filled with the enemies of the new state.[23]

The 'people's democratic revolution' and land reform

> Most people believe that the reforms accomplished in North Korea beginning in 1946 brought into being the 'socialist mode of production' there. Whether people like the North or not, the belief that North Korea is socialist has been a continuous feature of the last few decades [in South Korea]. Professor Kang Jeong-koo has gone as far as to state that 'if one does

> not recognise North Korea as a socialist state it is not possible to understand or investigate North Korean society'.[24]

But as Kim Ha-yong points out, there was never a workers' revolution in North Korea, and in the late 1940s Kim Il-sung himself did not talk much about socialism, but rather the 'people's democratic revolution', a theory that Lankov describes as 'specially designed for Soviet-controlled territories'.[25] The basic idea of 'people's democracy' was that the countries liberated by the Soviets after the Second World War would move gradually to socialism via 'people's democratic' reforms, without the need for a revolution like that experienced by Russia in 1917. But according to Kim Ha-yong, 'People's democracy was not the path of non-revolutionary transition from capitalism to socialism, but nothing more than the establishment from above of capitalism (a national economy)',[26] or what might also be termed an independent centre of capital accumulation.

One of the main elements of the people's democracy reforms was the North's land reform, much praised on the South Korean left. The reform took place in the space of only 20 days during spring 1946, and consisted of land confiscation without compensation and free land distribution to the former tenant farmers:

> Pro-Japanese landlords, those owning more than 500 hectares and other landlords not working their own fields had all their land confiscated, completely liquidating the tenant farming system in a stroke... Thus, by eliminating the old parasitic landlord class, the state bureaucrats were able to create the conditions for the effective exploitation of the peasantry and workers.[27]

This reform created a very big layer of small landowning peasants who were naturally averse to sending large amounts of their produce to market to feed the urban working classes. On the other hand, the advantage of the reform for the North Korean bureaucracy was that it produced a great deal of goodwill for the new regime among the peasant class and avoided the reliance on large farmers who might build up economic or social power. However, as Kim writes, while the North Korean bureaucracy chose the small-scale agricultural production path, 'they put in place measures that would subordinate agricultural production to the state capitalist economy'.[28]

In fact, Kim claims that, 'although the form was different, the North Korean peasants' legal position was really quite similar to that of the collectivised Russian peasants'. Supplying the cities with food required huge state intervention in agriculture, and the peasants were forced to give the government around 25 percent of their yield as a tax in kind that appeared little different to the portion of their crop they had given up to the landlords under the old sharecropping system or the exactions of rice by the Japanese colonial administration. Ultimately, this made it quite similar to the much less praised South Korean land reforms of the late 1940s, where the peasants had to pay for their allotments of land but then only had to give up around 15 percent of their crop in taxes. The bureaucracy also found other ways to squeeze the peasants—through various miscellaneous taxes, through the low prices paid for rice at the farmers' co-ops, and even through the continued use of corvée labour.[29]

The drive for rapid industrialisation

After liberation, factories and other industrial facilities formerly owned by the Japanese remained under the effective control of the Soviet administration until late July 1946, when the Korean-run government (now called the North Korea Provisional People's Committee) took them over and soon after announced their nationalisation. Further nationalisation happened rapidly, and by 1949 state-run industry accounted for 90.7 percent of total industrial production.[30] The nationalisation of industry and the commencement of a series of one-year plans in the late 1940s are one of the main developments that have led historians and commentators, whether hostile or friendly to the regime, to call North Korea socialist from this time on.

In opposition to this view, Kim Ha-yong puts North Korea's state ownership of industry into the context of the worldwide trend towards state capitalism, particularly in the period after the Second World War:

> It was very common, particularly in developing countries, for the state to take a direct role in planning and overseeing resources and means of production in order to achieve rapid industrial growth. Representative examples include China, Cuba and African countries such as Mozambique, but South Korea's economic development strategy under Park Chung-hee[31] cannot be excluded either. In the period immediately after liberation, even right wing

parties such as the Korean Democratic Party (Hanmindang) insisted that the main industries needed to be nationalised in order to overcome the society's backwardness. From this point of view, North Korea's nationalisation programme of 1946, far from being a break away from capitalism, was only an extreme manifestation of the trend towards the statisation of capital that continued from the 1930s through to the 1960s.[32]

Kim goes on to address two important aspects of North Korea's economic organisation that bring into sharp focus its character as a state capitalist economy oriented towards rapid industrial development rather than a workers' state. First, there was the complete separation of North Korean workers from ownership or control over the means of production. Not only were workers 'free' of the means of production in the Marxist sense, but there was also a complex labour market in the new state-run economy, with a great many gradations in wage levels and the active encouragement of competition between workers. Although there was an officially-sanctioned trade union federation and there were consultative councils including workers in the factories, in reality North Korean workers had no say in the running of factories or the overall planning of the economy and could not even organise themselves to improve their conditions and wages. In fact, organisations such as the North Korean Federation of Trade Unions and the 'production consultation councils' were really means for the state to better mobilise workers to meet production targets.[33]

The second aspect was the relentless drive for capital accumulation under the newly nationalised and planned economy of North Korea in the late 1940s. What this meant was a massive concentration of production into producing further means of production rather than consumer goods. As Kim Ha-yong shows, North Korea's concentration on producing means of production even outstripped what the USSR had managed after more than a decade of five-year plans, reaching 77.3 percent of total production in 1948, as compared to 61 percent for the Soviet Union in 1940.[34] North Korean industry was able to recover in the late 1940s and impressive growth was achieved, but only as a result of huge exploitation of the workers, spurred on by a continuous stream of Stakhanovite productivity campaigns and mass mobilisation movements.[35]

Kim also isolates the mechanism that drove the North Korean bureaucracy to rapid industrialisation and the primitive accumulation of capital. Not surprisingly, it was similar to that which drove the state capitalist economies of the Soviet Union and Eastern Europe. The economy of North Korea, like those of Eastern Europe, was subordinated to the needs of the Soviet ruling class and its military competition with the emerging Western bloc.[36] But a further element in the North Korean case was the proximity of the US-backed South and the military threat that it posed:

> Small-scale skirmishes began to arise in the border zone around the 38th parallel from early 1949. The economic strategy centred on heavy industry reflected this military competition between North and South. As the Communist Kim Il frankly pointed out at the time, the level of productivity would determine victory or defeat in a war... The North Korean bureaucracy was able to use this atmosphere of tension to force workers to make even bigger sacrifices.[37]

The importance of North Korea's past

In 1946 the bureaucracy were claiming to be carrying through the 'anti-imperialist, anti-feudal democratic revolution', and from early 1947 they claimed to have begun the 'transition to socialism', but as Kim Ha-yong says, 'what they had created had nothing in common with socialism—it was merely a state capitalist society in which the bureaucracy exploited the working class collectively.'

Although Kim Ha-yong's work focuses on laying to rest some of the myths expounded by the nationalist left in South Korea, confused ideas about North Korean history and society are by no means limited to Korea itself. The tendency to see North Korea as a form of socialist society or to view the role of the Soviet Union in its origins as fundamentally different to the US role in the formation of South Korea also exists in the English-language literature on the country. As we have seen, the most well known left-leaning US scholar on the subject, Bruce Cumings, has written that the Soviets created a regime that was (to paraphrase) 'responsive to the desires of the mass of Koreans', while both he and Martin Hart-Landsberg have described North Korea as a 'socialist-corporatist' state.[38]

The Korean peninsula is one part of the world where arguments over the true nature of a brutal regime that calls itself socialist still have great relevance. This recent writing from the South Korean internationalist left is therefore an important corrective to the prevailing views of a left that has not yet been able to disassociate itself entirely from Stalinism. For the Korean left, and the international left that takes an interest in this part of the world, a realistic understanding of the North's history and a clear analysis of its present character are crucial for political strategy today.

NOTES

1: Opinion poll reported in the *Munhwa Ilbo* newspaper, 5 May 2005. A more recent poll of 15 to 25 year olds produced a figure of 65.9 percent supporting the North in a war with the US (*Chosun Ilbo* newspaper, 14 August 2005).

2: For more on this issue see 'Prosecutors Trigger Roh's Anger and the Feeling Seems Mutual', *Joongang Daily*, 18 October 2005; 'Ideological Battle Polarizes Society', *Korea Times*, 18 October 2005.

3: A Lankov, 'Interpreting North Korean History', *Asia Times Online*, 18 August 2005.

4: Kim Ha-yong, *Kukche chuui sigak eso pon hanbando* (Seoul, 2002).

5: Juche is a sort of extreme voluntarist philosophy that places great emphasis on human will. It is also used to justify the absolute rule of a single 'great leader'. Kim Ha-yong describes it as a 'mutation of Stalinism' (Kim Ha-yong, as above, p213).

6: Quoted in Kim Ha-yong, as above, p232.

7: An example of this is the Korean language textbook, *Kugo*, published in 1956.

8: Kim Ha-yong, as above, p233; Andrei Lankov notes that although this rally is now officially known in the North as the 'Rally to Welcome Kim Il-sung' it was in fact a rally to honour the Soviet army at which Kim read a speech written for him in Russian and translated into Korean. He was only one among a number of Korean politicians participating and stood on the platform wearing a Soviet medal pinned on his chest—A Lankov, *From Stalin to Kim Il Sung: The Formation of North Korea 1945-1960* (London, 2002).

9: *Kulloja* [Worker], July 1987. Quoted in Kim Ha-yong, as above, p232.

10: A Lankov, 'Interpreting North Korean history', as above.

11: Kim Ha-yong, as above, p236.

12: As above, p238.

13: Immediately after liberation Nationalists and Communists who were in the country began to form provincial committees taking charge of administration and peace-preservation duties. Initially these had a variety of names, but were commonly called Committees for the Preparation of Korean Independence (CPKI, or in Korean *Kon'guk chunbi wiwonhoe*). Branches were quickly formed at levels below the provincial administrations and soon there were hundreds of these committees all over the peninsula at every level from provincial down to town and village committees. By early October 1945 these committees were uniformly known as People's Committees (*inmin wiwonhoe*). See B Cumings, *The Origins of the Korean War I* (Princeton, 1981); A Lankov, *From Stalin to Kim Il-sung*, as above.

14: B Cumings, as above, p426.

15: Kim Ha-yong, as above, p241.

16: As above, p243.

17: As above.

18: As above, p244.

19: Claims such as those of Pak Segil in his widely-read history of modern Korea, *Tasi ssunun han'guk hyondaesa* [Rewriting Korea's Modern History].

20: Kim Ha-yong, as above, p250. The Kang Jeong-koo quotation is from Han'guksa 21—Pukhan ui chongch'i wa sahoe (1) [Korean History, vol 21: Politics and society of North Korea] (Seoul, 1994), p102.

21: Kim Ha-yong, as above, pp250-253 and 319-322.

22: See A Lankov, *From Stalin to Kim Il-sung*, as above, p4.

23: Kim Ha-yong, as above, p257; see also C Armstrong, *The North Korean Revolution, 1945-1950* (Ithaca, 2003), pp62-63.

24: Kim Ha-yong, as above, p307.

25: A Lankov, *From Stalin to Kim Il-sung*, as above, p8.

26: Kim Ha-yong, as above, p310.

27: As above, p313.

28: As above, p315.

29: As above, p318. For a good summary in English of the extraction of surplus from North Korean farmers see C Armstrong, as above, pp144-148.

30: Kim Ha-yong, as above, p323.

31: South Korea's military dictator who came to power in a coup in 1961. He is often credited with creating the conditions for the country's rapid economic development during the 1970s. He was assassinated by the head of the Korean Central Intelligence Agency in 1979.

32: Kim Ha-yong, as above, p327.

33: C Armstrong, as above, pp160-163.

34: Kim Ha-yong, as above, p334.

35: As above, p336. Pak No-ja also discussed the nature of these campaigns at a recent talk in Seoul, pointing out how similar the techniques used by the North Korean bureaucracy were to those employed by the former Japanese colonial regime. A transcript of his talk (in Korean) can be found here: http://www.alltogether.or.kr/2005new/right/0702pnj/0702pnj.htm

36: Kim Ha-yong, as above, p341.

37: As above, p342.

38: See B Cumings, *The Origins of the Korean War 1*, as above; M Hart-Landsberg, *Korea: Division, Reunification, and U.S. Foreign Policy.*

There's no place like America today[1]

Neil Davidson

A review of V G Kiernan, ***America: The New Imperialism—From White Settlement to World Hegemony*** *with a preface by E J Hobsbawm and an epilogue by J Trumpbour (Verso, 2005), £15, and Neil Smith,* ***The Endgame of Globalization*** *(Routledge US, 2005)*

These two very different books are notable contributions to the debate over the nature and role of contemporary American imperialism. Both authors are Marxists, albeit from different generations, left wing organisations and academic disciplines. Both examine their subject from a longer historical perspective than is usual.

Victor Kiernan is, with Eric Hobsbawm and John Saville, one of the few remaining members of the Communist Party Historians Group. Born in 1913, of all his contemporaries he has been the most eclectic in his range of interests, as Hobsbawm notes in an informative preface (which itself contains some acute remarks on the continuities of US foreign policy).[2] Indeed, it may be that the very widespread nature of Kiernan's subject matter has contributed to his relative obscurity compared with—to take the most obvious example—Christopher Hill, whose reputation was based on work almost entirely about 17th century England. Even Hobsbawm, who has a comparable range of interests to Kiernan, is most identified with his great quartet on the history of capitalism since 1789. From 1948 until his retirement Kiernan taught at Edinburgh University, and it is perhaps for this reason that he was virtually alone among the British Marxist historians in showing any serious interest in Scottish history.[3] More important for our purposes, however, is the fact that he was also exceptional among them in paying sustained attention to imperialism, in a series of articles and books across three decades.[4] The book under review here, *America: The New Imperialism*, first appeared in 1978, in the aftermath of the catastrophic defeat for the US in Vietnam.

Neil Smith's *The Endgame of Globalization* is a different type of book. Smith comes from a much later generational cohort and stands in a different political tradition from Kiernan. He became active around the time *America: The New Imperialism* was originally written, and was for several years a member of the International Socialist Organisation in the US. Like his former supervisor and current colleague David Harvey, Smith is part of the radical geography tradition that emerged in the 1980s.[5]

The Endgame of Globalization is an angrier, more polemical work than those with which Smith first drew attention.[6] It is both a demonstration of how the Marxist theory of imperialism can be used to shed light on current events and an implicit rejoinder to those sections of the left which see the US as virtually invulnerable.[7]

Kiernan writes in a style quite unlike most modern academic historians, for which we can only be grateful. We gather an impression of how US imperialism developed through an accumulation of characteristic details, often derived from letters, diaries, novels and other examples of what are sometimes dismissed as 'literary sources' by those who believe that only quantifiable methods are valid. His canvas contains the whole of American history as such, which he treats as virtually co-extensive with the history of US imperialism. On this basis he begins his account with the Puritan settlers 'building in the wilderness the better society that the Levellers tried in vain to build in England'.[8]

The implication is that the process by which territory was acquired by colonisation, conquest or (that quintessentially America method) cash constituted the construction of an 'internal' empire. 'The great fact was that industrial capitalism, now firmly installed as arbiter of the national destinies, had a rapidly growing market and a spacious field of enterprise at home, without needing to look for colonies outside'.[9] This absence of a formal empire constitutes the 'newness' of the American Empire.

Kiernan comments with pungent irony on the crimes and follies which fill these pages, but without adopting the persona of the detached observer, judging from outside history. Instead he holds his subjects to account for transgressing their own self-proclaimed codes and values: 'In Washington's eyes, since the ultimate goal, preservation of democracy, was righteous, all means toward it were warrantable, including suppression of democracy'.[10] At the same time, we always know where Kiernan stands in relation to the peoples and classes whose fate he recounts. He treats the question of the Native Americans seriously, at a time when this was far from conventional even in left wing histories of the US. He devotes a substantial part of the book to recounting how they were killed or driven from what were once their lands, but he never romanticises them.[11]

The book is recommended then, but two cautions are in order. First, Kiernan's style, attractive though it is, can also be an obstacle to clarity.[12] It works well in relation to broad themes in social and cultural history, as he demonstrated in his masterpiece *The Lords of Human Kind*, a sweeping survey of how the Western merchants, soldiers and colonists regarded the non-European peoples they came into contact with.[13] But because it is illustrative of the ideological expressions of imperialism, it is less effective in dealing with its central political and economic aspects. Second, his refusal to privilege one historical moment over another has the effect of obscuring decisive turning points—the long view tends to present a flat landscape.

This is particularly noticeable in relation to Vietnam. Kiernan underplays both the seriousness of the resistance to the war within the US and the implications of the defeat for US power: 'Yet as soon as the risk of having to serve at the front was removed, agitation and concern over Vietnamese sufferings died down abruptly; a year or two more, and Vietnam was forgotten'.[14]

This judgement would certainly be a surprise to US strategists, since they have spent the last 30 years trying to overcome the 'syndrome' to which Vietnam gave rise.[15]

But there is a greater difficulty here, which springs not from style or method, but from the underlying theory of imperialism with which Kiernan undertakes his survey:

'Imperialism today...may be seen as a continuation or recrudescence within the capitalist era of the "extra-economic compulsion" which is the hallmark of any feudal dominion'.[16]

The classical Marxist definition of imperialism envisages it as a particular stage in the development of capitalism with two key characteristics: on the one hand, the fusion of financial and industrial capital with the state; on the other, the expansion of capital beyond the territorial boundaries of individual states. In this conception, although we can still refer to 'American (or whichever) imperialism' as shorthand for the activities of particular state capitals, it is the system as a whole which is imperialist, and which compels these states to act in certain ways. Consequently, imperialism in this sense is not necessarily concerned with the relationship between oppressor and oppressed states, as Kiernan believes, but with the rivalry *between* the oppressor states themselves.

In this respect, Smith has a surer grasp of what the Marxist theory of imperialism involves: 'Where many on the left have still not yet embraced [Lenin's] insight, and still treat colonialism and imperialism as the same phenomenon, the neo-cons who have embraced empire are, in this respect at least, the truer Leninists'.[17]

Given these theoretical differences, it is interesting to compare their respective accounts of that main episode in American history where the logic of imperialist rivalry manifests itself most clearly—the ultimately abortive colonial adventures in Cuba and the Philippines in 1898. For Kiernan:

'There was of course no rational need of mountainous exports; hence an irrationality tinging all the epoch of expansionism now starting... Here was both the curious logic of capitalism and the American obsession with destiny; a latter-day example also of how, as in the 17th century, Calvinist determinism could be fused with superabundant energy'.[18]

Smith is equally mindful of the ideological aspects of imperialism, but grounds them far more in the needs of an expanding capitalist economy, rather in a cultural metaphysics:

'It was a short-lived colonialism, however, not because of some liberal American antipathy to empire—quite the opposite—nor because it solved the questions of economic and liberal expansion. It was short-lived because it didn't solve these problems'.[19]

Smith's core thesis is that the current period is the third attempt by the US to establish a world order based on liberal capitalism.

It is within this overall framework that Smith discusses the specific reasons for the invasion and occupation of Iraq, in which he takes due account of the defeat in Vietnam: 'The rationale for the Iraq war emerged from the amalgam of...three elements: the geopolitics of oil, the dramatic loss of US political power after the 1970s, and the partial fragmentation of the delicate system of power inter-dependencies that had let the region's petro-capitalism flourish'.[20]

Powerful though the main lines of Smith's argument are, the book is not entirely convincing at every level. It bears some signs of having been written in haste, although, unlike Kiernan, Smith is of course trying to deal with these crucial issues while events are still unfolding. Nevertheless, some of his judgements are questionable. Two examples stand out.

One is his treatment of Israel. Where Kiernan simply expresses puzzlement at US support for Israel ('No nation in history has had a more expensive and more disobliging ally'[21]), Smith explains its origins in terms of domestic politics: 'It was in no way a principled response to the horrors of the Holocaust, but a cynical attempt to win Jewish votes at home, in a tight upcoming election, and it had global consequences.' In discussing the subsequent history, he broadens this out to include 'the need for oil' as well as 'a domestically inspired support for the Israeli'.[22]

Now, Smith is absolutely correct to connect the internal politics of the US to its external relationships with other states. The question here is the extent to which the pro-Israeli lobby is decisive in determining policy. If it had not existed, would successive US governments have taken a different attitude to Israel? It seems scarcely conceivable that they would have behaved any differently. From 1967 in particular, the American ruling class has regarded Israel as the only stable force representing the interests of US capitalism in the region, and everything that has happened since, from the fall of the Shah in 1979 onwards, has confirmed it in this view.

A more general issue is the distinction which Smith draws between 'global aspiration' and 'national self-interest' in determining American imperial policy. Running through his book is the argument that America's imperial ambitions have previously run aground on the shoals of nationalist isolationalism. This is a real division within the American ruling class, but surely the advocates of global intervention were also motivated by 'national self-interest'? This may simply be a question of Smith's presentation, but there seems to be a problem in elevating opposing strategies for advancing those interests into a fundamental political division.

Any criticisms which might be made of either book, however, must be set alongside the fundamental service to truth which, in their different ways, they perform. Members of the pro-war left are fond of explaining America's tendency to support murderous military dictatorships by claiming that this was an unfortunate by-product of the Cold War, and not an intrinsic part of the operation of American foreign policy.

However, the historical record set out by Kiernan and Smith makes it quite clear that American imperialism preceded the Cold War by a long way, and that current interventions have to be considered and understood in this context rather than as a new form of humanitarian militarism.

NOTES

1: With apologies to the late Curtis Mayfield.
2: E J Hobsbawm, 'Preface', in V G Kiernan, *America: The New Imperialism—From White Settlement to World Hegemony* (London and New York, 2005), pvii.
3: See V G Kiernan, 'A Banner with a Strange Device: The Later Covenanters', in T Brotherstone (ed), *Covenant, Charter and Party* (Aberdeen, 1989); and 'The Covenanters: A Problem of Creed and Class', in H G Kaye (ed), *Poets, Politics and the People* (London and New York, 1989).
4: His interest in imperialism was not only theoretical. As a member of the CPGB Kiernan was an active anti-imperialist, and he appears to have done work for the party in India (while in the British army) during the 1940s. As late as 1990 this reviewer remembers canvassing support among Scottish intellectuals and public figures for an open letter opposing the coming Iraq war which eventually appeared in *The Scotsman*—Kiernan was one of the first to respond. The essays can be found in *Marxism and Imperialism* (London, 1974) and H J Kaye (ed), *Imperialism and Its Contradictions* (New York and London, 1985). A companion volume to *America: The New Imperialism*, dealing with Europe, is *European Empires from Conquest to Collapse, 1815-1960* (London, 1982).
5: For David Harvey, see *The New Imperialism* (Oxford, 2003) and *A Brief History of Neoliberalism* (Oxford, 2005).
6: The contrast with the elegant but somewhat abstract formulations of his first book, *Uneven Development* (London, 1984), is marked. This important study is currently out of print.

7: See, for example, L Panitch and S Gindin, 'Superintending Global Capital', *New Left Review*, II/35 (September/October 2005), pp108-118, 121-122.
8: V G Kiernan, *America: The New Imperialism*, as above, p3.
9: As above, p75.
10: As above, p279.
11: As above, pp29-46, 70-104.
12: This writing style is not necessarily an obstacle to presenting a rounded picture of imperialism. For a work by a writer with a similar literary approach to Kiernan (albeit with a different political background) which succeeds in doing this, see A Calder, *Revolutionary Empire: The Rise of the English-Speaking Empires from the 15th Century to the 1780s* (London, 1981 and 1998).
13: V G Kiernan, *The Lords of Human Kind: European Attitudes to the Outside World* (London, 1969). By the second edition the subtitle had changed to *Black Man, Yellow Man, and White Man in an Age of Empire* (London, 1988).
14: V G Kiernan, *America: The New Imperialism*, as above, pp340-341.
15: See, for example, J Neale, *The American War: Vietnam, 1960-1975* (London, 2001), pp176-177. The slander that anti-war protesters in the US were only opposed to the war for reasons of their personal safety was attacked at the time in blistering style by a recently departed editor of this journal. See A MacIntyre, 'Le Rouge et Noir', *New Statesman*, 22 November 1968, p714.
16: V G Kiernan, *America: The New Imperialism*, as above, ppxv-xvi.
17: N Smith, *The Endgame of Globalization* (New York, 2005), p25.
18: V G Kiernan, *America: The New Imperialism*, as above, pp107-108. Kiernan is equally bemused by the internationalisation of capital: 'Over much of the globe today there is so complex a criss-crossing of US capital in Arabia and Japan, Arab and Japanese investment in the US, Dutch syndicates buying real estate in the Scottish Highlands, British in Germany, that Lenin would be hard put to say which is the imperialist, who is subjugating whom' (as above, p273). But since Lenin was one of the first theorists to identify one aspect of imperialism as the movement of capital beyond national borders, he would neither have been bemused nor reduced the question to one of 'subjugation' in the first place.
19: N Smith, *The Endgame of Globalization*, as above, pp48-49.
20: As above, p188.
21: V G Kiernan, *America: The New Imperialism*, as above, p312.
22: N Smith, *The Endgame of Globalization*, as above, pp114, 115.

Rigour against communal dogma

Talat Ahmed

A review of Romila Thapar, ***Somanatha: The Many Voices of a History*** *(Verso, 2005), £17*

On 6 December 1992 the Babri Mosque at Ayodhya in Uttar Pradesh, north India, was demolished by a mob organised by the Bharati Janata Party (BJP). This was the ruling party of India from March 1998 until May 2004. The BJP was led by Atal Bihari Vajpayee and L K Advani, both members of the Rashtriya Swayamsevak Sangh (RSS), a communalist organisation that promotes the notion of India as a 'Hindu' nation. From this stems a pernicious ideology, 'Hindutva', which calls for a 'return' to Hindu values based on sacred Sanskrit texts.

The mosque was destroyed on the supposed belief that it was built on the site of a temple that had been desecrated by the Mughal Muslims and, moreover, is the birthplace of Ram, a Hindu god. Two years before, Advani began his infamous journey to Ayodhya from the port city of Somnath in Gujarat. The choice was significant as the Somnath temple was subjected to a raid by a Muslim overlord from Afghanistan at the beginning of the 11th century. This is taken as proof of

Islamic zeal, demagogy and intolerance in the face of a passive Hindu majority.

The Hindutva creed promotes an account of India's past that is homogenous, monolithic and unmistakeably Hindu. All other religious and cultural traditions within India are viewed as at best marginal or inferior. In particular Islam is viewed with suspicion and presented as an alien and destructive force in Indian culture. While the BJP was in power attempts were made to rewrite the history curriculum and in 2001 the Indian Educational Council began deleting certain passages from school textbooks.

One person who has questioned this 'Hinduised' version of history is the eminent Indian historian Romila Thapar. She has written extensively on Early India, documenting the myriad traditions, languages and practices that have characterised Indian civilisation.[1] Her refusal to bow down before communalist dogma has led to her being vilified by the Hindutva brigade in the US and India. She has been accused of treason and the denigration of Hinduism. In November 1999 she was 'retired' from the Prasar Bharati Board in the BJP's opening salvo to 'saffronise' key institutions, and in 2001 Hindutva ideologues demanded that she be arrested.

Undaunted, Thapar has continued to research into different aspects of Indian history, employing diverse sources which she interrogates with rigour. This excellent book focuses on the raid of a temple in Somnath, Gujarat, in 1026. Thapar does not call into question the event itself. Instead her work probes how the event has been interpreted and remembered.

The temple in question was a Hindu shrine and the raid was orchestrated by a Muslim overlord from Afghanistan. This raid was undertaken by Mahmud of Ghazni, who is claimed to have come to India at the beginning of the 11th century as a conquering Turk and whose armies looted the temple, broke the idol inside and finally destroyed the temple structure in an act of religious frenzy against the infidel Hindus. This event has come to represent a rupture in Indian civilisation with the first 'invasion' of an alien presence in India, that of Muslims. It is also taken as the root cause of Hindu-Muslim antagonism on the subcontinent and all subsequent history is to be understood and interpreted accordingly.

The evidence for this is taken from Turko-Persian sources, many of which were composed during Mahmud's life, and their chroniclers were members of the Ghazni court. So there are the lyrical eulogies composed by the court poet, Farrukhi Sistani, who is claimed to have accompanied Mahmud on his expedition to Somnath.[2] Similarly, later accounts of the raid focus on the quantity of wealth that was taken but also praise Mahmud for destroying the idol and bringing the 'true' faith into India.[3] These tend to exaggerate the amount of booty taken and are full of embellishments about the extent of the raid and the size and importance of the temple.

As the centuries progress, new narratives are composed to describe other sultans conducting more raids on the site, destroying the idol yet again and building a mosque on the remnants of the demolished temple. As Thapar states, with each account fantasy and glorification of the exploits of reigning sultans multiplied as revisions were made to earlier narratives reflecting contemporary demands.[4] Despite the lack of coherency and logic these narratives have been accepted as the authoritative version of events and their re-telling has crystallised notions of the 'Hindu' as the injured party and the 'Muslim' as the invading zealous defender of Islam.

This version was accepted by colonial narratives as it conveniently fitted their periodisation of Indian history into three distinct phases: Ancient=Hindu; Medieval=Muslim; Modern=colonial. This arbitrary division allowed colonial officials of the early 19th century to emphasise hostility between Hindus and Muslims and in some cases present themselves as the protectors of Hindu culture.[5]

The subject of the raid and its apparent traumatic impact on the Hindu psyche was brought up in the House of Commons in 1843 by Lord Ellenborough who claimed that the gates of Somnath had been taken as a trophy by Mahmud to Ghazni and had to be returned by force in order to restore Hindu pride. The gates were brought back only to be found to contain no evidence of Indian workmanship and so they are locked up in some storeroom in the Agra Fort to avoid further embarrassment (pp172-173). These assumptions and prejudices were used by the colonial state to categorise Indians into their neat census surveys and present Indian history as one characterised by permanent conflict between two irreconcilable and distinct communities.

In interrogating this version of history Thapar not only questions the sources such assumptions are based on but also looks to other material from the period in order to gain a fuller picture of events. The real power of her book is her use of Sanskrit sources. Hindutva ideologues claim Sanskrit to be the root of all Indian languages (so Urdu is conveniently excluded for its Perso-Arabic script and vocabulary). As such Sanskrit texts are accepted as the unquestioned orthodoxy on Indian culture and civilisation. They are claimed to be authentic, indigenous and 'pure'. However, what Thapar finds in these sources reveals a very different account of the Somnath temple incident and a fascinating picture begins to emerge.

She shows how the area around Somnath was an active and thriving centre of trade and commerce. It was the heart of sea trade linking the Persian Gulf port towns with Goa and Cambay in South India and Somnath as the port in Gujarat. Consequently, city states and regional kingdoms developed as trade expanded and various temples were built to provide places of worship for pilgrims and as reflections of the importance of a place and its ruler or benefactor (pp22-24, 28-29). Taxes were collected from pilgrims and were a lucrative source of wealth for any kingdom. As trade declined and rival rulers fought over the wealth, raids were a systematic feature of the region.

The evidence for this is provided in Sanskrit sources such as inscriptions and texts, which reveal that looting by local rajas was a recurring pattern—this would include attacks upon temples (pp78-79). Early Buddhist texts such as biographies and chronicles by Jaina scholars depict regular confrontations between rival religious sects of Jainas and followers of Shiva. The temple becomes a contested site for Shiva and Buddha iconography and the texts exhort the superiority of Jainism over the older Vedic beliefs (pp109-111).

Conspicuous by its absence in these sources is any mention of the Somnath raid or, if it is mentioned, it is one raid among several, not worthy of any specific merit. These findings lead Thapar to conclude that this episode did not signify a trauma so great that it continues to wound Hindus today. Many inscriptions from the 12th century refer to the decline of the Somnath temple as stemming from its age, mismanagement and lack of maintenance (pp82-83). If there was a decline in pilgrims and traders this would explain its deterioration.

There is also a wide range of bilingual inscriptions dating from the 13th century which are in Sanskrit and Arabic. One shows a local raja, Sri Chada, granting a ship owner and trader from Hormuz land on the estates of the temple in order to build a mosque (pp84-87). The local ruler made provisions for the maintenance of the mosque and provided generously for teachers, daily worship, the reading of the Koran and celebration of festivals. What is more, these inscriptions show no evidence of animosity as a consequence of the raid on Somnath (pp87-92).

At the local level, popular ballads from the 13th and 14th centuries narrate stories of saints who were and still are revered by Hindus and Muslims alike (pp147-150). Thapar's work shows how temple desecration preceded the arrival of Islam to India. Moreover, when Mahmud returned to Ghazni he is reported to have attacked an Ismaili Muslim ruler causing much devastation in Sind. In Multan, the Ismaili mosque was attacked by Mahmud and replaced with a Sunni one, but when the ruler retracted from his conversion to Sunni Islam Mahmud's armies again attacked the town, this time murdered all the Ismaili Muslims (pp48-51). In the process of this raid Mahmud acquired greater wealth.

This demonstrates the hostility of Sunni Islam to sects of Ismailis, Shias and Sufis, who were all seen as heretics. As Thapar argues, there was no homogenised Muslim identity in this period any more than a fully formed, fixed, exclusive Hindu entity. Hindutva ideologues glorify Sanskrit knowledge and literature as representing the 'true' Hindu/Indian history. The fact that no major source of this type paints the incident as an epic of conquest or resistance for any homogenised grouping in itself proves the fallacy of Hindu communalism.

Thapar locates ideas of religion within a complex, nuanced narrative that incorporates political power, access to economic resources, and a mixing of cultural traditions in addition to religious iconography. Her work demonstrates how there were many layers of interaction, accommodation and integration in this period and she articulates most eloquently how reductive, crude and ahistorical fixed notions of religious identity were to early and medieval India.

This has immense relevance today. Not only was the temple rebuilt in 1951 based on the spurious claims to have occupied a special 'hurt' for Hindus, but the idea of temple desecration by Muslims is used by the BJP and its Hindutva acolytes to marginalise and oppress Muslims. It is also used to create a mythological community of Hindus that is far from reality. Thapar has done a great service in sifting through a range of historical sources to challenge accepted versions. We should admire Thapar for her courage and also salute her dogged commitment to academic rigour, honesty and refusal to bow before communalist hatred.

NOTES

1: See R Thapar, *Early India: From Origins to AD 1300* (Allen Lane, 2002).

2: R Thapar, *Somanatha: The Many Voices of a History* (Verso, 2005), p44.

3: As above, pp48-51.

4: As above, p71.

5: See J Mill, *History of India*, 6 vols (London, 1923).

Contested paths

Angie Gago

A review of James Petras and Henry Veltmeyer, ***Social Movements and State Power: Argentina, Brazil, Bolivia, Ecuador*** *(Pluto Press, 2005), £17.99*

Latin America is in turmoil. What is written today will be obsolete tomorrow. People's struggles to shift the course of a history of imperialist oppression, and to resist the attacks of the powerful and wealthy elite at home, have created movements that are reinventing themselves and adapting to new forms of exploitation. The continent is the best place to observe the impact of neo-liberalism, and to witness the development of what Antonio Gramsci called 'counter-hegemonic blocs' resisting this agenda.

This is the overall idea expressed in Petras and Veltmeyer's excellent account of recent events in Latin America. They provide a telescopic approach to the political changes in four countries—Argentina, Brazil, Bolivia and Ecuador—during the past five years. They show the expectations created on the left after the toppling of different presidents by mass movements. But in each of these countries disenchantment has grown as people realise that the new figures are continuing the neo-liberal policies of their predecessors. The detailed analysis of these policies helps us to get a great sense of the existing contradictions in Latin American politics nowadays.

The authors work within a Marxist framework to explain the tension between state power and the social movements. On the one hand, there is a political elite committed to the neo-liberal recipes of the international institutions such as the International Monetary Fund and the World Bank. On the other hand, there is a diverse mass movement that demands a radical transformation of society. Each of the case studies in the book offers certain specific features.

In Argentina, President de la Rua was overthrown in 2001 after two days of major demonstrations. A potentially revolutionary situation emerged. The authors argue that Nestor Kirchner (who became president) was aware that after the mass mobilisations the main challenge was to gain political hegemony among the movements. The application of policies aimed at delivering minimal social programmes had a devastating effect on the unity of the movement. And, only three years after the toppling of de la Rua, the *piqueteros*, the most militant group of the mass movement, was dispersed.

The situation in Brazil shows a different dynamic. Lula came to power in 2003 having already reached agreements with the US and the IMF over his planned economic measures. However, the close connection between his party, the PT (Workers Party), and important social struggles in Brazil assured him of popular support. Petras and Veltmeyer's view is that the PT was, by the time of the 2003 election, no longer a workers' party. They argue that this is not just due to the appointment of right wing ministers, but also to the transformation of the PT into an electoral party.

Moreover, Ecuador and Bolivia have experienced similar betrayals following recent mobilisations. The election of Lucio Gutierrez, an ex-army officer discontented with the armed forces who was supported by the main indigenous organisation (CONAIE-Pachakutik), was welcomed as a radical shift in Ecuadorean politics. The authors argue that it took only six months for Gutierrez to betray the movement and sign an agreement with the IMF. The pattern has been followed in Bolivia, where in the space of five years two presidents have been overthrown. The Movement Toward Socialism (MAS), led by Evo Morales, has played a contradictory role. It has benefited from the mass movement, but at crucial moments Morales has sought to hold the movement back. For example, during the mobilisation of 2003, which overthrew President Lozada, he offered critical support to Lozada's successor Carlos Mesa. But Mesa continued his predecessor's neo-liberal policies, leading to his overthrow in the June 2005 uprising.

What is the underlying cause for this phenomenon? Petras and Veltmeyer offer a sharp critical perspective of the problems that the social movements are facing. They explain that capitalism, in its neo-liberal form, has been accompanied by a process of disempowerment of the traditional grassroots movements. Since the 1980s the introduction of deregulation, privatisation and structural adjustment policies has had devastating consequences for living standards.

Therefore the introduction of concepts such as 'governability' and 'civil society' into liberal discourse was of major importance in counterbalancing the reduction of state services in aid of disadvantaged sectors. Furthermore, descentralisation strategies and 'participatory budgets' schemes were introduced. As the authors claim, the overall objective was the empowerment of the poor without the disempowerment of the rich. In fact, they argue that this process was 'designed to demobilise them, to divert the struggle for state power in one or more directions towards electoral politics, reformist social organisations or local development' (p9).

Which path, then, do the social movements need to take for the achievement of state power and therefore the radical transformation of their political and economic system? While the liberal discourse of civil society and the formation of 'no-power' was dominant for the last two decades, Petras and Veltmeyer argue that fashionable postmodernist perspectives are not relevant in the Latin American social movements' spectrum. That is clear in the levels of determination and militancy that we can observe through the struggles. Nevertheless, there is an important weakness that the social movements share in the different case studies—the lack of class consciousness. Examples of this thesis are abundant in the book—the splitting up of the movements in Argentina after the election of Kirchner when the middle class recovered their savings or the contradictory composition of the militancy of the PT are just two of them.

On the contrary, some indigenous movements such as the Movimiento Indigena Pachakuti (MIP) in Bolivia have shown far greater awareness of class (communal land rights, agrarian reforms, etc). In this case, Petras and Veltmeyer argue that they face a second major problem—the lack of a revolutionary political organisation that would lead them to achieve state power. The authors draw the following conclusion: 'Electoral politics are a trap and mass mobilisation is the only path to achieve political power and social change.' However, they affirm that the social movements have failed to deliver this change so far.

In conclusion, the book is a complete account of the complex relationship between the capitalist state and the building of a counter-power. Taking into account the failures of recent movements, the advice of the authors appears correct.

However, 'dry recipes' don't fit in Latin American politics—only rank and file struggles will ultimately define the strategies for a way forward.

Taking precautions

Mike Haynes

A review of Andrew Simms, ***Ecological Debt: The Health of the Planet and the Wealth of Nations*** *(Pluto Press, 2005), £12.99; Steven P McGiffen,* ***Biotechnology: Corporate Power Versus Public Interest*** *(Pluto Press, 2005), £15.99*

What is to be done about global warming? The greenhouse effect is caused by our pumping carbon dioxide into the atmosphere when we burn carbon-based fuels like coal, gas and oil. The atmosphere acts like greenhouse glass, trapping the heat we need to survive. But when the greenhouse becomes too hot, disaster beckons.

It is the advanced world that causes most of the problems and it is the poor world that suffers most as the number of 'ecological refugees' rises. Andrew Simms' *Ecological Debt* offers a vivid description of how this happens. The advanced capitalist states have plundered the world and continue to trap poor countries in a network of economic debt. But in any ecological accounting the debt would be the other way. The few owe the many because of their disproportionate use of resources and the disproportionate pollution that they cause. This is getting worse as competition for resources and energy grows. Two thirds of the anticipated increasing demand for oil in the next two decades will have to come from the Middle East, for example. This may not be the only reason for the US presence in Iraq but it is a powerful contributing factor.

Simms rejects the idea that capitalism has a self-correcting economic mechanism. Some claim that when prices rise the system will adjust and reduce the burden on the environment. For Simms, any such price signals would be too slow and distorted by dirty subsidies. They would also require unrealistic increases in technological efficiency. Inevitably the costs would again fall more on the poor. So far so good. Simms' account echoes what some on the left have argued. In two articles in the *Journal of Economic Issues* (34(3), September 2000 and 37(3), September 2003), for example, Rumy Husan and I have argued that even if the market argument worked (we don't think it does), then it could only equalise global incomes over huge time periods and with unsustainable environmental costs.

Is there an alternative? Simms suggests that if nothing changes the result will be chaos. Only a reduction and redistribution of resources makes any sense. This is what, following Aubrey Meyer, Simms calls 'contraction and convergence'. I would prefer to talk of restructuring, redistribution and convergence. But the key issue is, can we get either inside the system?

Simms' answer is by far the weakest part of this book. He veers towards the apocalyptic at one point, suggesting that 'global warming probably means the death of capitalism as the dominant organising framework for the global economy'. Yet much of the second half of the book is taken up with the idea that the international legal system can be used to control and moderate capitalism. Simms never seriously considers the limits to the law at the national level, let alone the international level. Nor does he ask who will enforce it.

To have an illusion in the law is also to have an illusion in the state and the ability of states to work together. In *Between Equal Rights* (reviewed in *International Socialism* 107), China Miéville has shown in terms of legal theory why international law cannot work in the way that its supporters hope. But even without this we might have hoped for a more sceptical position from an environmentalist like Simms. He uses the idea that the law needs to control the 'global commons'—the common land, atmosphere, etc, that we all share. But in England it was the rich who took the original common land from the people using the law and state together. Legal challenges have a place, but by themselves they are not enough and to the extent that they are effective they owe as much to the sound of noisy opposition beyond the courtroom walls as to 'legalistic thinking' inside.

Such arguments underpin Steven P McGiffen's *Biotechnology: Corporate Power Versus Public Interest*. McGiffen reviews the legal basis of the control of Genetically Modified Organisms across the developed world, in the developing world and through international treaties. Whereas Simms' writing is light, McGiffen's is dense. But he is the more realistic about what law and regulation can do. Corporate power, he argues, likes legal protection for some things—patents, for example, or forcing farmers to keep buying seeds from the company store. Corporate power dislikes regulations which conflict with its basic drive for profit and attempts to commodify increasing areas of life across the globe.

This undermines the possibility of the 'precautionary approach' whether it be to climate change or GM farming. The 'precautionary approach' is the argument that, since we cannot know exactly what climate change or genetic modification will bring but we suspect that any negative changes might be irreversible or only reversible over generations, we should err on the side of caution. In contrast, McGiffen argues that corporate power has no interest in a 'measured and considered' debate or measured regulation. Both are subject to 'the ferocious, self-interested lobbying of multinational corporations with a stake in biotechnology'.

This is justified by a GM science that makes vastly inflated claims. Companies prevent or denigrate independent tests.

One of the most interesting facets of global capitalism at the moment is the huge power of agribusiness. Hundreds of millions of people produce the food that feeds billions, but if it enters into the global economy then this food is funnelled through a tiny number of multinational companies. Ten pesticide companies, for example, control 84 percent of the global pesticide market and five of these (Du Pont, Syngenta, Bayer, Monsanto and Dow) control 25 percent of the commercial seed market as well. These same five companies control 71 percent of patents of agricultural biotechnology.

The problem is how to go beyond this situation. McGiffen argues that 'under pressure from a public increasingly aware of problems associated with biotech' in some places the law and elected representatives have gone some way to creating some controls. But elsewhere those who try to regulate the system 'have become nothing more than builders of the road along which the juggernaut of corporate-controlled biotechnology is moving, and crushing all that stands in its way'.

Scotland: almost afraid to know itself?

Neil Davidson

A review of Gregor Gall, ***The Political Economy of Scotland: Red Scotland? Radical Scotland?*** *(University of Wales Press, 2005), £19.99*

Macduff: Stands Scotland where it did?
Ross: Alas, poor country, almost afraid to know itself!
(*Macbeth*, act 4, scene 3)

Does Gregor Gall's new book help Scotland to 'know itself'? *The Political Economy of Scotland* is not a political economy of Scotland—the focus is too narrow for that. (In the acknowledgements, Gall still refers to the book by its current subtitle of *Red Scotland? Radical Scotland?* which suggests late interference by the publisher.) Nevertheless, it should be critically welcomed, if only because it subjects the claims about Scottish radicalism to sustained quantitative scrutiny for what may well be the first time.

Gall takes levels of trade union membership, activity, recognition and collective bargaining over the last 30 years (ie roughly since the Upper Clyde Shipbuilders work-in of 1971-72) as the main measures by which radicalism can be assessed. He establishes that, if we compare Scotland to the other 11 administrative regions of the UK, it has generally been in the top quartile by these criteria, but that 'workers in Scotland are not any more radical than the most radical or militant workers in the rest of Britain—these being found in Wales and the northern regions of England' (pp65-66). At one point Gall suggests that one reason there is more union activity in Scotland is because Scotland has more of the industries where unions are likely to be active—an unspectacular but sound conclusion supported by a series of detailed statistical tables which are among the most valuable features of the book.

In a preface Tommy Sheridan criticises Gall for treating what he calls 'our nation-state' as a mere region of the UK. Gall does no such thing. He simply points out that, given the differences in population, geography and economic structure between Scotland and England, it is legitimate to compare Scotland to particular regions of England. This has nothing whatever to do with Scotland's status as a nation, which is surely not in doubt. But it does lead us to ask what we are taking to be meant by 'Scotland'. If data for, say, Perthshire or Inverness, were made to stand for the whole of the country, the figures would look less impressive: 'When talking about Scotland we are really talking of the Central Belt and, in particular, Strathclyde' (p40).

Gall, glumly, but probably accurately, predicts that his work will nevertheless be received with 'shadow boxing and inaccurate representation' (pxvii), citing this reviewer's experience in 2003 as a precedent. It is therefore important to state that his attempt to quantify what is known about Scottish trade unionism gives his book a scientific rigour which is all too often missing in discussions of this subject.

But there is a problem with simply treating trade unions as a measure of radicalism. Unions will be crucial to the future of socialism, but only a minority of workers currently belong to unions and they may not necessarily be the most radical sections of the working class. Strikes can be passive, leaderships bureaucratic, collective bargaining compromised. There is, in other words, a limit to what can be understood from studying statistical tables.

The data also needs to be contextualised, and this is not done simply by adding the results of opinion polls. We need a method—the term 'dialectical' is inescapable here—capable of capturing the social dynamics at work and for this purpose the static models of empirical social science (Industrial Relations Branch) are simply inadequate. Broadening out the range of evidence might include the fact that racist attacks were, until the London bombings in July, higher in Scotland than England and this points to a less palatable aspect of Scottish identity which should not be avoided.

The main problem, however, lies in the latter part of the book. The discussion of trade unions is essentially a preparatory stage for Gall's central argument. Having dispensed with the more obviously exaggerated claims about Scottish radicalism, Gall attempts to establish its existence on a firmer footing. He claims that a broadly social democratic set of values has become bound up with the Scottish national identity, a process which he—correctly, in my view—sees as taking place through the Thatcher/Major years, when resistance to Tory governments took on a quasi-national character.

Gall sees Scotland as a special example of what he calls a 'community of collectivism' where there is a 'fusion of national identity and consciousness with...oppositionalism' (p177). National identity is a more powerful basis for this than the regional identity prevailing in areas which otherwise had similar political responses to Thatcherism:

'With a weaker form of identity... supported by less well-defined public institutions distinct to these regions, the associations with radicalism for these populaces within their geographical confines are often not so sharp or deep-seated' (p121).

Leaving aside the methodology (sources are almost all derived from opinion polls) and taking the conclusions at face value, I think there are three main problems with this analysis.

First, Gregor regards the strength of Scottish national identity as an advantage people in, say, Yorkshire do not possess. But the opposite is true. One of the greatest problems which faces the left in Scotland is precisely the way in which virtually every issue is viewed through the distorting lens of the 'national question', even when that has nothing to do with it.

Second, Gall does not attempt to define what he means by nation, national identity or any of the related terms. 'What we are discussing is not Scottish national identity per se, but obviously a certain manifestation or type of Scottish national identity which is of a progressive, radical and social democratic bent, for the other form of national identity in Scotland is conservative and reactionary' (p178).

But national identity is not a container which can be filled with a range of ideological contents. National identity can be more or less radical or conservative, but is always confined by the existence of actual or potential capitalist nation-states, which means that there are limits to how radical it can be. It is not compatible with revolutionary socialism, for example. (Indeed Gall points out that Scottish national identity is essentially a form of 'radical populism' (p156).)

At one point he writes that 'the strength of Scottish national identity is such that it can never be entirely disassociated so that it is believed by many (workers and non-workers) that workers in Scotland (or

Scottish workers) are more radical than elsewhere, this has a salience because it becomes not a "reality" as such but a significant socially constructed phenomenon for many' (p180).

We gather from this passage that Gall does not regard the possession of a readable prose style as obligatory for a writer, but I can assure readers that I have accurately reproduced the words as they appear in the book. What I think this incredibly convoluted sentence means is: 'People in Scotland may not actually be more radical than anywhere else, but they believe that they are, and this may influence their behaviour.' Well, maybe—but I think that it is just as likely that a genuine social crisis would shatter these cosy assumptions. A major conflict over public sector pensions, for example, would test the much-vaunted 'radicalism' of the Scottish middle class to destruction. It is more credible to see the radicalism of Scottish national identity as an *alternative* to or *substitute* for genuine socialist internationalism, born of a period of defeat from which we are only just emerging.

Third, Gregor's fixation with the trade union movement to the exclusion of all else blinds him to the fact that we are now moving into a different period. Many of the hundreds of thousands who marched against the Iraq war or to Make Poverty History in recent years were in trade unions, but many were not (although they would join if they had the chance, or they were asked)—surely their views also need to be taken into account? But these are outside the industrial relations frame of reference Gall imprisons himself in here. Nor are they compatible with a purely national narrative—displaying as they did the welcome beginnings of an international consciousness.

In conclusion, this is a deeply frustrating book. At various points Gall himself raises virtually all the problems that I have done here, but never pursues them or integrates them into his account. His refusal to follow through the more sceptical aspects of his analysis will win him no friends on the hard or even soft nationalist wings of the SSP, who do not want a politics of ambiguity. The book stops, rather than concludes, without any clue as to what he thinks socialists should actually *do* in relation to the identity he describes. Should socialists in Scotland frame their arguments in terms of a supposed radical national identity or not? The answer to this question is one of the most important facing the Scottish left today. In so far as this book begins to tackle the issue, it is to be welcomed. In so far as it avoids the question, it represents a missed opportunity.

Brain food

John Parrington

*A review of Steven Rose, **The 21st Century Brain** (Jonathan Cape, 2005), £25, and Terrence Deacon, **The Symbolic Species** (Norton, 1998), £8.99*

Understanding how the human brain works is one of the biggest unsolved questions in biology, and it is also the subject of Steven Rose's most recent book. *The 21st Century Brain* is a book of two halves. In the first half Rose maps out the current state of the neurosciences, and in particular he discusses how new developments in genetics and brain imaging techniques are affecting our understanding of the processes going on within the brain. In the second half he takes up the question of whether this new found knowledge is leading to new cures and treatments for brain disorders, or to new, possibly sinister, ways to control human behaviour.

For Rose the past is the key to understanding the present. In the case of the brain, this means taking us through a tour of human evolution starting from the origins of life in the primeval soup that existed on this planet 4 billion years ago, through to the changes in brain structure that accompanied our divergence from the apes. There are a variety of alternate explanations for how life originally evolved. Some favour the idea that it all started with DNA, or its chemical cousin RNA, because of the roles these molecules play as the so-called 'blueprint' of life.

But as Rose points out, it is far more likely that life began within a protective bubble, the precursor to the cells that are the building blocks of our bodies. It is a pertinent point to make in the context of a discussion about the brain because it stresses the importance that cell membranes play in creating a specialised micro-environment that is different both in its chemical composition and its electrical potential from the surrounding fluid that bathes the cell. It is the dynamic changes in these two components, powered by movements of charged atoms, or ions, that underlie the electrical impulses that sweep across the brain when we think a thought, or move a muscle, or indulge in any other activity that requires the action of nerves.

In adopting an evolutionary perspective, Rose is very careful to distinguish himself from a recent school of thought, spearheaded by people such as the linguist Steven Pinker, called 'evolutionary psychology', which sees human behaviour as being rigidly determined by the genes. Two defining features of evolutionary psychology are firstly that it sees the mind as being composed of a series of modules, each one mediating a different facet of human behaviour, and secondly that these modules, and the resulting behaviour, are presumed to have originated, and become fixed, in the early Stone Age, anywhere from 600,000 to 100,000 years ago. Under such a guiding philosophy its exponents have sought to explain everything from rape and aggression, through why women tend not to rise to the top in large corporations, to children's tendency to dislike spinach, in terms of genes and natural selection.

There is much that is laughable about evolutionary psychology, not least the fact that the picture it paints of early hunter-gatherer society as one where hunter-dad brings home the sabre-toothed tiger steaks, while gatherer-mum tidies the cave and looks after the children, seems more based on *The Flintstones* than on any serious anthropological studies. But the most serious problem from a scientific point of view is evolutionary psychology's complete unwillingness, or inability, to relate its proposed mental modules to the biology of the brain.

In fact, recent studies suggest that, while there is undoubtedly some localisation of function at the lowest levels of brain activity, the more sophisticated and complex the behaviour, the more likely it is to be a global process involving many different brain regions. While it is not something Rose spells out in his book, the scientific findings emerging from the human genome project, and those of other organisms such as the chimp, also argue against the idea that different aspects of human behaviour, even something as apparently clearly defined as language, originate in specific brain modules, each one determined by a different gene. If such were the case, then one might expect that humans would have a much greater number of genes than so-called 'simpler' organisms.

Indeed, this was originally thought to be the case, with estimates prior to the human genome project predicting 100,000 genes. It was quite a shock when the 'first draft' of the human genome, completed in 2001, indicated that there were only likely to be 30,000 to 40,000 genes. This figure has since been revised downwards even more dramatically, with current estimates suggesting that we have only have 20,000 to 25,000 genes, about the same as a mouse or a rat, and hardly more than the lowly nematode worm, which has 19,000. Most recently the sequencing of the chimp genome has indicated that the differences between ourselves and our closest relative are unlikely to be due to gross differences in the genes themselves, but instead probably represent alterations in the way certain genes are turned on or off during embryo development.

So if the evolutionary psychologists are wrong, how does the human brain work? Currently neuroscience draws on two main resources. We have learned much about the human brain from studying how its thought processes are affected by injury and disease, or even by stimulating brain regions during surgery and seeing how this affects the behaviour of the person who has volunteered to take part in such an experiment. However, these are all very indirect routes to knowledge. By necessity, most of what we know about basic brain processes comes from experiments on animals. Rose himself studies the process of memory in chicks. Much of the rest of neuroscience involves experiments on mice or rats, or to a lesser extent on primates, while important insights about the development of the brain and nervous system have emerged from studies of fruit flies and zebrafish.

Rose's descriptions of the similarities in brain chemistry between different species show that animal rights supporters' arguments against the value of animal experiments for the study of such processes are not based upon any valid scientific premise. However, Rose does have reservations about the 'reductionism' that guides many such studies.

Rose describes how there is currently a great deal of excitement in the neurosciences because of new technologies, by-products of the human genome project, that allow scientists for the first time to study which genes are turned on or off within brain cells on a global scale. He mentions proteomics, which allows scientists to make a catalogue of all the proteins within a particular cell, but there are also DNA microchips, which can be used to create such a catalogue for the RNA messages that act as an intermediary between the genes and the proteins that they code for. In addition, there now increasingly sophisticated 'imaging' techniques that allow the chemical changes taking place in brain cells to be visualised in real time. Finally, a large number of mutant mice have been created that have defects in genes involved in important cellular processes. By studying such mice, scientists hope to decipher their function within the brain, as well as gaining insights into how defects in these genes in humans might underlie certain types of mental illness or degenerative brain disorders.

According to Rose, one of the problems with proteomic approaches is that they only provide a static snapshot of the proteins in the brain, not their changes and interactions over time. In this respect, he may be unaware of important new developments in proteomics that mean it is now possible to record not just the presence or absence of a particular protein in the cell, but also the chemical changes that modify its activity in response to cellular signals. Meanwhile, in what can be seen as a fusion of genetic engineering and imaging technology, it is becoming possible to add fluorescent 'tags' to proteins of interest so that their interactions within the living brain cell can be studied in real time. Another exciting development is that genetically engineered mice are being created in which the control region of a gene of interest is fused to the gene coding for a fluorescent 'reporter' protein, so that when the normal gene is turned on within the brain this registers as a fluorescent signal that can be studied in the living animal.

Rose also has some serious criticisms of mutant mouse studies—for instance, that the effects of such mutations are often masked by the redundancy and plasticity of the developing brain which ensures that the gene defect is compensated for by other genes. Conversely, he argues that because many genes are involved in a variety of different processes, deleting them from the genome may result in a vast range of diffuse consequences. These are valid criticisms, but I feel that here Rose overstates his case.

Firstly, despite their deficiencies, scientists have learned an enormous amount about some of the basic cellular processes taking place in the brain from studying such mutants. Secondly, increasingly sophisticated genetic engineering techniques mean that it is now possible to delete genes in only a small subset of cells in the brain, or even to turn selected genes on and off by the addition of a special chemical, thus allowing neuroscientists to avoid some of the problems of redundancy and compensation inherent in traditional mutant mouse studies.

Nevertheless, despite the increasing sophistication of such research tools, I would agree with Rose that a key unsolved problem for neuroscience is how to integrate the increasing amounts of information emerging from such studies into a coherent global picture of how the brain works as a whole. According to Rose, this is because we lack an appropriate theoretical framework to accommodate all the mountains of new data. As a consequence, while we may increasingly know which genes are turned on where and when in the brain, and even the cellular signals that regulate them, we still lack the basic concepts to explain such fundamental properties of the brain as learning and memory, even in animals.

Undoubtedly the biggest unsolved question about the brain is that of our own human consciousness, the material roots that it springs from, and what it is that makes us unique compared to other animals. Surprisingly, some neuroscientists seem to have a problem recognising that human consciousness is a unique phenomenon in its own right, and instead have defined it by such narrow limits that it makes you wonder whether they have ever really sat down and thought about the miraculous events going on in their own heads. So Rose describes how one brain researcher has compared consciousness to an electrical dimmer switch, brightening as more neurons are engaged, darkening when fewer are active, while another believes that consciousness is what abandons you every night and returns to you next morning upon waking!

What these scientists seem to be confusing is the ability that we share with other complex animals of being able to feel and be aware of the world around us, and even to unconsciously react back upon it to an extent, with the specifically human attribute of self-conscious awareness that allows us to reflect upon the world around us, rationalise and analyse it in abstract terms, and having made sense of the world in this way, use the information to plan and carry out future actions, as well as communicating what we have discovered to other human beings. Some scientists have grasped this point but, having recognised that there is something unique about human consciousness, they then try and model it as analogous to a computer.

But as Rose points out, this misses another crucial feature of the human brain. Unlike a computer, it has not been designed but has evolved over millions of years. This has the consequence that sophisticated and specifically human forms of cognitive processing are present together in the brain with far more primitive functions that we share with less complex organisms, the two existing together in a complex, layered manner. Another important reason why we can't just consider brains as 'wetware', analogous to the hardware of a computer, is the role of emotional responses in mediating the functions of the brain. Negative emotions such as concern, stress, fear and alarm, but also positive ones such as contentment, joy and euphoria, are conveyed by hormones, which interact with receptors in the brain as well as in other parts of the body. The importance of emotions for cognitive responses is illustrated by a study described by Rose in which a set of volunteers listened to stories, some of which contained fearful elements. The stories that were best remembered were the scary ones, but not when volunteers were also given a drug that blocked their response to adrenaline. The steroid hormones that regulate sex and stress also seem to have important effects upon cognition.

Any explanation of human consciousness will have to incorporate all these different elements. But before such an explanation can even begin, surely a crucial remaining step is to identify what it is within the human brain that underlies our specifically human form of consciousness.

One of the distinctive features about human beings is our capacity for language. Is this where the key to human consciousness lies? Rose has some thoughts on this matter, primarily in reference to the work of Terrence Deacon, who has carried out some important studies in this area. In his book *The Symbolic Species*, Deacon made the important point that what is distinctive about human language is its reliance upon symbolic representation, words being abstract symbols with no need to reflect the properties of the objects they represent. It is by manipulating this system of abstract symbols that we rationalise the world around us. In many ways Deacon is merely updating the insights of Lev Vygotsky, the psychologist who did so much to develop a theory of the mind along Marxist principles in post-revolutionary Russia. What is exciting about Deacon's work is that he is exploring a similar explanatory framework to Vygotsky but within the context of modern neuroscience.

A key issue that now needs to be addressed is how the emergence of language during human evolution has affected the other functions of the brain. One of the important points that Deacon makes is that because language is not just a means of communication, but also a way of symbolically representing the world around us, it has the potential to transform all aspects of the ways in which we interact with the world, for instance our emotional responses. Although emotions have an important role to play in shaping cognitive function, it is equally true that it is very hard to imagine a human emotion that is not deeply affected by the social context in which it occurs, whether this be sex, or hunger, or fear. This raises the question of what physical changes in the brain underlie such a transformative capacity.

The ease with which children learn to speak suggests that innate biological features must underlie our language abilities. However, in terms of evolutionary timescales, the evolution of language is still a very recent phenomenon. This means that the differences that exist between our brains and those of our closest relative, the chimpanzee, may be incredibly subtle. What most surprised Deacon when he first began to study the regions of the human brain thought to be involved in language was that the same regions in the brains of other primates seemed to be incredibly similar. In his book, Rose mentions some examples of genes that appear to be involved in language formation in humans. However, there is no clear evidence for a 'language gene' as such, but rather the suggestion that language in humans is the result of a variety of genes subtly affecting the position of certain nerve cells and the time at which they appear in the developing brain.

We might have more idea about how language shapes human consciousness if we knew more about what factors triggered the emergence of language during evolution. Rose doesn't really address this issue, while Deacon suggests that it was due to the increasing size of the human social group. But this doesn't explain why language only evolved in humans and not other apes. For me a far better explanation is that put forward by Frederick Engels in his essay 'The Part Played by Labour in the Transition from Ape to Man', which he wrote in 1876. Engels saw the development of the use of tools for social labour as being one of the key moments in our evolution. For him, language was the next major development because social labour 'brought society closer together by increasing cases of mutual support and joint activity and by making clear the advantage of this joint activity to each individual. In short, men in the making arrived at the point where they had something to say to each other.'

Recent studies have shown that not only humans but also apes and even some birds can make and use tools, and this has led to the argument that there is nothing unique about our capabilities in this area. However, this argument misses the fact that these instances of animal tool use are all deeply rooted in the innate biological responses of the animal. In contrast, human tool use became both all-pervasive as our way of interacting with the world, and at the same time is constantly revolutionising itself, so that over a period of only a few hundred thousand years we have progressed from living in caves to sending rockets into outer space. Obviously this must have involved an interactive process between tool use and language, with each one stimulating the evolution of the other.

The final part of Rose's book is concerned with how our increasing knowledge of the brain, but also our continuing confusion about how it really works, has influenced the development of new drugs and treatments for mental disorders. He describes how unusual and abnormal mental conditions have been recognised since ancient times, but only began to be classified as distinct 'illnesses' with the start of the industrial age. While acknowledging the advances that have been made in the diagnosis of neurological conditions such as Huntington's, Parkinson's and Alzheimer's diseases, what also emerges from Rose's account is how little we still know about many disorders of the mind.

This is particularly true of personality disorders such as manic depression and schizophrenia. It has become very fashionable recently to claim that schizophrenia is caused by a genetic defect. However, despite successive claims that a new gene 'for' schizophrenia has been discovered, there is little in the way of evidence to suggest any of these supposed genetic determinants have anything but the loosest of associations with the condition. Meanwhile, as Rose points out, one of the more striking features of schizophrenia is how much it is influenced by social conditions, with the consequence that working class people are twice as likely to be diagnosed as schizophrenic as those who are middle class. Even more striking is the fact that black people of Caribbean origin living in Britain are far more likely to suffer from schizophrenia than in their country of origin.

Rose is critical of many of the drug treatments for mental disorders. He mentions the examples of Ritalin, which is being increasingly used to control the behaviour of children in the classroom, and Prozac, used to treat depression. It is clear that these drugs do change behaviour in some quite drastic ways, but whether they are anything more than chemical straitjackets remains to be shown. Children treated with Ritalin are said to be suffering from attention deficit/hyperactivity disorder and it is claimed that they have a defect in the response to dopamine, a neurochemical in the brain, rather than the other possibility which is that they are rebelling against a rigid and unstimulating school system. Yet since 2004 a new drug, Strattera, has been marketed as a cure for this supposed disorder, despite the fact that it has an entirely different target site in the brain, with no explanation provided for the discrepancy.

In this context, it is difficult to know how seriously to regard some of the future possibilities that Rose discusses at the end of his book, of the development of methods for mind control by the military, or the use of gene therapy to treat disorders of the brain. What does seem clear is that while we lack a proper framework for how the mind works we will be stumbling in the dark. Equally, as long as the pharmaceutical industry is primarily guided in its research activities simply by how much money it can make from its drugs, we are likely to see more reliance on chemical straitjackets rather than any real attempt to treat the real, actual basis of disorders of the mind.

Shedding new light on the Dark Ages

Chris Harman

*A review of Chris Wickham, **Framing the Early Middle Ages: Europe and the Mediterranean, 400-800** (Oxford, 2005), £85*

The period from the 5th to the 11th centuries in Europe has traditionally been treated in Britain as the 'Dark Ages'—of little interest. Roman civilisation is seen as disappearing beneath the assault of 'barbarian invasions', and nothing significant happens thereafter, except perhaps the efforts of Charlemagne (at the turn of the 8th and 9th centuries) to reunite Western Europe in a shortlived caricature of the Roman Empire.

In recent years academic study has undermined part of this picture, even if this has not filtered down into the popular history of television documentaries or the unpopular history of school syllabuses. Chris Wickham draws together all the new material, particularly that from recent archaeological studies, and sets out to interpret it through a framework influenced in an unashamed manner by Marxism. He presents a picture in which Roman civilisation did not simply disappear with the conquests. The 'barbarian rulers' (Goths, Visigoths, Franks and so on) who took control of the different parts of the old empire were from societies that had interacted across its borders for centuries, absorbing and accepting many of its cultural values. They ruled as the Romans had ruled in most places (England was the exception, not the rule), imposing themselves on top of the old aristocracies which they left intact. As a result, the change of rulers did not mean the immediate qualitative transformation of society which the usually emphasised litany of dates for the different invasions suggests.

The break-up of the empire did, however, have important longer term consequences leading to eventual qualitative change. The 'civilisation' of the empire had been based upon an aristocracy centred on Rome, and later to an increasing extent on Constantinople (present-day Istanbul), extracting massive amounts of tribute from Sicily, North Africa and Egypt. The break-up of the empire into separate kingdoms, each based on its own version of the old civilisation, ended the flow to Italy from North Africa and Egypt, and then from Sicily. Rome itself ceased to be a focus for the aristocracies of Western Europe and the Mediterranean, and its population fell within a couple of centuries by perhaps half a million to around 20,000.

The effects of disintegration were not confined to the centre. It also reduced trade between the former provinces. Trade in bulky goods (grain or pottery, for instance), Wickham argues, had only ever been profitable when it could use the state-subsidised transport conveying the imperial tribute. Once the tribute stopped, the commerce declined. At the same time, the fragmentation of the empire meant warfare between the former constituents—and further threats from outside the borders. There was a militarisation of the aristocracy and a gradual erosion of its old cultural values.

The impact of the changes, Wickham explains, varied enormously from region to region. The Frankish kingdom ('Francia') briefly established over present-day France and southern Germany split into segments. In Spain a central Visigoth monarchy based in Toledo only managed to maintain a weak hold over a regionally fragmented aristocracy through a combination of military threats and patronage. By contrast, a Rome-derived civilisation flourished in most of North Africa for another three centuries, under first the Vandals and then the Umayyad Islamic Empire.

The eastern wing of the old empire (Byzantium) based on Constantinople remained virtually unchanged, continuing to provide for itself with grain from the immensely fertile Nile Valley. It was only with the loss of the southern provinces of Syria and Egypt, first to the Persian Empire and then to Islamic armies from the Arabian Peninsula, that the rump Eastern Empire suffered a decay of urban life. And towns and cities continued to flourish in the regions conquered by the Islamic armies, with the old ruling classes continuing their old lifestyles for another century, until the replacement of the Umayyad dynasty by the Abbasids shifted the centre of the Islamic Empire from

Syria to Iraq and encouraged the conversion of the old elites to Islam.

The disintegration of the Western Empire had the long-term effect of depopulating many of its cities and tarnishing the veneer of civilisation on fragments of what had always been a brutal ruling class, but it was by no means a disaster for the peasants who made up the great bulk of its population. The burden on them of taxation tended to fall (although to different degrees in the different regions), and the weakening of the state lessened the capacity of the aristocracy to enforce the extraction of rents from them. Although there were regions where forms of serfdom prevailed, in others freeholding peasants ('allodists') were in the majority. Meanwhile, in the regions which had never been conquered by Rome or where the old state had disintegrated completely (England and Wales, for instance) there were forms of 'tribal organisation' (Wickham uses the term to make a comparison with more recent pre-state societies studied by anthropologists), where high status individuals and families might exist, gathering a surplus into their hands to redistribute to the population at large, but not an exploiting ruling class.

The two sorts of societies tended to converge over time, with the 'tribal' societies witnessing the slow crystallisation out of new aristocracies and with them new state structures. In this they were influenced by the impact of contact with the successor states—and with the network of Christian religious institutions that increasingly provided the rulers of Western Europe with their administrative personnel and a single ideological framework. By the 8th century the wealth of these rulers laid the basis of a new long distance trade in luxury items and the growth of new trading towns, 'emporia', alongside the depleted administrative cities left over from the old empire.

What was the character of the post-Roman class societies? Wickham writes of 'the feudal mode of production', thereby confronting a number of long debated theoretical issues.

First he disentangles the feudal mode of production from the specific pattern of aristocratic rule in Europe from the 11th to the 16th centuries, with its hierarchies of kings, lords, abbots and knights, and so on. The mode of production, he says, depends on the way the direct producers are exploited. And there are only three forms this can take—the exploitation of slaves, the exploitation of waged ('free') workers, and the exploitation of dependent peasants forced to hand over a portion of their produce to their exploiters.

This leads him to break with a common view (which he himself used to hold)[1] that there is a different mode of production if the ruling class receives revenues from taxing the peasants as opposed to extracting rents—one an 'Asiatic' or 'tributary' mode of production, the other the feudal mode.

He accepts the argument of the Turkish Marxist Halil Berktay that the differences in the superstructural relations between members of the ruling class cannot be equated with differences in the mode of production.[2] In passing, it should be said that the empirical material he provides shows that the post-empire aristocracies depended on taxes and rents to varying degrees in different places and at different times. To say that taxes meant one mode of production and rents a different one would be to say there was a continual swinging in relatively short periods of time from one mode of production to the other and back again.

His material also leads him to confront two other popular views. One is that medieval feudalism emerged as a fully formed system out of the villas of the Roman Empire as aristocrats settled peasants on their land as 'colloni' under their control. He shows that, although the colloni existed, in many regions they were a minority among free 'allodial' peasants. It was not until half a millennium after the collapse of the empire that feudal exploitation became so widespread as to be near-universal. There was no simple continuity between what existed in the 5th and the 11th centuries.

Secondly, he challenges forcefully the notion that the 'slave mode of production' survived right through until the 11th century. Slavery persisted as a category denying people a range of legal rights, but he argues that the slaves were, in the great majority of cases, exploited in the same way as other sections of dependent peasants, even if to a greater extent. They were settled on plots of their own or working in the households of others who were settled on such plots. 'Plantation slavery', a completely different way of organising exploitation in which the toilers were compelled to work by the overseer's whip, had, he argues, virtually died out in the early centuries of the empire.

Wickham's distinction between 'slavery' as a juridical category and a mode of production is correct.[3] But it leaves open the questions as to why slave trading remained so widespread in the period, and why 'slaves' as a separate juridical category virtually ceased to exist in north western Europe after the 11th century.

Wickham's book is historical analysis in which class plays a central role. It is not meant to be a full account of the societies of the period. The 'framing' deliberately omits any detailed account of the cultural and intellectual changes which occurred (for these, readers would do well to look at the excellent books by Peter Brown *The World of Late Antiquity* and *The Rise of Western Christendom*).

There is, however, one problem with the 'framing'. There is little in the book about the actual process of physical production—the means the peasants used as they toiled to produce the wealth that kept the state, the aristocracy, the warrior bands and the religious hierarchies going. As a result it is not clear why the surplus and aristocratic wealth starts rising in the 8th century, or why the classes begin to crystallise out in the peripheral regions. Wickham stresses the importance of exchange networks, but as John Moreland has argued (in a book co-edited by Wickham), the exchange networks were underpinned by changes in production in the towns around which they were built.[4] And there is considerable evidence that by the 8th and 9th centuries there was the gradual adoption in agriculture of new techniques, some known but rarely used in the Roman period, others spreading westwards across Eurasia. An examination of these would seem to be a precondition for providing an understanding of the dynamic of history in this period that goes beyond simple description.

The overall result is that the book undermines some of the evidence used by older attempts to provide a dynamic understanding, for instance Perry Anderson's *Passages from Antiquity to Feudalism*. But it does not succeed in producing a new, fully dynamic account of its own.

The merit of this book is that it is an invaluable source of raw material, based on a vast range of primary and secondary sources. This does, however, mean that it is very long—831 pages. General readers may want to wait for Wickham to complete his promised volume for the Penguin 'History of Europe' series.

NOTES

1: See his contribution to the debate on the issue in H Mukhia (ed), *The Feudalism Debate* (New Delhi, 1999).

2: Also in H Mukhia (ed), as above.

3: It is the same distinction I made in reviewing Guy Bois, *The Transformation of the Year 1000*, in this journal some years back (see International Socialism 62, Spring 1994).

4: J Moreland, 'The Significance of Production in 8th Century England', in I L Hansen and C Wickham (eds), *The Long 8th Century* (Dill, 2000), pp69-75.

Pick of the quarter

The Bolivian election was due to take place two days after we went to print. But the country seems likely to be in turmoil in the months ahead, whatever the outcome. Two recent articles are a useful complement to Mike Gonzalez's piece in our last issue. Forrest Hylton and Sinclair Thomson provide an account of the last two uprisings in the October issue of **New Left Review** (available on www.newleftreview.net/NLR26903.shtml), while Robert Albro writes on the country's indigenous movements in the October issue of the **Bulletin of Latin American Studies**.

Anyone prone to write off workers' struggles in Third World countries should read the fascinating account of the strikes against the privatisation of Pakistan's telecoms corporation by Aasim Sajjad Akhtar in the October **Monthly Review** (www.monthlyreview.org/1005akhtar.htm).

The November issue also contains two pieces of some interest. Chinese-born Yiching Wu grapples with developments in his homeland from a critical Marxist point of view in 'Rethinking China's "Capitalist Restoration"' (www.monthlyreview.org/1105wu.htm), discussing, among other ideas, those put forward by myself and Mike Haynes.

John Mage and Nepalese revolutionary Parvati provide an account of the guerrilla struggles to overthrow Nepal's monarchy, described by Parvati as a struggle for 'people's power' to 'build a national capitalist economic base with a socialist orientation' (www.monthlyreview.org/1105mage.htm and www.monthlyreview.org/1105parvati.htm). Those with memories of the over-glowing accounts of guerrilla movements against imperialism in places like Mozambique, Guinea Bissau and Angola 30 years ago will identify with the resistance to the monarchic dictatorship, but will be wary about taking at face value all of the articles' claims about the popular movement.

Africa is becoming a continent of increased interest to the imperialist powers because of oil, and growing competition between China and the US. Sandra T Barnes argues in a very useful article in the **Review of African Political Economy** (July-September 2005) that this is leading to 'strategic philanthropy' on the one hand and a proliferation of US bases on the other.

In the same issue, Tim Jacoby shows how the notion of 'failed states' is being used to justify such intervention.

Some years back the American Marxists Anwar Shaikh and Ahmet Tonak produced an analysis of the statistical development of the US economy in terms of Marxist economic categories such as the rate of profit and the rate of exploitation (*Measuring the Wealth of Nations*, 1984). Simon Mohun provides a corrective update of some of their figures in the September issue of the **Cambridge Journal of Economics**. He concludes that the rate of surplus value on productive labour is around 2.9, as opposed to their estimate of 2.3.

Readers wanting to follow up our coverage of present day China should look at the September issue of the **China Quarterly**. It centres on culture today, with particularly interesting articles by Jeroen de Kloet on social comment in popular music and by Deborah Davis on consumption in the cities, with a breakdown of social differentiation and consumption levels in Shanghai. Few readers will be able to afford the journal—but some will be able grab the chance to read it in university libraries.

Supporting the struggle of a country against imperialism does not necessarily mean ignoring the way the local rulers exploit the workers and peasants. Readers who understand this will be interested in an article by Tuong Vu in **Communist and Post-Communist Studies** (September 2005). Based on archival research in Hanoi, it looks at the way workers struggled within what claimed to be a socialist state.

The last two issues of **Historical Materialism** for 2005 contained a number of articles taking up issues debated in **International Socialism**. Among them are Neil Davidson's polemical Isaac Deutscher memorial prize lecture on bourgeois revolutions; Paul Blackledge on the late Brian Manning and Manning on the Levellers; Rick Kuhn on Henryk Grossman; Daniel Bensaïd on John Holloway; and Ian Birchall on books on Trotskyism.

CH

'Imperialism and global political economy'—a reply to Alex Callinicos

Leo Panitch and Sam Gindin

We appreciate the attention that Alex Callinicos is giving to our work (*International Socialism* 108), and are especially pleased that he sees it as a 'useful corrective' to his earlier 'mistaken claim' that the end of the Cold War would see a return to the old inter-imperial rivalries. Our argument, he acknowledges, helped him see the error in expecting, after 1989, 'a simple repetition of earlier historical patterns without taking into account the effects of the concrete forms taken by economic and geopolitical competition' in the post-1945 era (p116).

Unfortunately, Callinicos's critique of our work makes it rather clear that the theoretical mistakes that led him to make this earlier claim have not been corrected. Despite beginning by admitting the 'serious defects' of the classical theory of imperialism, Callinicos seems mainly concerned to defend it as an 'indispensable instrument for understanding the contemporary world'. He borrows from Harvey and Arrighi a notion of 'two logics of power'—economic and territorial—to try to revive the classical theory.[1] Defining imperialism as 'the intersection of economic and geopolitical competition', he explains this as deriving from the internationalisation of capital, and the interpenetration of private capital and the nation-state by the late 19th century, which gave rise to the 'merger' of the two previously distinct logics of power: economic competition between capital and geopolitical competition among states. Their 'contradictory fusion' continues to define imperialism today.

By contrast, our argument is that there was a fundamental transformation in capitalist imperialism in the last half century along the following lines: (a) the closest linkages among capitalist states were now between the American state and the other states of the West, rather than with the South as in the old imperial era; (b) the internationalisation of capital was fundamentally different in the second half of the 20th century than in the 19th and early 20th, based as it now was on foreign direct investment and the multinational corporation; (c) the interpenetration of production and finance in the contemporary era dissolved the coherence of the old national bourgeoisies that was the basis of the earlier inter-imperial rivalries; (d) what Marx in the *Grundrisse* called 'many capitals' came to depend on *many states*; and (e) the internationalisation of the state reflected this in terms of the responsibilities states took on for managing the contradictions and crises of global capitalism, while still trying to make their territorial spaces attractive as sites of accumulation for foreign as well as domestic bourgeoisies.

Callinicos appears to accept our argument on how capitalist imperialism was transformed. As he puts it, 'Thus the historic achievement of the American state during the 1940s was the construction of a transnational economic and geopolitical space that unified the entire advanced capitalist world under US leadership' (p117). But he contends that we are 'insufficiently sensitive to the strains' to which this new imperial system was 'increasingly subjected' by the late 1960s. His entire argument in this respect appears to be founded on the claim that the economic crisis of the 1970s has never been resolved. Yet we show that it was precisely through the neo-liberal resolution of that crisis that global capitalism's dynamism and the structural power of the American empire were reconstituted over the last quarter of a century.

Callinicos misunderstands our argument when he says that we see class struggle from below as the sole cause of the crisis of the 1970s; we make it very clear that renewed economic competition was also at the root of this. Our main point is that it became impossible to resolve the crisis of the 1970s without breaking the back of labour, not least through opening up the world to the free flow of capital and restructuring the world's states to that end under the new form of social rule that is neo-liberalism. Far from the 'strains' of the crisis of the 1970s undoing the new form of capitalist imperialism, we show that American hegemony not only remained unchallenged through that decade, but the trade competition that emerged from the revived Japanese and European economies did not lead on to anything like the old rivalries. This was so precisely because of the integration in production and finance that had already taken place and continued apace amid this revived competition. Callinicos does not challenge this, nor does he dispute our argument that it was after the US applied neo-liberal discipline to itself under the Volcker shock that the international authority of neo-liberalism was established, emulated and generalised. It was this that resolved, for capital, the crisis of the 1970s.

Callinicos offers no evidence himself that the crisis of the 1970s remains with us to this day, and totally ignores the evidence we offer to the contrary, including our refutation of the 'plentiful evidence' he seems to think the sources he mentions provide.[2] Insofar as Callinicos is arguing that there are structural tendencies to crises in capitalism that operate behind the backs of class and state actors, we don't disagree at all. In fact, we think that uneven development and financial volatility under neo-liberal globalisation significantly reinforce those tendencies. But we argue that the capacity to manage and contain crises also needs to enter into the analysis, and we stress not only the coordinated management under the American imperial aegis, but also the difficulties involved in having to manage global capitalism through relatively autonomous states.

Despite his *mea culpa* for his earlier mistakes on this, Callinicos still seems to believe that the end of the Cold War, reinforced by the ongoing economic crisis that began in the 1970s, should have removed the structural underpinning of 'the transnational economic and geopolitical space constructed in the 1940s'. Insofar as he now says the disintegration of the latter proved to be 'in no sense inevitable' after 1989, he seems to think this was only due to 'the creative political intervention of the American state, particularly under the Clinton administration' (p118). He thus fails to appreciate that the international economic integration and the coordinated management of global capitalism were not a mere addendum to the Cold War; and he also gives far too much weight to the primacy of American state actors in making what he calls a 'genuinely global capitalism' happen in the 1990s. This is rather ironic, given that he accuses us of not giving primacy to economic determinants and paying too much attention to the imperial capacities of the American state.

Whereas we see the theoretical importance of stressing the relative autonomy of the state in terms of the role many states play in fostering and reproducing a dynamic global capitalism, Callinicos seems to mainly see the importance of states in terms of their role in 'geopolitical competition'. This loose notion of 'geopolitical competition' acts as a stand-in for the concept of inter-imperial rivalries, and it is this that allows him to cling to the classical theory of imperialism as 'an indispensable instrument for understanding the contemporary world'.

The evidence Callinicos adduces to make his case for 'the development of centrifugal tendencies within the Western geopolitical bloc' (p118) strikes us as very weak, especially since the whole implication of his argument is that this is suggestive of a return to inter-imperial rivalries. All he points to are certain concerns among some American elites to prevent the emergence of effective rivals to US military dominance. This is hardly surprising, and only confirms that the American state wants to develop further capacities to reinforce its dominance. The very fact that Callincos speaks in terms of American elites having 'a *longstanding* preoccupation...to prevent the emergence of a hostile Great Power' (p118, emphasis added) is evidence that there is nothing new here. And even if we granted that this preoccupation alone could explain the American invasion of Iraq, it would no more indicate the likely re-emergence of inter-imperial rivalries than the war on Yugoslavia over Kosovo did. We explicitly argued that the latter was mainly directed at making it clear to the Europeans that NATO would remain the policeman of Europe—and Callinicos admits it was successful in this respect.

There were of course greater tensions over the war on Iraq, but Callinicos makes far too much out of what transpired in this respect in the early months of 2003, and ignores the significance of the German and French endorsement at the UN in the spring of 2004 of the American occupation of Iraq. As Dominique Moisi explained, the main reason for this accommodation was that 'when the US finds itself bogged down, it poses a big challenge to the rest of the world. If America simply pulled out [of Iraq] now...concern would quickly switch from the perils of US global domination to the dangers of a world deprived of US international engagement... America is in a mess but so are we'.[3] This sustains our argument that 'what is at play in the current conjuncture is not contradictions between national bourgeoisies, but contradictions of "the whole of imperialism", implicating all the bourgeoisies that function under the American umbrella'.[4]

We may also note in this context the French defence minister's reassurance that even the 'Defence Europe' initiative would 'strengthen NATO's capacities and benefit the trans-Atlantic link. We are not in competition. We complement each other'.[5] No less notable is the French government's advertising campaign (inaugurated in late 2004) in publications like the *Wall Street Journal*, *Harvard Business Review* and *Time Global Business* trumpeting 'The New France' (in obvious contrast with 'Old Europe') as the savvy investor's place to do business.[6] More than a short-term concern with profits is involved here. Very much at play is the belief by European capitalists that neo-liberalism can remain strong in Europe only insofar as it remains strongly tied to an America-led global capitalism. Indeed, the class alignments in relation to the yes and no votes in the referendum on the European constitution sustains our argument that 'the most serious contradictions and conflicts are located not so much in the relationships between the advanced capitalist states, as *within* these states, as they try to manage their internal processes of accumulation, legitimation and class struggle'.[7] Of course, as we also argued, this is no less true of the American state as it tries to manage and cope with the complexities of neo-imperial globalisation while also overseeing the social forces and social contradictions in its own social formation.

What all this suggests is that, even by replacing the concept of rivalry with the vaguer one of 'geopolitical competition', Callinicos cannot make the old classical theory of imperialism 'indispensable' for understanding European-American relations today. Callinicos offers nothing at all to challenge our central argument that the asymmetric power relationships that emerged out of the penetration and integration among the leading capitalist countries under the aegis of informal American empire were not dissolved in the wake of the crisis of the Golden Age or the end of the Cold War, but rather were refashioned and reconstituted through the era of neo-liberal globalisation. And he only caricatures our argument (and to recognise this one does not need to read our own extensive critique of Hardt and Negri[8]) when he contends that we arrive at the same conclusion as Hardt and Negri 'that geopolitical competition has largely been transcended in contemporary capitalism' (p111). It is only because he wants 'geopolitical competition' to act as a stand-in for inter-imperial rivalry that he can suggest this. For unlike Hardt and Negri we reject the notion that borders are being erased and states are being bypassed in global capitalism, and we insist on the very large role of states in the making of global capitalism; we also explicitly say that the relative autonomy of states within the American informal empire allows for divergence in many policy areas.

Indeed we would even agree with Greg Albo's important argument that the precise nature of hegemony is that you expect different tactics to be put forward by the integrated field of forces but that they do so in a way that reproduces the overall structural relation and power.[9] In a world of states, you would expect different states to exhibit different approaches to what is needed for global capitalist development and security. The problem is to think that every conjunctural expression of this should be taken as proof of fundamental divergences within the imperium, and to draw the conclusion that this constitutes a geopolitical fault line that will spill over into rivalry for world dominance. Neither of these reductions is necessary theoretically, and they are wrong empirically.

The weakness of an argument that must rely on inflating instances of strain or tension among the advanced capitalist states far beyond what they deserve is especially seen when Callinicos points to the EU's plans to end the arms embargo on China as 'perhaps the most serious row since the invasion of Iraq'. The EU has, of course, backed down on this since he penned these words. What this type of argument makes clear is that Callinicos is still too easily tempted to slip back into making the same mistake he made in earlier writings—he remains on the lookout for 'a simple repetition of earlier historical patterns' that will sustain the old classical theory of inter-imperial rivalry. The attention he pays to China as a putative new player in these patterns might seem more plausible than the attention he gives to Europe in this respect. But the case he tries to make to counter our argument that China will remain very far from reaching the status of an inter-imperial pole for a good many decades relies again on quotations from American security elites that express their concern to prevent China from acquiring this status. He himself provides no historical materialist analysis of the capacity of China to do this.

Callinicos returns at the end of his article to the question of the underlying economic factors that are allegedly undoing the American Empire. He focuses primarily on 'the role played by China in particular and Asian capitalism in general in financing the US deficit'. From this, he draws a parallel with Britain having become 'financially indebted to the United States during the First World War even if took another 30 years into the definitive displacement of one by the other as the leading capitalist power' (p124). He thus slips here yet again into 'a simple repetition of earlier historical patterns', and this is especially troubling insofar as it encourages people to pay insufficient attention to the need for careful historical materialist analyses of what has distinctively changed by way not only of the names of the state players in the global capitalist economy but in the relationships between them over the course of the last century.

All this makes it rather ironic that Callinicos should chastise us for not giving primacy to economic determinations. By virtue of our 'not setting the development of capitalist imperialism in the context of the structurally determined crisis tendencies of the capitalist mode of production', he is emboldened to ask: 'If economic primacy doesn't figure somewhere in the argument what is the point of calling oneself a Marxist?' (p116) This betrays a number of fundamental theoretical problems. On what basis does giving primacy to economic determinants get translated into crisis tendencies alone? What are we to understand by 'economic primacy' if the structural determination involved is read off from contradictory versions of crisis theory and that plays down the balance of power in social relations of production at both national and international levels? Isn't it a version of the monetary illusion to read structural crises off from such indicators as deficits and debts?

It is significant in this respect that Callinicos fails to address our theoretical as well as empirical argument regarding the relationship between finance and empire in global capitalism, nor our explicit explanation of why the relationship between the US and its creditors today is so different than that between Britain and the US yesterday. Our explanation of the American ability to finance its massive deficits over the past quarter century, and our argument that this has reflected imperial strength rather than weakness, has fundamentally to do with the 'economic primacy' we give to production and finance in our analysis, although we show that these can never be separated from their class and institutional moorings.[10]

We said of Lenin in 'Global Capitalism and American Empire' that he had a proclivity for over-politicising theory. We expect Alex Callinicos will not be overly upset if we say—in what is perhaps yet another example of 'repetition of earlier historical patterns'—that he is also like Lenin in this respect. Unfortunately, this proclivity all too often gives rise to a search for evidence of economic crises on the basis of an overestimation of the political fragmentation and instability that such crises must bring. This tends to be accompanied by a type of politics that is premised on the expectation that economic crises and war among capitalist states will provide the setting for revolutionary opportunities. And the underestimation that necessarily follows from this of the strength and cohesiveness of global capitalism today unfortunately also gives rise to an underestimation of what the left needs to do politically and organisationally to develop the revolutionary capacities to challenge capitalism in the 21st century.

NOTES

1: It ought to be pointed out that Harvey's notion of the territorial logic in his *The New Imperialism* (Oxford, 2003) is explicitly derived from Arendt rather than Lenin; and Arrighi has long dismissed as 'irrelevant' the old classical theory of imperialism for 'interpreting accounts of world-historical events, trends and developmental tendencies since the Second World War'. See *The Geometry of Imperialism* (London, 1978), p160.

2: We have shown, for instance, that Brenner's data generally distorts the upturn in growth and profitability by including the crisis decade of the 1970s and leaving out the decade after 1996; the picture looks very different if one takes the period of neo-liberalism proper from 1983 to the present. As for the 'plentiful evidence' of the other sources he mentions, Dumenil actually agrees with us against Brenner about neo-liberalism's resolution of the crisis of the 1970s and the upturn in profits this gave rise to; his recent work points to the possibility of a new crisis now based on finance's excessive appropriation of the revived profits. In addition to our essays in the 2004 and 2005 volumes of the *Socialist Register*, see also S Gindin, 'Turning Points and Starting Points', *Socialist Register* 2001, and L Panitch and S Gindin, 'Rethinking Crisis', *Monthly Review* 54:6, November 2002, and 'Euro-Capitalism and American Empire' in D Coates (ed), *Varieties of Capitalism, Varieties of Approaches* (Basingstoke, 2005). Most recently, see L Panitch and S Gindin, 'Superintending Global Capital', *New Left Review* 35 (September/ October 2005).

3: *Financial Times*, 12 November 2003.

4: 'Global Capitalism and American Empire', *Socialist Register* 2004, p32.

5: Michele Alliot-Marie, *Wall Street Journal*, 9 March 2005.

6: www.thenewfrance.com

7: 'Global Capitalism and American Empire', as above, p24.

8: 'Gems and Baubles in Empire', *Historical Materialism* 10:2 (2002).

9: See G Albo, 'The Old and New Economics of Imperialism', *Socialist Register* 2004.

10: See our 'Finance and American Empire', *Socialist Register* 2005, esp pp67-75.

Transport and climate change—a reply to James Woodcock

Mark Thomas

In *International Socialism* 108 James Woodcock took issue with some of Paul McGarr's arguments about the role transport under capitalism plays in the growing threat of climate change (see *International Socialism* 107). In particular, James offers some sharp criticisms of the idea that public transport is the solution to the environmental and other costs of transport under capitalism. In doing so, James challenges many of the solutions that most socialists, and by no means just revolutionaries, have looked to as the basis of a radical transport policy.

James instead proposes that walking and cycling rather than public transport form the centre of the transport solutions we should propose. He makes a number of arguments for why this should be the case, but the one I consider the most important and which I will focus on is the implication for greenhouse emissions and hence climate change.

Renewables

The thrust of James's case is that the focus on public transport is misplaced as it will fail to achieve the necessary reductions in emissions. His argument is that any motorised transport will use fossil fuels or nuclear power until sufficient sources of renewable energy are available, and that this can only be achieved in the long term, while the threat of climate change is urgent. Yet is it the case that the barriers to the extensive introduction of renewable energy are so steep as to preclude their rapid introduction? Paul McGarr offered a strong case why this is not the case, which James does not challenge. In other words James is mistaken when he separates the battle for renewable energy from the task of transforming our transport system.

Surprisingly, some environmentalists are equivocal about renewable energy sources, and I suspect that what lurks behind this is a belief that industrial societies per se are ecologically unsupportable. Reservations about the viability of renewables also disarm us in the face of the growing campaign to persuade us that nuclear power is the only solution to the climate costs of fossil fuels.

Patterns of employment and provisions

As James points out, if we wish to place pedal and foot power at the centre of the transport system, then patterns of employment and provision (at the very least the location of food outlets) need to be radically altered. He is right to point to the way capitalism rips up jobs, forcing people to commute long distances, or the way the growth of out of town supermarkets reachable only by car has both increased pressures on many workers and contributed to rising greenhouse emissions. He is right to suggest we should fight for the availability of both jobs and provisions near where people live. There are battles which can be fought in the here and now over these issues, and James gives some good examples.

But is it possible to conceive of a complete reorganisation of the economy and society along these lines? Surely under capitalism, with its relentless logic of capital accumulation and constant restructuring of employment patterns, increasingly of course on a global basis, we would be fighting at best defensive battles. But even in a future society the level of democratic control and conscious planning required to realise James's vision would not be available overnight. A communist society would initially inherit the employment and residential patterns of capitalism, and this would take time to unpick.

Now, all this might seem like the ABC of Marxism, but in the absence of such a reorganisation workers will be faced with the need for motorised transport to get to work and shops, etc, let alone visit friends, family and leisure facilities. The demand for walking and cycling as an immediate and overall solution to our transport needs as opposed to an expansion of public transport then becomes merely utopian and risks lapsing into a moralistic cry of what we 'should' do without providing the material basis for its realisation.

Now, of course, this is certainly not to oppose fighting to extend and improve cycling facilities, as indeed Paul does in his article (contrary to what James claims). But to counterpose this to fighting for better, cheaper and environmentally cleaner public transport is mistaken. James is left suggesting that renewable energy is a long term demand, yet completely reorganising employment, housing and retail structures is a short term goal. This seems untenable to say the least.

Localism

James's article also seems to contain too many concessions to ideas of 'localism', an idea widespread inside large parts of the environmental movement. The thrust of these arguments is to seek an answer to the problems created by globalisation in the existence of an internationalised economy as such rather than in capitalism as a specific mode of production. The remedy is sought in calls to minimise international trade and to seek to establish economies based on 'local' self-sufficiency only.

But one of the great gains of capitalism is its welding together of different societies into a single world system, and this development is central to the huge transformation in human productive power wrought by the rise of capitalism. This is not to accept the prevailing international division of labour and inequalities of course. Alex Callinicos makes the point in his book *An Anti-Capitalist Manifesto*:

'Why should international economic connections be treated as *a priori* undesirable? It is undoubtedly an obscenity that farms in Zimbabwe produce flowers and mange-touts for export while millions of local people go hungry. But, equally, why should rural producers return to the vulnerability to vicissitudes of weather and disease that was their unavoidable fate in premodern times?'[1]

The question is whether an internationally organised economy is necessary for what Marx called the material preconditions of communism. In other words, the kind of expanded democracy that we place at the heart of our vision of communism depends on the enormous gains in human productivity that capitalism has created but cannot place at the benefit of the majority of humanity. It is difficult to see how this is compatible with a locally based self-sufficient economy in anything like the foreseeable future, and we need to direct our attention to the internal transformation of the global economy, not its break-up into smaller units.

Limitless growth?

Now, does a commitment to abundance as an essential precondition of communism imply limitless economic growth, which is ecologically unsustainable? As Paul Burkett points out in the October 2005 edition of Monthly Review, although this is certainly what many ecological critics of Marx hold to be the case, it involves a fundamentally mistaken view of Marx's vision of communism.[2]

For Marx, abundance is not the complete satisfaction of all conceivable material needs (it is hard to see how that would be possible) but the eradication of all basic and most of what we might call our secondary needs. So, even on the basis of what capitalism has developed we could reasonably aspire not just to feed everyone on the planet, but also provide a varied and interesting diet. However, luxuries—caviar, say—could not be made universally available. But the point for Marx is that capitalism makes it possible for humanity's fundamental needs to be addressed, thus removing the material basis for the division of society into classes.

But Marx's real focus is with the free and all-round development of human capacities, not with the growth of material production and consumption for its own sake. Central to that is the expansion of free time to explore those capabilities. Thus beyond a certain point of material satisfaction, further rises in productivity would involve not greater material consumption, but reductions in the amount of labour time required to satisfy the material necessities of life. There is no reason to hold that Marx's vision of communism and a sustainable environment are in conflict.

I make this point not because I think James rejects it, but because some environmental writers and campaigners do reject it and use it to question whether any form of industrial society is ecologically sustainable. James's arguments weaken our response to those claims.

Waste and energy efficiency

Equally, it is not just a question of taking over and reproducing the existing form of economic organisation as it exists under capitalism. So, for example, another crucial part of any serious programme addressing climate change is the eradication of the huge amount of waste generated by capitalism. In an essay written over 30 years ago a former editor of this journal, Mike Kidron, looked at the US economy for the year 1970 and suggested, on a conservative estimate, that over 60 percent of output was waste. These figures need to be handled with care, as Kidron was interested in estimating what was wasteful from the point of view of capitalism, not from the vantage point of a future socialist society. Nonetheless, it is very suggestive, and certainly the scope for eradicating enormous socially unnecessary waste—from advertising, through the built-in obsolescence of goods, to military production and so on—is surely very great.[3]

The massive use of renewable energy sources, the wholescale eradication of waste and widespread adoption of energy efficiency savings point to the solutions for climate change. James's emphasis on an immediate reorganisation of work and provisioning to place walking and cycling at the centre of our transport system leads us away from focusing on these political battles, and is in danger of leaving us with little to say to the real needs of millions of workers who face chronic transport problems.

Partial demands and revolution

Tackling climate change means demonstrating that the solution requires the reorganisation of society, that we face not technical but political barriers. It means raising demands in the here and now that can begin to address these problems, and can win workers to seeing their capacity and interest in fighting for things that will improve their lives and make the environment more sustainable. Of course, any partial demands under capitalism run the risk of being subverted by capitalism. So James argues that improvements in public transport simply encourage the rich to use their cars more as traffic congestion is alleviated. But this simply suggests further measures are required to discourage car use. Ultimately it points to the limits of reforms under capitalism and the necessity of a revolutionary transformation of society. James's arguments, despite his intentions, are in danger of taking us away from the direction of a real onslaught on the political structures of capitalism and towards the cul-de-sac of focusing on individual behaviour.

NOTES

1: A Callinicos, *An Anti-Capitalist Manifesto* (Cambridge 2003), p131.
2: P Burkett, 'Marx's Vision of Sustainable Human Development', *Monthly Review*, vol 57, no 5 (October 2005), pp34-62.
3: M Kidron, 'Waste: US 1970', in *Capitalism and Theory* (London, 1974). I owe this point to Pete Gillard.

Still available...

The following issues of International Socialism are available for the prices shown. Please send a cheque payable to ISJ to PO Box 42184, London SW8 2WD, or phone 020 7819 1177 to pay by card. Issues 58 (Spring 1993) and 65 (Special issue on Engels) are available on cassette from the Royal National Institute for the Blind. Tel: 01733 370 777.

International Socialism 108 *(Autumn 2005) £5*
Europe—birth of a new left: Stathis Kouvelakis on France | Stefan Bornost on Germany | Pepijn Brandon on the Netherlands after the referendum | Poland: the workers' movement 25 years after Solidarity | Respect: the view from below | Irfan Habib on Edward Said | Bolivia's rising | Lula's crisis | Imperialism and global economy | Making sense of socialism today | Consciousness in the 1905 Russian Revolution

International Socialism 107 *(Summer 2005) £5*
How the G8 is strangling the planet: aid, trade, debt and governance | Paul McGarr on climate change | French referendum campaign | Jean Paul Sartre | Claudio Katz on Latin America's new 'left' governments | Dragan Plavsic on the new 'democratic revolutions' | China's strikewave

International Socialism 106 *(Spring 2005) £5*
Britain after eight years of Blair: Jane Hardy on the changing structure of the econom | Jacob Middleton on the working class | Terry Wrigley on Blair's vision for education | Alex Law and Gerry Mooney on urban landscapes | Charlie Kimber on Labour's shrivelling roots | The elections and the resistance in Iraq | Tensions in Egypt | John Holloway and Alex Callinicos debate taking power | John Molyneux appreciates the work of Tracey Emin

International Socialism 105 *(Winter 2005) £5*
Iraq: the rise of the resistance | An interview with Iranian activist Elaheh Rostami Povey | Marxists and the 1905 Revolution | Gregor Gall and Martin Smith debate industrial perspectives | Debates in Rifondazione on entering bourgeois governments | Interview with the people behind the Marxists Internet Archive

International Socialism 104 *(Autumn 2004) £4*
Anti-capitalism five years after Seattle: Chris Harman on spontaneity, strategy and politics | Giles Ungpakorn on NGOs | Mike Gonzalez on Venezuela | Neil Davidson on Isaac Deutscher's biography of Trotsky

International Socialism 103 *(Summer 2004) £4*
Charlie Hore on China | Chris Harman's rough guide to the Indian elections | Michael Bradley on D-Day | Judith Butler in perspective by Rachel Aldred | Obituary for Brian Manning by James Holstun | Alfred Rosmer on Tony Cliff

International Socialism 102 *(Spring 2004) £4*
Antoine Boulangé on the Hijab, racism and the state | François Chesnais: Globalisation against development | Chris Harman on the rise of capitalism

International Socialism 101 *(Winter 2003) £4*
Women's liberation today by Lindsey German | The politics of food by Carlo Morelli | In the middle way: an extended review of Geoff Eley's *Forging Democracy* by Colin Barker

International Socialism 100 *(Autumn 2003) £4*
Socialism in the 21st century by John Rees | Global and local echoes of the anti-war movement: a British Muslim perspective by Salma Yaqoob | Murray Smith replies to John Rees on the broad party, the revolutionary party and the united front | Stephen Jay Gould in perspective

Some older issues are still available at £3 each (inc p&p). Please call 020 7819 1177 or email isj@swp.org.uk for details.

Notes on contributors

Talat Ahmed is working on the history of the All-India Progressive Writers Association

Joseph Choonara is a journalist with *Socialist Worker*

Neil Davidson won the 2004 Isaac and Tamara Deutscher Memorial Prize for his *Discovering the Scottish Revolution*

Neil Faulkner is author of *Apocalypse: The Great Jewish Revolt Against Rome, AD66-73*

Angie Gago is a student in south London

Abdellali Hajjat lives in France and is author of *Immigration postcoloniale et mémoire*

Chris Harman is author of *Explaining the Crisis*, *A People's History of the World* and *The Prophet and the Proletariat*

Mike Haynes is author of *Russia: Class and Power in the 20th Century* and *A Century of State Murder?*

Owen Miller is active in Respect in south London and doing research at the School of Oriental and African Studies

Chris Nineham is a on the steering committee of the Stop the War Coalition and a member of the Socialist Workers Party

Leo Panitch and **Sam Gindin** are the authors of *Global Capitalism and American Empire*

John Parrington is a lecturer in molecular and cellular pharmacology at Oxford University

Sami Ramadani is a senior lecturer in sociology at London Metropolitan University and writes on Iraq

Roberto Robaina was formerly a leading member of the Brazilian Workers Party and is now on the executive of the new Party of Socialism and Liberty, PSOL

Mark Thomas works for the Bookmarks bookshop in London

Jim Wolfreys is co-author of *The Politics of Racism in France*

Haifa Zangana is an Iraqi novelist and anti-occupation activist